The Making of the Royal Pavilion, Brighton

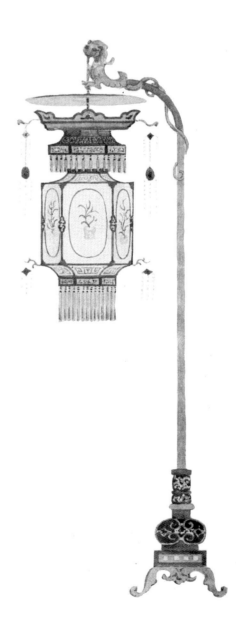

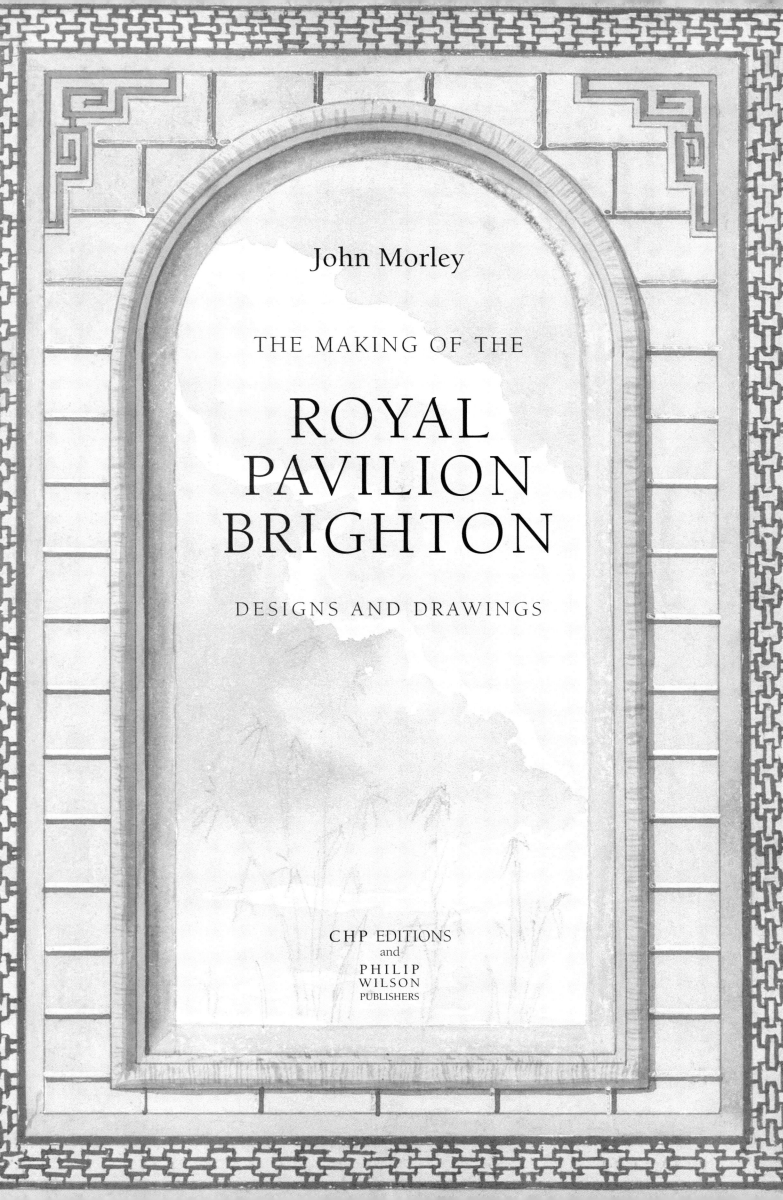

John Morley

THE MAKING OF THE

ROYAL
PAVILION
BRIGHTON

DESIGNS AND DRAWINGS

CHP EDITIONS
and
PHILIP
WILSON
PUBLISHERS

NOTE In the text, the designs, drawings and prints are
referred to by the numbers of the illustrations,
between square brackets. Full documentary details
are given in the 'Catalogue of Illustrations'.
Interpolations by the author in quoted excerpts
are also enclosed between square brackets.

*This new paperback edition has been
produced for the benefit of
The Friends of the Royal Pavilion,
Art Gallery and Museums
with generous assistance from
The Hazen Polsky Foundation*

First published as a paperback edition in 2003 by
Philip Wilson Publishers Ltd.,
7 Deane House, 27 Greenwood Place,
London NW5 1LB

Originally published in 1984 by Sotheby Publications

ISBN 0 85667 557 1

Distributed in the United States and Canada by
Palgrave Macmillan,
175 Fifth Avenue, New York, NY 10010

Distributed in the UK and the rest of the world by
I.B. Tauris & Co. Ltd,
6 Salem Road, London W2 4BU

Cover designed by Norman Turpin
Original text design by Gillian Greenwood

Printed by Craft Print International Ltd., Singapore

Contents

Foreword

This book brings together, in as comprehensive a manner as possible within the publisher's patience, all the important known surviving original designs for, and depictions of, the Royal Pavilion before 1830; ordinary topographical views have not been included. The date 1830 has been taken as the terminus ad quem because it was in that year that King George IV, whose tastes ruled his architects and decorators, died; after that came anti-climax, diminuendo, and disaster.

For thirty-five years or so the Pavilion was the favourite plaything of a Prince as sophisticated and cultivated, if as erratic, as any who have occupied the throne. His purpose at Brighton was less consistent than at Windsor Castle, Buckingham Palace, or with that vanished and lamented masterpiece, Carlton House. A royal palace does not usually begin as a 'genteel farmhouse' on a site so confined as to be, in Repton's words, 'deemed by every body too small to admit of any improvements', nor, in the course of expansion, does its style usually borrow forms and motifs from quite so many civilisations. It is remarkable that the final result of this lurching progress is so consummately successful, so coherent – and so unforgettably sumptuous; as the author of a *History of Brighton* of 1827 wrote with some complacency, 'the splendid decorations of the palace, in the aggregate considered, afford the most pleasing testimony, that John Bull, with suitable encouragement, has it within the scope of his own powers, to excel all the boasted frippery ornaments of the continent.'

A mass of material, in the shape of drawings and designs, remains as evidence of the evolutionary process that preceded and accompanied the creation of the final work of art. The various architects principally concerned with the Pavilion – Holland, Repton, Porden, and Nash – have all left samples of their labours, or of their aspirations, in pictorial form; there exist also well over three hundred designs for the interior produced by, or in association with, the Crace firm, the Prince's principal agents in the production of the later interior decorations. The great majority of these are in the Chinese or Indian styles, or in a mixture of both; the fanciful magnificence of the later designs would be impossible to surpass.

An attempt has been made, with the help of archival evidence, to place the designs for the interiors in their destined context; simple in some cases, but not always an easy task when the nomenclature, and even the walls, of the rooms have shifted so many times, and the vacillations of the patron have sometimes led to one room being decorated four times within a year. The author has, perhaps rashly, not been deterred from speculation; those who speculate today are as liable to error, and to the later lash of correction, as were the early Fathers, but there seems little alternative. There has, on the other hand, been no attempt to elucidate the exotic sources of the designs, a task that seems likely to occupy almost as much space as the present book.

Ground plans are given of the building at the three major stages of its development: the Holland villa of 1787; the Holland enlargement of 1801–2; the Nash enlargement from 1815 onwards. The reader is recommended, despite their dry contours, to peruse them closely; they greatly help to elucidate the text, more especially because it has proved sensible, in order to preserve the vein of continuity, to tell the history of the interior decorations (through the designs) independently of that of the structure; the Saloon, for example, remained virtually unaltered in basic inner form from 1787 to the end of the period dealt with here.

A word should perhaps be said of the post-1830 history of the building. Stripped, and sold by Queen Victoria in 1850 to the Corporation of Brighton (which saved the palace from demolition), it was at first most sensitively treated, and the return of many of the original decorations in 1864 saw most of them put back in their original places. But gradually the impetus was lost, and in the later years of the century increasingly inappropriate treatments were devised for the interiors (some under the hands of the same Crace firm that devised its splendours). By 1935 Sir John Summerson could describe it thus: 'a curiosity which rouses only a vague, transient wonder in the visitor. Its ornaments are scarcely more extravagant than those of the roundabouts at Hampstead, which they closely resemble; for singularity of form it has long ago been surpassed by the Crystal Palace and the White City; and for richness it compares unfavourably with the Granada Cinema at Tooting. Its intrinsic beauty is small; surprise and novelty were the great things about it, and the thrill of such ephemeral virtues is not easily recaptured . . . it is simply a minor historical monument . . .'. Not all agreed with this opinion; Sir Osbert Sitwell, also in 1935, wrote that 'even now, as it stands, forlorn and degraded by popular festivals, what other buildings exist in England, or, as for that, in Europe, to compare with it in individuality and exotic beauty? . . . to this singular dwelling undoubtedly attaches something of the dreamlike quality which is often found to infuse great poetry. . . .'

Unfortunately as many agreed with the former as with the latter; in the same year powerful voices at Brighton were raised urging demolition. Three factors appear to have preserved the building. One, undoubtedly, was the strong local sentiment that has always existed in its favour; another was the prestige in Brighton of the formidable personality of the then Director of the Pavilion, Mr Henry Roberts; most important, perhaps, was the buttress provided by the interest and support shown by Her late Majesty Queen Mary, which were well known in the town.

The forces of light prevailed; after 1946 Dr Clifford Musgrave, as Director, with the invaluable aid of Mr Roy Bradley, as Decorative Artist, was able to set the Royal Pavilion on the course it has since followed of restoration, replacement, and refurnishing, a course made easier by the permanent loan in 1955, from Her Majesty The Queen, of many original pieces of furniture, which made it possible to set out parts of the Pavilion in a style resembling that so carefully worked out by King George IV. Mention should be made of the invaluable support given to the writer, since he became Director in 1968, of two leading members of Brighton Corporation: Alderman Dr Stanley Deason, who succeeded in limiting smoking in the building (a great victory!) and Councillor Dudley Baker, MBE, whose building firm played a part in the construction of Porden's great Stables, and who has steadily guided the present structural restorations, the most thoroughgoing and extensive ever attempted.

The battle is not yet won, but the beauty and interest of the building, especially when fully furnished (as it is during most of the summer season), are powerful advocates, which one feels in the end must prevail.*

What *is* the significance, the value of this extraordinary building? It obviously has the power both of repelling and of capturing the imagination. The guiding spirit of the post-war restoration of the Royal Pavilion gave his own testimony (in his book on the building) in 1951, when he declared that it 'equals in evasive loveliness even Shah Jehan's own creations', and that in the Pavilion 'the Chinese taste had now attained to a vast exotic grandeur that made it confederate with the ultimate kingdoms of the romantic imagination'. The author is emboldened to add his own interpretation.

Stendhal once spoke of 'having enough sense, or, if you prefer, good taste in music not completely to be deceived by the whipped cream and swagger of Rossini'. It is with the music of Rossini, who himself played in its Music Room and aroused, with his familiar treatment of the King, the snobbish ire of Lady Granville, that it seems to the present writer that the Royal Pavilion may fitly be compared. Neither expresses the highest form of its respective art; in both a certain inflation excludes true nobility. But, in common with the music of Rossini, the Royal Pavilion has wit, exhilaration, invention, splendour, a superb and breath-taking beauty; it has its comic pomposities, its arpeggios, its magnificent crescendos and its melting coloratura. One might perhaps oppose to its fascinations a rigid armour of architectural propriety, and reject the 'whipped cream and swagger'. But at what a cost!

King George IV (1762–1830) is referred to, wherever possible, by the title appropriate to the period under discussion: Prince of Wales (1762–1811), Prince Regent (1811–20), King (1820–30). Where the context is general, he is referred to as King George IV or George IV.

---

*Brighton Corporation has now decided that the building shall be open fully furnished throughout the year.

List of Sources and Short Bibliography

The main sources of original information, and the abbreviations (where applicable) used in the references, are as follows:

The Royal Archives: RA (followed by number)

The Crace Ledgers (a typed transcript in the Royal Pavilion Collection, Brighton Corporation): CL (followed by page number)

An abstract of various Royal Pavilion accounts, at present in the possession of the East Sussex County Library: A of A (followed by page number, where it exists)

An Inventory of the contents of the Royal Pavilion, spanning the years 1815–39, at present in the possession of the East Sussex County Library

Jutsham's Day Books, recording the movements of furniture and other objects to and from the Royal Pavilion; in the Office of the Lord Chamberlain, St James's Palace, London

The Public Record Office: PRO

A book of drawings by Frederick Crace, owned by Mrs J.F.Crace: CB (unpaginated)

The number of books that refer to the Royal Pavilion is legion. Here are included only those that are essential reading, or that have important references to the building or its contents. For Nash's *Views of the Royal Pavilion, Brighton* (1826), which contains no continuous text, see the introduction to the Catalogue.

Attree, H.R., *Topography of Brighton*, London, Longman, Hunt and Co., 1809. This book is referred to many times in the text; the Pavilion is treated on pp. 6–12. Individual page references are not given in the References

Bellaigue, Geoffrey de, John Harris, Oliver Millar, *Buckingham Palace*, London, Nelson, 1968. Contains information on many pieces of furniture and objets d'art at one time associated with the Royal Pavilion. See also the various catalogues of exhibitions given at The Queen's Gallery

Brayley, E.W.A., *Illustrations of Her Majesty's Palace at Brighton*, London, J.B.Nichols and Son, 1838

Cooper-Hewitt Museum, New York, *The Royal Pavilion at Brighton*, 1977. Catalogue of an exhibition of original Royal Pavilion material

Dinkel, John, *The Royal Pavilion, Brighton*, London, Scala/Philip Wilson, 1983. The present book was written concurrently with Mr Dinkel's book, and the author was unable to consult it. He has since seen the text, and it is clear that it contains invaluable references

Laking, G.F., *The Furniture of Windsor Castle*, London, Bradbury, Agnew & Co.; undated, published by command of King Edward VII

Musgrave, Clifford, *Royal Pavilion, An Episode in the Romantic*, London, Leonard Hill, 1959; first published 1951

Repton, Humphry, *Designs for the Pavillon at Brighton*, London, J.C.Stadler, 1808

Roberts, Henry D., *A History of the Royal Pavilion, Brighton*, London, Country Life, 1939.
  Despite inaccuracies, still the most detailed account

Smith, Clifford, *Buckingham Palace, Its Furniture, Decoration and History*, London, Country Life,
  1931

Stroud, Dorothy, *Henry Holland, His Life and Architecture*, London, Country Life, 1966

Summerson, John, *The Life and Work of John Nash, Architect*, London, Allen and Unwin, 1980

In addition, the annual catalogues issued by the Royal Pavilion, Art Gallery and Museums,
Brighton, contain much information, including a detailed post-1830 history of the building
by Mr John Dinkel, Deputy Director.

Acknowledgments

This book depends, more than most, on the readiness of owners to allow their possessions to be illustrated. The Repton and other drawings kept in the Royal Library at Windsor are reproduced by gracious permission of Her Majesty The Queen, as are quotations from documents in the Royal Archives. Others who must be thanked include Mrs Lisa Taylor, Director of the Cooper-Hewitt Museum, New York, for permission to study and illustrate the unrivalled designs in its possession; Mrs J.F.Crace, who gave the author and photographer unlimited access to her book of Crace drawings; the Corporation of Brighton, which has both a large group of drawings given by Mr John Crace and many of the studies made by Augustus Pugin for the 'Nash' book; and the Victoria and Albert Museum, which allowed study of its Crace material and reproduction of drawings.

The author thanks Mr Derek Shrub, who manoeuvred him into a position where he had no alternative but to write this book, and Mr Geoffrey de Bellaigue, cvo, who undertook the labour of reading it in typescript – the errors that remain after the latter's searching inquest are the author's. The author has found most useful the discussions he and the Hon. Mrs Jane Roberts have had on various points. Mr C.E.Crace, to whom the author was introduced by Mr Michael Sherrard, supplied a copy of the Crace genealogy. Miss Joanna Warrand began the trail that led, through the Rev. Alan Crace, to the discovery of Mrs J.F.Crace's book of drawings by Frederick Crace. Miss Jane Langton, mvo, Registrar of the Royal Archives, has been unfailingly helpful; Sir Robin Mackworth-Young, kcvo, has allowed frequent intrusion into the Royal Library. Mrs Elaine Evans Dee, Curator of Drawings at the Cooper-Hewitt Museum, was generous of her time.

Others who have helped in material ways include Mr Ian Askew, Miss Elaine Baird (formerly of the Brighton Reference Library), Lord Briggs, Mr John Harris, Lady Johnston, Colonel A.J.P.Lincoln (Clerk to The Worshipful Company of Painter-Stainers), Miss Henrietta McBurney, Mrs Joan McDowell, Dr Clifford Musgrave, Miss Merribell Parsons (The Metropolitan Museum, New York), Mr Derek Rogers, and Mr Dudley Snelgrove. The author thanks his own staff for support – Mr John Dinkel, Miss Caroline Dudley, Dr Patrick Conner, and Miss Jessica Rutherford; he is especially grateful to Miss Marion Waller who brought, through the agency of Mrs Mavis Batey, Repton material to his notice, and to Mrs Batey herself, who allowed him to use the result of her researches into the Pavilion gardens. He thanks Mr Clive Wainwright, Mr Simon Jervis, and Mr John Hardy for having thrown down an Ariadne's thread through the labyrinth of the Victoria and Albert Museum, the Paul Mellon Centre for Studies in British Art for a grant for travel to New York, and Brighton Corporation for permission to write this book (in his own time).

Last, but not least, he wishes to thank his wife for her unfailing support and help, and for her removal of solecisms from the text.

Outline of Events and Relevant Plans

The plans that follow demonstrate the extent of the growth of the Royal Pavilion, and the altered disposition of rooms within it, from 1787 to 1826; they are here given in a group to enable the reader easily to take up the references to them within the text. Full documentary details of the plans are given at the beginning of the 'Catalogue of Illustrations'. Also, it may suit the reader's convenience to give here, very briefly, the main stages in that evolution, which are greatly expanded in the text:

October 1786
    First lease taken of the farmhouse later to become the Royal Pavilion

April–July 1787
    The farmhouse enlarged and rebuilt by Henry Holland as the 'Marine Pavilion'

1801–4
    Enlargement of the Marine Pavilion by Henry Holland and P.F.Robinson; Crace firm employed on the interior

1803–8
    Building of the Stables and Riding House by William Porden

March 1815–1823
    Enlargement and rebuilding of the Royal Pavilion by Nash; Crace firm employed on interior

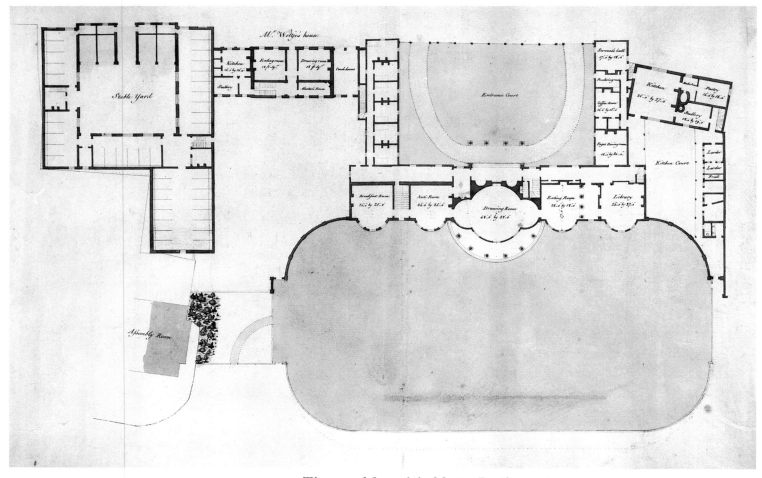

A *The ground floor of the Marine Pavilion, 1787.*

B *The first floor of the Marine Pavilion, 1787.*

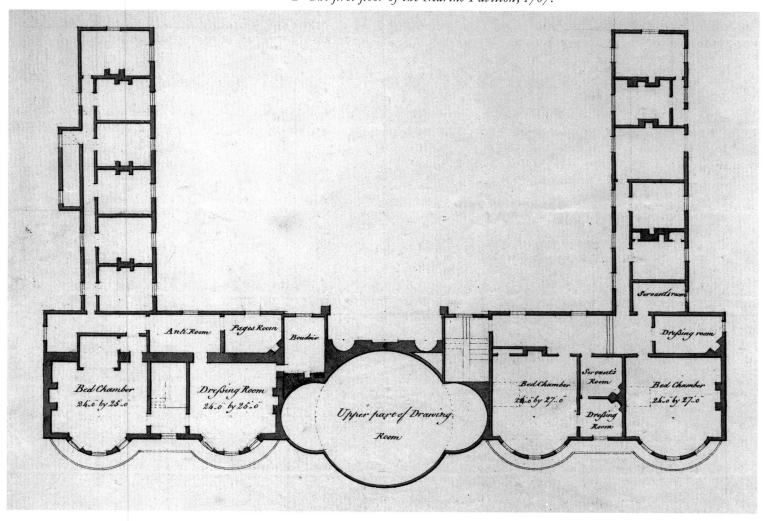

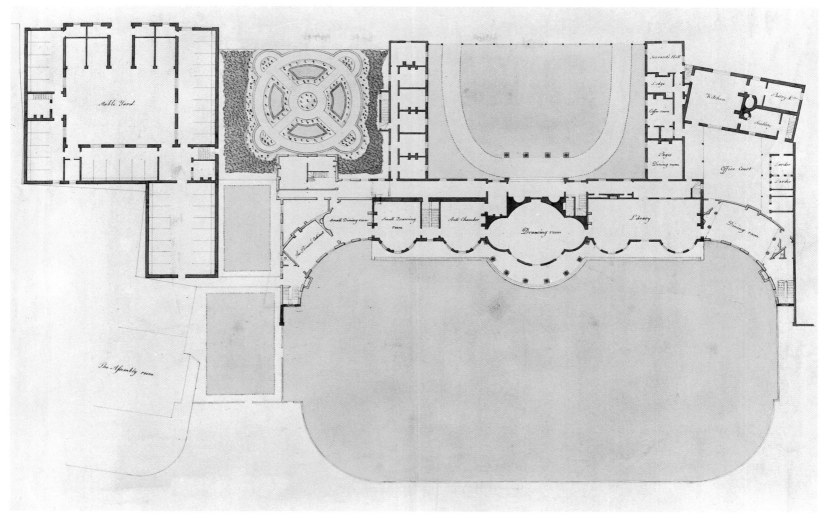

c *The ground floor of the Marine Pavilion, 1795, with proposed alterations.*

d *The first floor of the Marine Pavilion, 1795, with proposed alterations.*

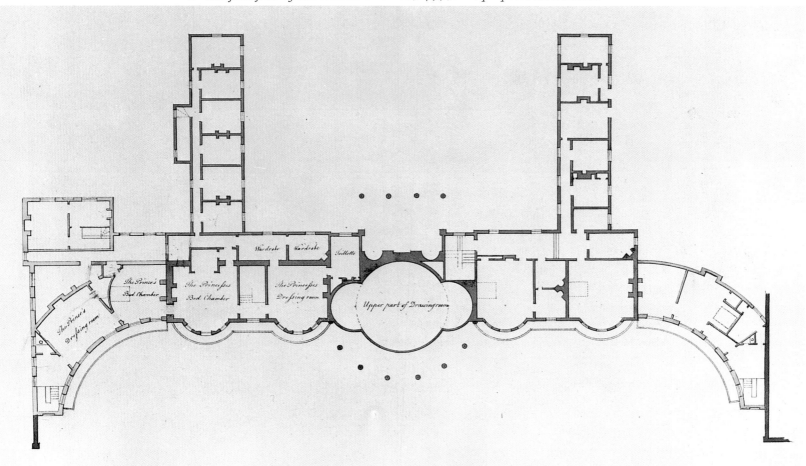

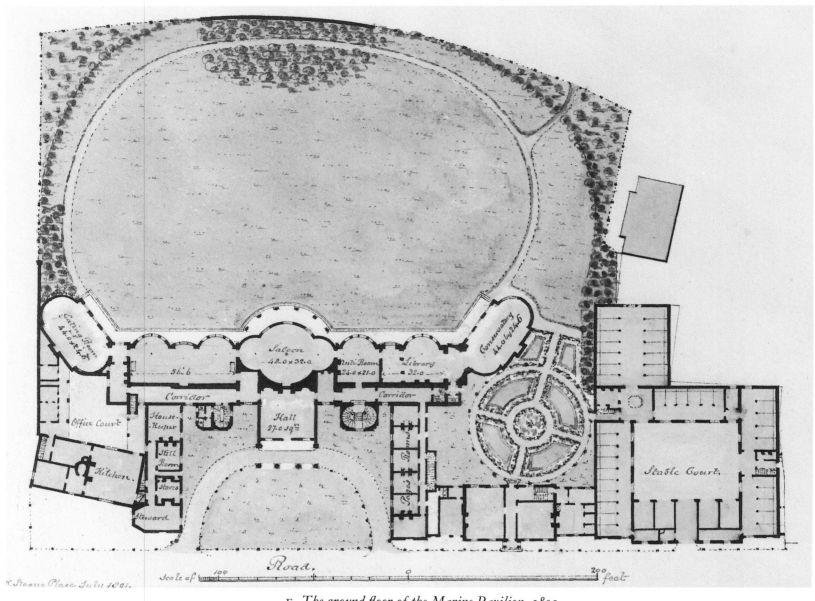

E *The ground floor of the Marine Pavilion, 1801.*

F *The first floor of the Marine Pavilion, 1801.*

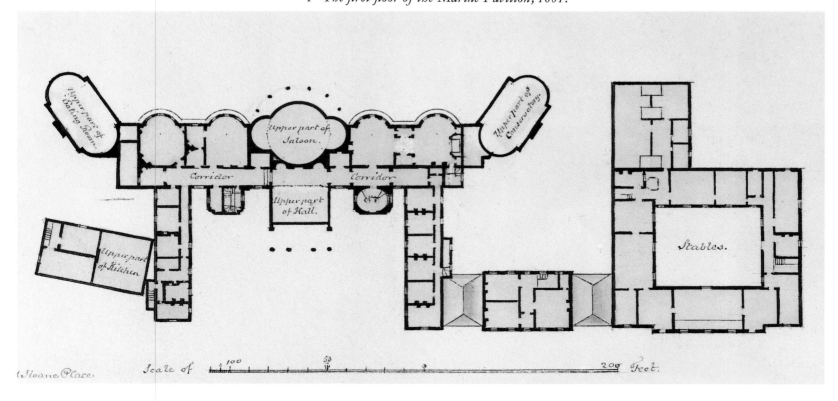

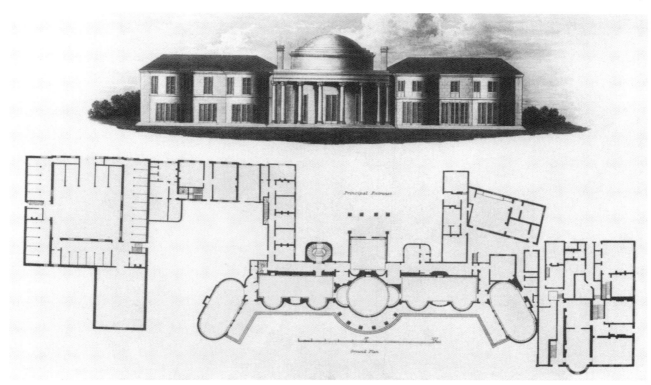

G *The ground floor of the Pavilion and East Front elevation, 1815.*

H *The ground floor of the Pavilion, 1815–22, and a design for the Gardens.*

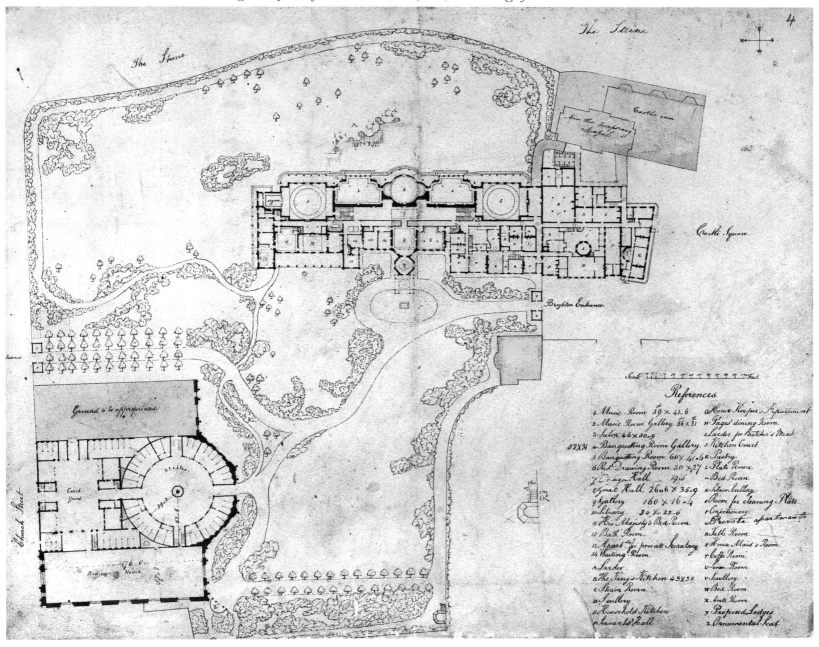

HIS ROYAL HIGHNESS GEORGE PRINCE of WALES

R:dus Cosway. R:A:et Primarius Pictor Serenifsimi Walliæ Principis delin:t et Excut

L. Sailliar Sc.

THE PATRON

His royal status apart, the principal begetter of the Royal Pavilion was not an ordinary man. King George IV was, in the original sense of the term, a monster: 'a prodigy, a marvel, a portent; something abnormal, out of the ordinary course of nature; compounded of incongruous parts.' That such monstrous terms can be applied with justice to his favourite creation, the Royal Pavilion, is hardly surprising.

From all that we know of George IV, the likelihood emerges that this extraordinary character was to some extent the result of a deliberate act of will, and that he formed for himself a style that influenced every action. An examination of character and style illumines his aesthetic intentions, and consequently the nature of his relationships with artists, decorators, and architects.

A prominent element in his character was that of the masquerader; it is likely that he saw himself, as an actor sees himself, filling the role of a prince or king. He was a spectator of his own actions; sometimes he so moved himself that he wept, a trait shared with other self-spectators. He played the royal actor directly, as well as indirectly; it was his habit to mimic people as he quoted them, and at times he acted them, and 'actually made himself look like the parties'.[1] His powers of sympathetic intuition, allied to the actor's power of judging the temper of his audience, are evident in a discussion between Croker and the Duke of Wellington in 1828 of the King's 'wonderful knowledge of character and his art of guessing what any one is about to say to him' (they agreed also that he was unequalled in his power of exhibiting in his imitations 'the mental character')[2].

These interests extended to private theatricals, a taste he shared with Nash and Lawrence; an inborn sense of the dramatic is to be seen in the careers of all three. Masquerades gave opportunities for the exotic; in 1791, for instance, he found Mrs Bristow at Fulham dressed as the Queen of Nourjahad, smoking her hookah in her drawing room, 'very beautifully fitted up with cushions in the Indian style' – a description paralleled in Cruikshank's cartoon of thirty years later, showing the King seated amongst the Chinese delights of his Pavilion.[3] He himself designed masquerade clothes; a sketch of 1783 or earlier exists in his own hand, a figure in a yellow uniform with flowered blue sash and jewelled sword (does one already see the liking for complementary colours?).[4] It may seem a long step from these frivolities to his demeanour at the funeral of Queen Charlotte in 1818 – or perhaps not. On that occasion, his majestic carriage, and fine commanding figure dressed in an 'inky cloak' of 'a great amplitude of folds', appeared most striking, as did 'a star of brilliants, shining most resplendently among his sables, above which he wore four collars of knighthood. Thus did his love of show and splendour accompany him even to the grave of his mother.'[5] He would have deemed this aulic splendour appropriate to the event; whether it were a masquerade, a funeral, a Coronation, or a Pavilion, the same careful planning and execution, and the same actor–manager's attention to details of gesture, costume, and scene, are alike evident.

To the talents of the actor was added the self-preoccupation of the narcissist. George IV saw the impedimenta of living – palaces, horses, carriages, and dress – as part of himself. A perceptive critic has said, 'If one wanted to make a list of the great narcissists of history, I dare say one would discover that all of them liked the most sumptuous and elegant in decoration.'[6] Of none was this more true than of George IV. A metaphor drawn from his own world seems apt; his personality resembles that optical effect of which he was so fond, and which one encounters in so many of the brilliant interiors he brought into existence, whereby the placing of one mirror diametrically opposite another causes every image, person and surroundings to be reflected into infinity; for the illusion to be perfect, the spectator has himself to be placed squarely in the centre of the glass. George IV did that as a matter of course.

This narcissism was compounded by another quality present in his composition; a certain exaggeration, emotional and aesthetic, that has in it a tincture almost of madness. The excesses in which this exaggeration was manifested were often destructive; they were often intensely creative. They were magnified by his position as heir apparent, as king – the apex of the hierarchical pyramid. The effect on his character was profound, accentuated by the archaism always present in a royal court.

George IV, born in 1762, was thirty years of age by the time the French Revolution had consumed the most famous dynasty of Europe. *Ancien régime* by style and temperament, he became increasingly so, a process hardly discouraged by his growing self-identification with Louis XIV, to whom he was likened in a eulogy published in 1815.[7] Archaism began with his own person; the 'Maecenas of tailors'[8] had as absorbing an interest in dress as in decoration (his majority was celebrated by his invention of a shoe buckle,[9] then a focus of fashionable interest, and later in his career he was considered an expert on 'fit' – he himself invented the 'button stand', employed to this day).[10] But fashionable though he desired to be, his style less and less accommodated itself to prevailing tendencies. His rich and elaborate clothes, his curled wigs, paint, stays and perfumes attracted ridicule, although the artifice often worked; as late as 1829 Madame du Cayla, the mistress of Louis XVIII, expressed astonishment at 'ses belles jámbes et sa perruque bien arrangée'.[11]

In a similar fashion, archaistic attitudes affected his aesthetic preferences. Not only in detail, as his passionate assemblage of French furniture and objets d'art, 'old-fashioned' in his day, but in, for instance, his transformation of the drawing rooms at Windsor into those of the grandest French châteaux, or in his rejection of the doctrinaire neo-classicism that had been tainted with republicanism. Even his adoption of the Chinese idiom at Carlton House and Brighton can be viewed in this light; far from being the *dernier cri*, it had been in and out of fashion for well over a hundred years; he himself, at the age of twelve days, had been first contemplated by the populace through the screen of a Chinese lattice,[12] and the New Japan Room at Buckingham House, decorated in the year of his birth, had been familiar to him from early years.[13] His mother and sisters themselves had indulged in the amateur art of japanning.

It is a revealing idiosyncrasy that he was the last of England's kings (before the age of safari parks revived the fashion) to keep a royal menagerie. Various strange beasts were maintained; towards the end of his life he fell in love with the strangest – a giraffe. The infatuation became notorious; the cartoonists who parodied his bulk, his mistresses, his dress, his buildings, included the giraffe as an object of humour. Is it really remarkable that such a man loved such an animal, the fabled 'camelopard' of earlier times, an animal in which unbelievable exaggeration is united with extreme distinction of style?

One thus sees in George IV a potent combination of narcissism, archaism, exaggeration – and royalty; together with an exacting sense of style that informed all he did and extended to the most trivial details (in 1829 the victor of Waterloo and Greville spent half an hour endeavouring to 'fold a letter to His Majesty in a particular way – for he will have his envelopes made up in some French fashion'.)[14] It made a remarkable mixture. Added to it was aesthetic sensitivity and an absorbing passion for building, decoration, and collecting; the result was dazzling.

By the 1790s he was at his apogee; his 'elegance of manners, his superb person, his exquisite taste in dress, as well as in the fitting up of his palaces, his equipages and entertainments, were the theme of general praise and the objects of imitation'.[15] So wrote a hostile critic; these multiplied as time went on, and as with age and self-indulgence the façade crumbled. Princess Lieven, one of his most intelligent friends, described him, in a remarkable piece of analysis, as he appeared in the 1820s: 'Unquestionably he had some wit, and great penetration; he quickly summed up persons and things; he was educated and had much tact, easy, animated and varied conversation, not at all pedantic. He adorned the subjects he touched, he knew how to listen, he was very polished. For my part I had never known a person like him, who was also affectionate, sympathetic, and galant. But he was full of vanity and could be flattered at will. Weary of all the joys of life, *having only taste* [my italics], not one true sentiment, he was hardly susceptible to attachment, and never I believe sincerely inspired anybody with it. . . .'[16]

The picture that emerges is consistent. It is that of a man completely self-absorbed; a man with fine sentiments but a cold heart, who none the less had the gift and the desire to create an illusion not only for himself but for others; a man of great 'tact' ('perception', in modern parlance) and subtlety, well used to having his own way; a man to whom style was everything. This self absorption and style remained when all else had fallen away; in 1826 in the King's composition were to be found 'general disgust, boredom, and superlative vanity. His portrait would be the strangest in the world.'[17]

As a builder, George IV was in the same league as Catherine the Great or Ludwig of Bavaria; as a collector, he was the equal of Cardinal Mazarin or King Charles I. He brought, to the business of patronage, a mind as original and as venturesome as those of Burlington, Beckford, and Hope; none could have been more exigent or more particular in their demands than he; none could have been less concerned at the cost, in time or money, of attaining them.

An eclectic period like that of the late eighteenth and early nineteenth centuries gives the patron more choice, and therefore more power, than one in which the rule of taste is stricter. The first and most influential choice exercised by the patron is that of an architect, and perhaps a decorator, to carry out his wishes (it was during this period that the two became separate – Thomas Hope was the first to use the term 'interior decoration'). The architects patronised by George IV were not, Holland excepted, amongst the most discriminating of their period, but they were flexible and open to suggestion.

Flexibility was necessary to conjure up an opium dream beside the English Channel, or the most obsessively overgrown Cottage in existence, or even the most romantic castellated silhouette – on a huge scale – in the world at Windsor. There is no doubt that the common element in these uncommon productions sprang, fully armed, from the personality of George IV himself, and that his architects and decorators were used as instruments; it is strikingly evident that the buildings produced for him were not typical of the usual work of their architects, although naturally they bear their impress. It seems as if, in working for George IV, architects were impelled to push their respective styles to their limits, to exaggerate them to a point that stops just short of where excess becomes caricature (in the case of the original east front of Buckingham Palace it *did* become caricature, and was pulled down as a result.)

This exaggeration is as evident in the interiors, in the breathtakingly daring later chinoiserie interiors of the Pavilion, or in the 'Louis' and mediaeval revivals of Windsor – as it is with the exteriors; it is even true, as far as one can discern, of the fripperies of Holland's Chinese Drawing Room at Carlton House, and it is certainly true of the voluptuous redressings of that 'chaste palace' under the influence of Walsh Porter. Such exaggerations are a mark of high style and boundless confidence; they had become more difficult to stomach in the mercantile times of George iv; Stratfield Saye, in its patched up form, was the Blenheim of the early nineteenth century. Patrons such as Beckford and Hope invited, and often received, ridicule, as did George iv.

It is almost as interesting to consider which architects George iv did not select as those whom he did. His long avoidance of Chambers, for instance, may have been the result not only of the latter's involvement with his father; he probably found him too sober and masculine in style, despite his Chinese essays. That could not have been said of Wyatt, whose temperament and abilities seem of a variety congenial to George iv, but Wyatt also became involved with the old King, who suffered an architectural mania in the first years of the new century in which vast sums were wasted. When George iv did, as Prince Regent, finally capture Wyatt for his purposes at the Pavilion, the latter was almost immediately killed in a carriage accident; the Prince paid him the tribute of tears. One regrets the missed opportunity of seeing the results of their collaboration; Wyatt had a certain finesse lacking in Nash. As had other architects, unfortunately not in the Prince's idiom. Of these one of the most distinguished was Soane; his austere and pared down neo-classicism was not likely to appeal to the Prince; the same is probably true of such less individual architects as Wilkins and Smirke.

The variety of styles encompassed within his patronage indicates, in the King himself, a catholicity of taste that carried to an extreme the tendencies of his age; it demonstrates, despite the beauty of individual productions, the frivolity of a decadent taste. His buildings and interiors have every virtue save that of nobility. This last quality might have been given by the major styles that he did *not* employ – the Egyptian, the extreme neo-classic, and the full-blown French Empire. All may have been open to some political objection, for him if not for others. The fact that he was alive to such meanings is apparent in his often quoted witticism to Lady Bessborough, that he chose the Chinese style at Brighton because he was afraid that his French furniture would be accused of jacobinism.[18]

This was all the more a renunciation in that George iv remained, throughout his life, in matters of taste a convinced francophile; the constant wars with France did not, despite his heartfelt patriotism, shake that taste one iota. He was an eclectic in francophilism as in everything else. The grandeurs of Louis xiv boulle (accurately copied by Louis Legaigneur), the verve of Louis xv rococo, and the sophisticated restraint of Louis xvi neo-classicism were all to be found, in various versions and with other ingredients, in the North Drawing Room at Brighton (see p. 139). He patronised the Jacob family, and his attempts to purchase the sumptuous, high Empire 'Table des Grands Capitaines' prompted Louis xviii to offer it as a gift;[19] the superb desk in his bedroom at Brighton (see p. 228) was another trophy. French furniture of one kind or another was at the heart of most of his decorating schemes. Although he spent lavishly, his advanced taste meant that often he spent wisely; for example the jewel cabinet of the Comtesse de Provence, a Louis xvi piece by Riesener of unsurpassed luxury which was said to have cost 80,000 francs to make and which was rejected in 1811 by Napoleon as old-fashioned, was bought by George iv in 1825 for £420.[20] Most of the French furniture he acquired came considerably cheaper than this.

Other pieces were made especially for him, and again in a variety of styles.

Some of the heavy giltwood furniture made by Tatham and Bailey, and by Morel and Seddon, for Carlton House and Windsor in the last two decades of his life, seems proto-Victorian in weight and solidity, although it never becomes so floridly coarse in detail. The chinoiserie furniture made for the Pavilion between 1802 and 1822 ran the whole gamut of taste, and he did not hesitate to place, next to the delicate Frenchified chinoiserie cabinets of Marsh and Tatham, a set of Indian ivory-veneered chairs and settees, in the Chippendale style, bought at the sale that followed the death of Queen Charlotte. Boulle, rococo, and neo-classical clocks, many in gilt bronze, and many given new movements and sometimes additional ornaments by Vulliamy, jostled on chimneypieces and cabinets with thronged examples of oriental and French porcelains, also mounted in gilt bronze. On the dragon-wreathed sideboards and on the large centre table in the Pavilion's exuberant Banqueting Room stood silver gilt vessels in strict Empire taste. The mixture makes up an extraordinary ensemble, but the result was the reverse of aesthetic chaos. Unlike other eclectic collectors, such as Walpole, or even Soane, George IV rarely bought objects only for associational meanings; aesthetic attraction usually played a part.

His taste in paintings was catholic, but less adventurous; he showed the special fondness for Dutch and Flemish cabinet pictures that was a feature of the most luxurious strain in mid-eighteenth century French taste, and that was shared with other contemporary collectors of old French furniture (he was well aware of a truth enunciated – in another context – by Mrs Proudie, that 'large rooms when full of people and full of light look well . . . small rooms are those which require costly fittings and rich furniture'.)[21] Oddly enough, he was not interested in French rococo painting. The Pavilion at Brighton, with its complete and utter absence of easel paintings, is a striking illustration of how single-minded George IV, who passionately loved painting, could be in pursuance of stylistic unity. The blank walls – except for gilding – of the two drawing rooms are eloquent of the fact that George IV, whose stylistic fault was profusion, could accept restraint.

For his judgment was not perfect; the strengths and weaknesses of the royal patron are appropriately caught in the portraits, 'tawdry and beautiful' (the phrase is Thackeray's),[22] by Lawrence. The glitter and artifice of the theatre was brought, beyond the footlights, to a proximity too near to the spectator. It was an age when magnificence easily became overblown, and George IV, on whose yacht 'even the blocks carrying the ladders and the rigging are fully *gilt*',[23] was not the man to escape infection.

As a collector, he preferred rich and elaborate objects and furniture; the design of his interiors was influenced by these objects, which were often placed in context at an early stage; the series of designs for the private apartments at Windsor, for example, shows individual pieces placed in appropriate settings.[24] The *Pictorial Inventory of George IV*, a series of watercolours of objects in inventory form compiled in the 1820s, was probably a useful tool in deciding how things were to be done. Everything was seen as a whole; the paintings hung in the Corridor at Windsor, one of the grandest schemes executed by George IV, were especially enclosed in Crouzet frames as an aid to unifying the scheme. There is evidence at Brighton that, quite apart from the instances where new furniture was expressly made for a particular room, as with the magnificent giltwood seat furniture for the Music Room, or Robert Jones' exotically inventive cabinets for the Saloon, there was also an express intention stylistically to integrate old furniture and objects into new settings; this is most clearly seen in the gilded wall decoration of the two Drawing Rooms, drawn from the Weisweiler wall furniture and other objects to be placed in them (see p. 129), but is present also in such little touches as the repetition on the walls of the Saloon of the sunflower from the 'Kylin Clock', as amended by Vulliamy.

George IV used every source possible to acquire objects, and every kind of agent. Some, such as Sir Charles Long, afterwards Lord Farnborough, were friends who influenced his taste: 'the Prince Regent saw through Mr Long's spectacles.'[25] The Prince haunted the sale rooms with Lord Yarmouth, another devotee of old French furniture: he used dealers, English and French, especially the Parisian *marchands merciers*; members of his own household, many, like Benois, of French birth; diplomatists, many of whom were aware of his tastes and would write from Rome, Naples, Paris or elsewhere with news of some 'find' that might be added to his collection. He himself frequently bought from shops and auction rooms, attending the latter himself. A great amount of the furniture and decorative accessories for the early chinoiserie schemes at Brighton was imported directly from China, and one must admit that the lists of miscellaneous objects seen in the Crace accounts at this time give a sense of a wholesale and indiscriminate rage for acquisition. The means used were not always beyond reproach: 'in bribing the Hoppos and their underlings in China, for conniving at the bringing out of pictures of their customs and particularly the Emperor's Court — Armour of all kinds — Mandarine Dresses — flags . . . and wrought metal of every description — Lanterns, etc. etc.'[26] The use of such material declined as the schemes for the Pavilion became richer and more sophisticated, and the interiors finally shown in Nash's *Views* contain only the scantiest remains — the ivory ship models seen in the South Galleries, for instance (see [274]).

George IV was always in direct intercourse, on more than equal terms, with his architects and decorators — constantly at their elbows (see p. 120); designing (see [240]); making technical suggestions (see p. 110); ordering, and no doubt cajoling with his well known 'condescension'; often rejecting, as is seen over and over again in frequent changes of mind and changes of scheme (see p. 119). He perhaps divided in order to rule, as has been tentatively suggested of the ambiguous Daguerre/Holland relationship at Carlton House;[27] this may be equally the case with the Nash/Crace/Robert Jones relationship at Brighton. Accepted designs often bear, on the margin, his signed approval, or other pertinent comments. His own designs, or the few that remain, have a nervous, broken line that never assumes any fluency of expression.

There is a remarkable lack of letters in his own hand to architects and decorators. This may be due to some detail of protocol, or it may, more simply, have been the case that he was in such constant personal communication with such people that letters were unnecessary.

The situation for patronage appears near ideal, given such lofty station, such abilities, and such inclinations. It was not, for at most periods of his life he was straitened for money. When, in 1783, he came of age, the King his father — who already distrusted the heir whose brilliant and flamboyant character was in such contrast to his own domestic virtues, and whom in course of time he was to hate 'with a hatred scarcely consistent with the supposition of a sound mind'[28] — asked for an allocation for the Prince of Wales of £50,000 a year. This was half of the £100,000 allocated to the Prince's grandfather as Prince of Wales. The King gave the Prince an establishment to maintain that was far beyond his income: 'it was a maxim of the King and Queen to keep their sons out of vice by keeping them poor, and to retain them in obedience by making them dependent.'[29] This simply did not work, and led to disaster. Extravagant and expansive by nature, and with

1 Longitudinal section of the Pavilion.

From John Nash, Views of the Royal Pavilion, Brighton *(1826).* CAT. NO. 37.

no aversion to disorder, the Prince of Wales succumbed to all the allurements of a polished and corrupt society; paid far less than his predecessors, he was placed in the same situation and exposed to the same expense. Far more than any non-royal magnate, he was expected to be, and was prepared to be, fashionable, hospitable, and to lead society. He went further; he 'carried magnificence to profusion'.[30]

The great aristocrats of the 1780s and 1790s, having inherited, had usually some £40,000 to £50,000 a year to spend.[31] The Prince of Wales, with his sense of the need of a splendid setting, had to find the money to pay for it. Even had he taken the most extreme care, £50,000 a year would hardly have sufficed; for a man of prodigal temperament it was impossible. This was a period (1779) when Lord Grosvenor could spend £7000 a year on racing[32] (a great passion with the Prince at this time): building (another, and longer lived passion) was even more expensive. Beckford spent £400,000 or so on Fonthill; Lord Ailesbury (in 1821) spent £250,000 on Tottenham Court; the Duke of Bedford (in 1810) spent £70,000 to £80,000 on Endsleigh, a cottage ornée of no great size.[33] The Prince Regent, in 1819, refused to attempt to build a new palace in the metropolis with the £150,000 that Lord Liverpool informed him might be found[34] on the grounds that it was insufficient. It has been estimated that the grand total of moneys spent on the Pavilion, for all building and decoration purposes, during George IV's lifetime, amounted to at least £502,000.[35]

George IV's household and ministers were, throughout his career, conscious of the incompatability of his building and furniture mania with the need to keep within his income. The theme is constant. In 1784, the year after the Prince's majority, Colonel Hotham wrote of his grief and vexation at seeing His Royal Highness 'totally in the hands, and at the mercy of your builder, your upholsterer, your jeweller and your tailor'.[36] By 1792 matters had got completely out of control, and the great crash came; the Prince's debts were taken into parliamentary care. Indebtedness in the eighteenth century was common; indebtedness to the point of crisis was rare, and especially reprehensible in a royal personage. The crisis was never forgotten.

At the beginning of the final, and most ambitious, programme at the Pavilion, an especially determined effort was made by Lords Liverpool, Castlereagh, and Vansittart to stop it; in March 1816 they referred to the fact that 'no subject is viewed with more jealousy and suspicion than the personal expenses of the Sovereign...'; they deplored the 'expenses incurred at Brighton in the course of this last year...'; they foresaw disturbances, and declared that the only means of 'weathering the impending storm is by stating ... that all new expenses for additions or alterations at Brighton or elsewhere will, under the present circumstances, be abandoned'.[37] Fortunately for posterity, the sage advice of the politicians went unheeded. One point of the tirade was that the Pavilion was, and had always been, a private venture. All the work done by Holland had been paid for from the Prince's privy purse; lack of money meant that the building already on the site in 1787 was converted, and not entirely rebuilt, and was thereafter added to in a piecemeal fashion. When a completely fresh start was made, as with Porden's Stables, agonising shortages and even suicides were the result. Lack of supervision by the Lord Commissioners of the Treasury did not mean that the ministers abandoned all efforts at control; after 1816, however, the enterprise had been launched, and expostulation was really the only recourse left open to them. In a sense, the dénouement came after George IV's death, when Nash was subjected to the hostile questioning of the parliamentary investigation into the overspendings on Buckingham Palace.

The clamour and the tumult now survive only in the researches of historians and in the unattractive (and fast decaying) bundles of invoices in the Public Record Office. The buildings remain; not in their first splendour, but splendid enough to excite wonder by that very contempt for the established rules, and that lack of restraint, that incurred such censure in the past. The Prince himself must have been much aware of the 'unofficial' nature of his Brighton enterprise; a marine caprice paid for from the private funds of an elevated gentleman on holiday by the sea.

This knowledge may possibly have contributed to the complete insouciance with which he embarked on so extraordinary a building in so 'unofficial' a style; it displays his virtues, and perhaps his faults, to an unexampled degree. Its utter lack of restraint; its wild minglings of various exoticisms, a soufflée of Chinese, Indian, French and English motifs; its daring and extreme colour harmonies, which give the frisson of approaching discordance; its lavish use of gold in every form and in every material; its sybaritic luxury; its brilliant and witty use of *faux* surfaces: all seem a reflection of the character, a summation of the personality, of George IV himself, even to the slightly dubious flavour that now and then escapes, causing one to question, with some trepidation, its nature. An extraordinary person had reproduced himself in an extraordinary building, a building of which the delights, as he reflected on them, made him 'cry for joy'.[38]

2 The Marine Pavilion, East Front, 1788. CAT. NO. I.

THE EXTERIOR

3 *The Marine Pavilion, West Front, 1788.* CAT. NO. 2.

Henry Holland and the Marine Pavilion

The Marine Pavilion, the first of the structures erected on the site that was later to bear the more grandiose Royal Pavilion, was erected between April and July 1787 [2, 3].

The charms of Brighton, described as a place where 'the sinews of morality are so happily relaxed, that a bawd and a baroness may snore in the same tenement',[1] had seduced the Prince on his first visit, in 1783. In October 1786 the plot of ground on which the Marine Pavilion was to stand first came, vicariously, into his hands, when his general factotum, Weltje, took a three year lease of a 'genteel farmhouse' that stood on the Steine, an open area where fishermen dried their nets within sight of the sea; the building was immediately sublet to the Prince (it was purchased only in 1807, some years after Weltje's death).[2]

The 'farmhouse' is not pictured, although a later source called it 'a pretty and picturesque little fabric, in a small piece of ground, where a few shrubs and roses shut out the road, and the eye looked unobstructed over the ocean'.[3] (This original house, short though its life in the Prince's possession was to be, may have had an appeal; he later built his own Cottage, and even a sophisticated foreigner could confess to having been moved by this 'insipid style of architecture', and that 'little houses . . . decorated with rose trees . . . had a genuinely elegiac quality'.)[4] Its basic structure of flint, with two bay (not bow) windows, still exists within the present palace.

The architect of the new Marine Pavilion was Henry Holland (1745–1806), the most fastidious and refined of all the architects who worked for George IV. He was much influenced by contemporary French architecture, which excelled in those qualities. His style, as he aged, progressively discarded decorative motifs in favour of a pared down elegance that relied much upon proportion and understatement for effect. His development did not, in this, keep pace with that of the Prince of Wales. Moreover, his buildings did not have the attribute of bravura, or indeed triumphalism, that is so noticeable in the taste of George IV. The latter found he was expressing himself architecturally through, so to speak, a Mozart, or at least a Gluck, whereas a Rossini would have better suited him.

Holland had, from the end of 1783, remodelled Carlton House for the Prince of Wales; the work received the applause of the fashionable world. The Prince had seen his own part in the work as far from passive: 'I am hard at work upon my mansion at Carlton House . . . I . . . hope on your return you will not think me a bad architect.'[5] He was pleased enough with the results to employ Holland at Brighton, in the year (1787) when the interior decorations at Carlton House had just begun.

The new enterprise was fairly modest: the cost, including £5850 for buildings on the site and adjacent, is given in an undated, abstracted account as a total of £20,841;[6] this included various sums of expenditure on interior decoration and

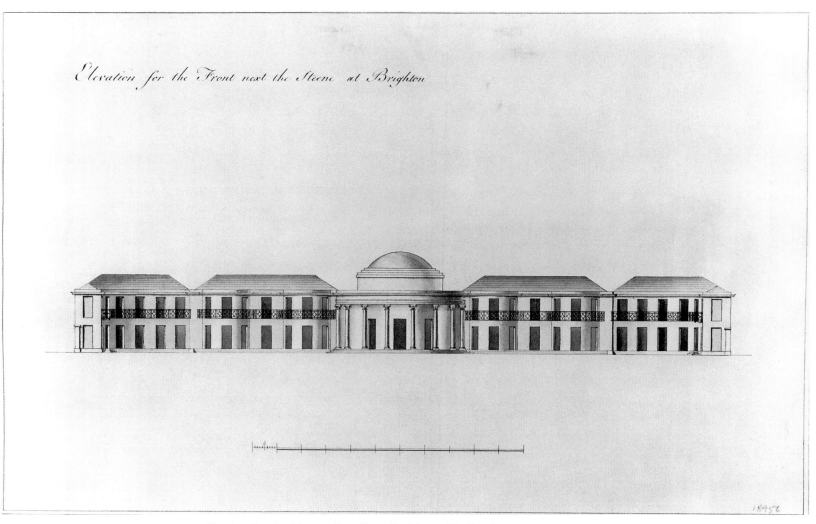

Elevation for the Front next the Steene at Brighton

4 Design for the Marine Pavilion. By Henry Holland, 1795. CAT. NO. 3.

furniture. Plan A shows the disposition of the ground floor as built. The formal
pivot of the design was a circular room, extended in semi-circles to the north
and south; known originally as the 'Drawing Room', its ceremonial function was
soon to be recognised by the adoption of the term 'Saloon' (it was thus named
in the plan of 1801). South of the Drawing Room lay the original farmhouse;
it was remodelled and divided, on the ground floor, into two rooms known as
the 'Breakfast Room' and the 'Anti Room'; a staircase divided them. North of
the Drawing Room, a duplicate wing balanced the composition; it contained an
'Eating Room' and a 'Library'. On the west side, ranges of other rooms formed
two wings enclosing a courtyard; along the western side of the main range ran
a corridor, interrupted by an entrance hall, from north to south. Saloon, corridor,
and east front alike were to survive to become major ingredients of the Nash
building.

    The first floor (plan B, inscribed 'Hertford Street Nov. 1787' – *after* the building
had been erected) shows how simple, and how limited in accommodation, the
Marine Pavilion was. The Prince's bedchamber and dressing room lay south of
the Drawing Room. A bill, rendered by Holland after alterations in 1801, makes

clear that the Prince's rooms on the upper floor were regarded as en suite with those on the ground floor beneath them, with which they were connected by a staircase; the 'Anti Room' was the ante room not to the Drawing Room but to the Breakfast Room, which must have been used as the Prince's 'cabinet'.

The external appearance of the early Holland building is amply recorded. A major contribution to the total effect came from the cream-glazed Hampshire tiles that faced the walls, some of which still exist under the stucco of the Saloon. These were being used in that same year (1787) at Althorp and on Holland's own house, Sloane Place; the use of such tiles had become more common after 1784, when a brick tax was imposed from which tiles were exempt; they were not particularly cheap, although they went further in use. One's impression is that Holland liked them for their own sake.

The views of the East [2] and West [3] fronts of the Marine Pavilion have the air not of architectural drawings but of depictions of a building actually erected; the first has half curtains at all the windows save those of the Saloon (a custom continued throughout royal occupation), whilst the second shows some blinds open, some closed, with a rather strange mass of vegetation in the portico that, surely, no architectural draughtsman ever invented. On the roof are placed eight statues. The drawings are undated.

The earliest dated print of the east façade, by Charles Middleton (June 1788; not illustrated) has an intriguing detail – the statues were inserted (in etching) at a later date than the rest of the print (in engraving); also the top line of the platform is visible through the bases of the statues (this was first noticed by Mr Derek Rogers). Moreover, a Coade catalogue published in 1799 notes that six statues were placed on the outside of the Pavilion in 1788.

It may have been that the haste with which the building was erected (April to July 1787) made it impossible to obtain the statues in time. However, a royal order would perhaps have been given some priority, and it seems just as possible that the statues were an afterthought. The question may have some bearing on the theory that 'an echo of the Hotel de Salm' [in Paris] 'was also to be found in the Prince's villa at Brighton. . . . This was given a domed bay on the garden side, with Ionic columns supporting an entablature over which were placed statues very much in the manner of the French mansion.'[7] It is interesting that the Hotel de Salm has been seen as an influence also on Buckingham Palace, which enjoyed a different architect (Nash) but the same patron.

The use of statues in such a position as at Brighton was not uncommon in France; it never became an obvious Holland motif, despite his francophilism, and the statues are omitted from Holland's design of 1795 [4]. There was, however, somebody else concerned in the matter who was just as francophile as Holland, and with a cast of mind considerably more addicted to bravura ornament – the Prince. If the statues were an afterthought, were they perhaps a royal afterthought?

If so, it seems that the Prince may have regretted them. Their omission from the design of 1795 could hardly have occurred had disapprobation not been expressed, and they were removed in the alterations of 1801–4. And indeed, on close scrutiny the combination of the formal central portico, its formality increased but its restraint contradicted by the statues, with the easy simplicity of the bow-windowed wings, does give one some unease, the feeling of a dichotomy of styles in one building.

It is possible that the distinction between the central domed portico and the wings helped in the adoption of the term 'pavilion' for the whole building; Chambers defines pavilions as 'sometimes also projecting pieces in the front of a building, marking the middle thereof'.[8] This does not, of course, mean that general francophilism may not have assisted the use of the word.

The structure later gave trouble; damp and dry rot occurred, and it is possible that the encasement of an older building did not make Holland's task any easier. However, it must be said that the Conservatory, added by Holland in 1801 as an entirely new building, caused more concern than any part of the older building. Nash, who was himself not disinterested, wrote in the early 1820s that the Holland buildings 'were of the slightest kind being constructed with timber placed on a few courses of brick upon the damp soil without cellars or excavation under the floor so that they were subject to the rot, generated by stagnant exhalations from the ground'.[9] The present tortuous network of cellars underneath the oldest portion of the building testifies sufficiently to the ad hoc nature of their construction.

In February 1795 Holland produced plans (plans C and D) and an elevation [4] for an enlargement and alteration of the Pavilion. In June the Prince's debts were settled, but no alterations were made.

It may have been that the plans, at the time, did not find favour; a letter of July 1795 from Princess Elizabeth to the Prince of Wales hints that he may have been casting around for another architect: 'Mr.Wyatt . . . having heard that you had dismissed Mr. Holland . . . inclined to recommend his nephew.'[10] However, it is possible that the catalyst for the plans may not have been any general desire of the Prince to build, but an event of another kind entirely. On December 30 1794, the intended marriage of the Prince to Princess Caroline of Brunswick was announced to Parliament; the plans followed in February 1795; in April that year the marriage took place.

This necessitated a larger establishment and different arrangements; the 'Plan of the Bed Chamber Story at Brighton, with Alteration' (plan D) shows the construction of curved additional wings: to the south the Princess was to take the Prince's present Bed Chamber and Dressing Room, whilst equivalent rooms for the Prince, with direct communication, were to be added in the new southern wing. It would have been a gallant gesture on his part, since there is no doubt that the Princess' rooms would have been superior. Alas, it never happened. And it seems that the Prince, even at this early stage, may have had misgivings; the plan for the ground floor (plan C) includes, at the southern extremity, beyond a 'Small Dining Room', the 'Prince's Cabinet'. From this cabinet he could have ascended to his dressing room; it was intended to take the place of the 'Breakfast Room' (also called the 'Small Drawing Room') as the Prince's inner sanctum, admission to which was a high favour.

One anomalous feature may have an explanation in the Prince's complicated amatory life – apparently no communication was planned between the new bedroom in the north wing and the rest of the 'Chamber Story'; the only access was via the staircase adjacent to the new Large Dining Room. In the event nothing was needed. By the time of the Princess of Wales' expected visit in June 1796, which did not materialise, the separation was a confirmed fact. Since Mrs Fitzherbert never lived in the Pavilion, and other attachments of the Prince were even more unofficial, the planning of the rooms remained as for a bachelor establishment.

The comparatively trifling nature of the alterations proposed in 1795 lends colour to the view that they were the result of a foreseen need for practical provision; the Prince was perhaps too preoccupied, and even too agitated, to indulge in stylistic experiment. But it is puzzling that when major alterations *were* made, between Midsummer 1801 and Midsummer 1803, they were not more innovatory.

Elevation to the Steyne as executing.

5 The Marine Pavilion, East Front. By Henry Holland, 1801.
CAT. NO. 4.

Four drawings exist of and for this project, in a little book now kept at Windsor.
They are in the following order: a plan of the ground floor (plan E); a plan of
the first floor (plan F); a drawing of the East Front [5]; a design for the East
Front [6]. Only the first (plan E) is dated: July 1801; the others are undated.
The book itself is dated on its cover, July 1801. The accounts indicate that the
work was the responsibility of Holland himself, although there is a tradition that
P.F.Robinson, his pupil, undertook the major part.[11]

It is difficult to tell exactly when work started; certain of the early accounts
appear to have been inscribed '1801' at a slightly later date. An account from
Holland of July 24 1801[12] refers to the fact that the Prince wished to build two
wings; a letter of October 16 1801 mentions that 'The Prince and Mrs.F. have
been here all this season, he is making great alterations to the Pavillion and building
Wings. . . .'[13] A bill of October 31 1802[14] gives Holland's account of the principal
alterations: 'For sundry works done at the Pavilion at Brighton, in general repairs
and painting and whitewashing, in building a new Hall, and bringing forward
the Portico, Building three Staircases, a large new Eating Room and Conservatory,

A Design for the Elevation to the Steyne

6 *Design for the East Front of the Marine Pavilion in chinoiserie style. By Henry Holland, 1801.*
CAT. NO. 5.

and the communication to them, three water Closets and a Stewards Room, –
fitting up a Confectionary, forming a long room out of two Rooms; altering the
plan of His Royal Highness' rooms on two stories altering, adding to, and repairing
the out side fences: stuccoing part of the North Front and painting it in fresco
. . .'. The cost of this came to £13,358.

The character of the building that emerged from these alterations was peculiar,
and far removed from the severe harmonies of Holland's usual style. The most
eccentric feature was the two rooms, a dining room and a conservatory, added
as angled pavilions at the north and south ends of the façade. They approached
the older building in height, but appeared higher in proportion because they contained one storey only: the windows seemed elongated out of reason. One can
hardly believe that they were designed deliberately in such a form.

A possible explanation is that their height, and the fact that they were of one
storey only, may have been dictated by the exigencies of interior decoration; they
may, so to speak, have been designed from the inside out, not the outside in.
It may be that the drama of contrasting ceiling heights had begun already to seize

the Prince's imagination, and these rooms may, in that sense, have been the rehearsal for Nash's Banqueting and Music Rooms; it is perhaps not strange that the latter rooms, during construction and before being clothed with concealing screens, had a brand of ugliness not unlike that of the Holland extensions. The difference was that Nash's ultimate solution was brilliantly successful, with no hint of the strains successfully overcome.

It is obvious that there were changes of mind, and probably improvisations, during the rebuilding; the East Front was not completed exactly as seen in [5]. The exterior of the two pavilions appears to have been amended, with a somewhat more successful effect. The gaunt ends were given green metal canopies, as was the main East Front, and treillage helped to disguise awkwardness. The outside of the building was painted in 'fresco' by Louis Barzago.[15] It seems more than possible that some of these changes may have been derived from the chinoiserie design [6].

A hint of what possibly happened may lie in the different natures of these two depictions, quite apart from the different styles they illustrate. The first is not a design, it is a drawing. No attempt is made to conceal the architectural infelicities, especially those of the skyline; the description 'Elevation to the Steyne as executing' [5] has, when followed by 'A Design for the Elevation to the Steyne' [6], the flavour almost of a criticism followed by an alternative. It is true that the colour and treatment of [5] lend the drawing charm, but had the Prince acted as his own architect a certain tact might have been thought necessary. Is it possible that the latter, a true design, was at the same time a silent comment on the infelicities of the former, and a suggestion of how the irregularities of skyline and proportion could be turned to picturesque effect by the adoption of the Chinese style? One cannot believe that [5] and [6] were ever conceived, or presented, on one occasion as alternative designs. Everything about them prohibits that idea; as does one's own knowledge of the Prince's nature – it seems unlikely that, having seen a chinoiserie design that promised an exciting new departure (however unsatisfactory the actual design), he would have chosen a scheme that was substantially a clumsy adaptation of one presented in 1795.

Given the indication in Princess Elizabeth's letter of July 1795 (following the production of the design of February 1795) that the Prince may not have been satisfied with his architect, it seems at least possible that in 1801 that design was tampered with, in a way that proved unsatisfactory, at the instigation of the Prince; that Holland's drawing [5] records the result; that Holland then suggested a chinoiserie 'trim' to harmonise the building, from which a few suggestions were adopted.

In this context, the date and circumstances of the appearance of chinoiserie in the interior are relevant. Unfortunately, one does not know precisely when this happened, apart from the fact that the Crace accounts for chinoiserie decoration begin in the summer of 1802, and that neo-classical hall chairs in Holland's style were still being produced in the same year.[16] The catalyst as given by Brayley (see pp. 104–5) seems unconvincing, and if the gift, the famous gift of Chinese wallpaper, *did* occur, it was probably peripheral in effect – it might just as easily have happened as the result, rather than have been the cause, of the Prince's interest in chinoiserie. Holland himself was, of course, an old hand at chinoiserie, and his account, dated '1801' (but possibly so marked at a later date), speaks of 'making Designs for Chinese Decorations and directing the execution for Works and Furniture by Messrs. Saunders, Hale & Robson, Marsh and Tatham, Morell, Crace etc etc.'[17] Taken at its most obvious, this appears to say not only that Holland

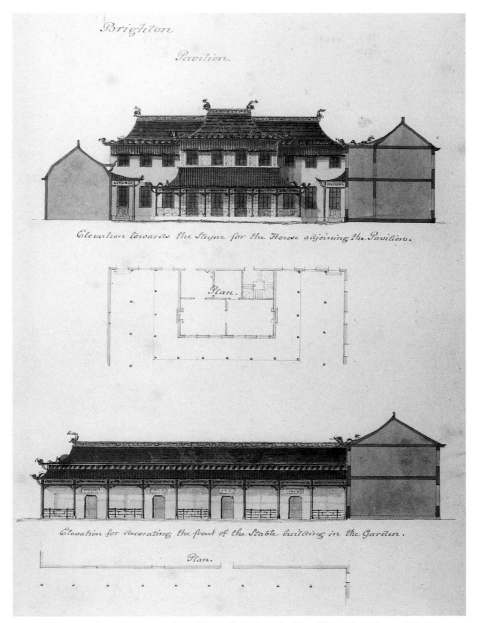

Brighton

Pavilion.

Elevation towards the Steyne for the House adjoining the Pavilion.

Plan.

Elevation for decorating the front of the Stable building in the Garden.

Plan.

7 Designs for a house and stables adjoining the Pavilion. By Henry Holland,
1802. CAT. NO. 5.

designed 'Chinese Decorations' – schemes for interior decoration in the Chinese style – for the Pavilion, but that they were executed, and that he supervised the execution. The fact that Holland himself appears to have designed and installed Chinese schemes within the building (see p. 90) would seem to indicate the possibility that chinoiserie ideas for both exterior and interior evolved at an early stage, and probably more or less simultaneously – although had earlier precedent been followed the likelihood would have been that the interior came first.

Holland's chinoiserie design for the East Front [6] is at once extremely pretty and extremely old fashioned (that alone should indicate it as his own), 'dix-huitième', and fussy. It is very different from Porden's Chinese designs (see below). The central pagoda, especially, looks like a design of forty years earlier.

Two other chinoiserie designs, on one sheet of paper, exist; signed 'H H Sloane Place Nov[er] 1802'. They are an 'Elevation for decorating the front of the Stable building in the Garden', and an 'Elevation towards the Steyne for the House adjoining the Pavilion' [7]. The 'Garden' mentioned must be the formal garden that, in one guise or another, is depicted at the south end of the Pavilion, adjacent to the Stables (plan E). The designs appear meant to bring the west side of the garden (made up of the house adjoining the Pavilion) and the south side (made up of the Stables) into conformity with the Pavilion itself, or rather into conformity with a chinoiserie design for it.

There are difficulties. The internal plan of the house was nothing like that given in [7]. However, it may be that the intent was not only to dress the house in exotic guise, but to replan or rebuild it – it does not appear on the 1795 plan (C), its site being occupied by extended garden. The house, built in 1787, had belonged to Weltje, who had lived in it; for the 1795 plan to have been executed, the Prince must have intended by some means to acquire the house (in 1793 abortive negotiations had been carried on to buy both house and Pavilion). Weltje had died in October 1800, and it appears that for some time before that the Prince had been paying him rent for the house as well as the Pavilion.[18] There is a mysterious entry in Holland's account,[19] dated 1801 (at a possibly later date) which mentions 'the Estate, purchased of Mr. Weltje and agreeing with him for the same ... £240. 0. 0'. It is something of a puzzle to know to what this could refer; if it is to the house, it seems a low figure. On the other hand, the Crace ledgers show that between Christmas 1803 and Midsummer 1804 a sum of £581 16s 9½d was paid, presumably by the Prince, for decorating the inside of 'Weltzee's House'.[20] The house does not appear to have been included in the final transactions in 1807 whereby the Prince exercised his option of purchasing the Pavilion itself.[21]

The date of [7], November 1802, is interestingly late. By that time not only were the interior chinoiserie decorations well under way, but in August 1802 the 'Promenade Grove', on which Porden's Stables (see below) were to be built, had been acquired by the Prince.[22] It is true that the intervening land to the west of the Pavilion, the 'Dairy Field', was not purchased until December 1803, but the Prince had had a lease on it, and long-term plans could have been made. It is not beyond the realms of possibility that the author of [7] was not in the Prince's confidence at the time his design was made. In any event, the Stables were within a very short space of time from November 1802 to commence rebuilding on a completely different site, on a completely different scale, and in a completely different style.

William Porden's Chinese Designs and the Royal Stables

The three designs by Holland for the Pavilion and its environs in the Chinese style are balanced in number, if in nothing else, by three Chinese designs for the Pavilion itself by William Porden (1755–1822). In the event, Porden became architect of the Stables, designed in the Indian style, where building began probably in 1803.

One of the Chinese designs for the Pavilion [8, 9, 12] was exhibited at the Royal Academy in 1806; it is not known which. It was shown together with Porden's Indian 'Designs for the Stables, Riding House and Tennis Court now building for H.R.H. the Prince of Wales at Brighton' and an 'Elevation of a house lately built for Mrs. Fitzherbert at Brighton'.[23] Taken together, they provided for Porden impressive evidence of royal patronage.

The date of the Chinese designs is somewhat problematical; the fact that one of them was shown in 1806 does not necessarily mean that any of them were produced in that year. It appears that, in a reply to questions put to him probably in 1809, Porden said that the Prince was pleased to employ him as architect and surveyor, and that he 'made several designs for altering, enlarging and embellishing the Pavilion, and for converting the old Stables into a suite of offices. . . .'[24] The fact that he was, at the Prince's behest, making designs for the Pavilion itself, seems to indicate that the use of the Chinese style had been requested by the Prince. But when?

The first question that one asks is whether Porden's Chinese designs show an awareness of the difficulties caused by the massive grandeur of his own Stables, difficulties which were certainly uppermost in the minds of Repton and Nash. The scale of the Stables meant that any building contiguous would have to be sufficiently extraordinary, in size or in some other feature, successfully to compete. It is hardly possible that the very architect who produced that grandeur would not have realised the problems it posed.

The three Chinese designs give some evidence of having perhaps been produced in different circumstances. Two [9, 12] are recognisable adaptations and enlargements of the existing building, set out as formal large-scale designs. The other one [8] seems unrelated to any existing building, and the drawing is given a naturalistic setting. It has been suggested[25] that this third drawing may reflect a comment, quoted by Brayley in 1838, that the Prince had in March 1805 expressed approval of the Stables and had added that 'he should like to have a palace built on the same plan; the central area to be a vast hall of communication to the apartments ranged around, with four staircases';[26] the theory is that the enlarged central hexagon of [8] may have been prompted by the Prince's words. This seems quite possible, and is perhaps reinforced by two other considerations – that Repton's plan [18] contains at its heart a Music Room that could have given similar opportunities, and that the Octagon Saloon at Fonthill, which forms the pivot of that most famous building, had something of the same arrangement.

The three designs are certainly on a larger scale, and are more broadly and grandly conceived, than is Holland's chinoiserie design [6]. The polychromatic brilliance of red, blue, and gold would have attracted the eye. But one doubts whether, had they been implemented, the building would ever have appeared as more than a toy, albeit a quite large toy, beside the mass of the Stables; perhaps it would have been impossible for any architect to produce a design capable of relegating the Stables to their proper station in life, unless he had the advantage, as Nash had, of more land; or unless he ignored, as Repton ignored, all the practicalities of ownership.

One minor puzzle presented by the history of the Royal Pavilion estate is how the Prince could so swiftly have switched his enthusiasm from a recent preoccupation with chinoiserie interiors to stables in an Indian style and an alien grandeur; perhaps one is being unhistorical in expecting consistency in such a context. A patron as didactic as Thomas Hope could place a Pannini in his Indian room, and speak of the 'unavoidable intermixture of other productions of art'.[27] It would be neat to suppose that the chinoiserie interiors were regarded as interior decoration and ephemeral in character, that Porden's Chinese designs came at a time when the Prince was contemplating a complete Chinese exterior, and that he then rejected exterior chinoiserie for his palace, perhaps on the 'light and trifling' grounds on which Repton rejected it, and turned decisively to India. The fact that Repton himself retained a Chinese exterior, perhaps reluctantly, for the East Front, would seem to refute this, as does the style of the Pavilion as rebuilt by Nash; overwhelmingly Indian, it yet displays two pagoda roofs of unmistakeable Chinese inspiration.

If Porden's design [8] were produced in 1806, it is hardly surprising that it was rejected. Its monotonous fenestration and vacant lack of a central feature below the lantern do not make for the hectic excitements promised by an exotic style. The 'Design for embellishing the East Front of the Pavilion in the Chinese Style with the Upper Part of the New Apartments in the West Front appearing over it' [12] is better; it has pomp, movement, and vivacity, in addition to the colour mentioned above. It manages, as does the later Nash building, to be both picturesque and symmetrical, a combination thought difficult by the theorists but repeatedly achieved. It incorporates and transforms the Holland additions, and the multiplicity of shapes gives the impression almost of a small Chinese town.

The third design [9] is of the west front glimpsed at the back of [12]; it will have been noticed that the hexagonal lantern tower seen in both is different from that in [8], with which, however, it has elements in common, including the statues set in niches.

Despite their virtues, the Porden designs, compared even with the Holland design [6], seem pedestrian; they lack the sense of fantasy which seems to have informed some of his Gothick designs – and which in some of his furniture is united with a most satisfying sense of weight. They do not meet the challenge of the Stables, and were bound to be rejected.

In 1797 Porden had exhibited, at the Royal Academy, a 'design for a place of amusement in the style of the Mahometan architecture of Hindustan'.[28] The Stables that he built at Brighton in the same style were greeted with a general, if guarded, approval; Repton described them in unrestrained terms (it suited his general thesis to do so; see below) as 'a stupendous and magnificent Building, which by its lightness, its elegance, its boldness of construction, and the symmetry of its proportions

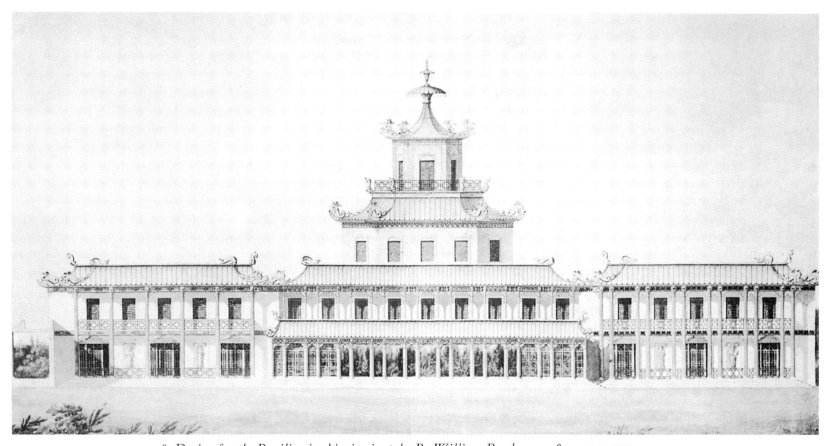

8 Design for the Pavilion in chinoiserie style. By William Porden, c. *1805.* CAT. NO. 7.

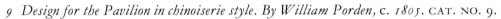

9 Design for the Pavilion in chinoiserie style. By William Porden, c. *1805.* CAT. NO. 9.

10   The Stables, the Garden Front. From John Nash, Views of the Royal Pavilion,
Brighton *(1826)*. CAT. NO. 10.

does credit both to the genius of the Artist, and the good taste of his Royal
Employer.'[29] The boldness of construction is evident enough; the dome, which
is eighty feet wide and sixty-five feet high, is only twelve inches thick at the base,
and nine at the top.[30] A letter from Porden to his daughter, written on November
29 1804, is reputed to have said, 'The cupola is now on, and the workmen are
swarming about it like jackdaws. The whole proves fully equal to expectation.
The dome now supports itself, without assistance from the scaffolding, and has
not yet fallen.'[31]

   The designs for the Stables seem unfortunately to have disappeared; they are
recorded as having been possessed in the nineteenth century by Joseph Kay,
Porden's assistant and son-in-law.[32] However, the contemporary appearance of
the splendid group of buildings is preserved in a watercolour, drawing and
aquatints [10, 11, 13–15] made for the 1826 edition of Nash's *Views*, as well as
in Repton's proposals for the Pavilion and its grounds.

   The structure was built of yellow brick and Bath stone; the ornament crowning
the dome was gilded. The circular form of the Stables was said to be 'in imitation
of the famous Corn Market at Paris which was burnt in 1803'.[33] This Cornmarket
had been built in 1782, and one notices how, despite the foreign detail, the Stables

11 The Stables and Riding House, seen from Church Street. From John Nash, Views of
the Royal Pavilion, Brighton *(1826).* CAT. NO. 11.

convey an impression of neo-classic or Empire solidarity. One notices also, in
the interior [14], that without any direct quotation the handling of the space is
reminiscent of the Pantheon at Rome. The Riding House, a hundred and seventy
eight feet long, is almost as impressive; it, unlike the Stables, retains much of
the original interior to this day, albeit unsympathetically treated [15].*

The central rotunda within the Stables [13,14] is beautifully composed and must,
despite the effluvia of such places, have given an exhilarating sensation; Repton's
delight, quoted above, sounds spontaneous and genuine. The movement of the
arches towards the dome apex is effortlessly handled. The detail is not as purely
Indian as might at first appear. The panelling of the pilasters has a faintly Gothic
air, and the iron railing around the first-floor arcade is more of a Chinese fret
than anything else.

By its completion in April 1808 the whole block had cost £54,783 12s 5d.[34]
The strain of paying for the work had caused great distress, both to the architect
and to the tradesmen he employed. The Prince complained of delays; in October

*In 1983 the Riding House interior was repainted in a scheme devised for it in 1933 which, although
not 'correct', has its own beguiling character.

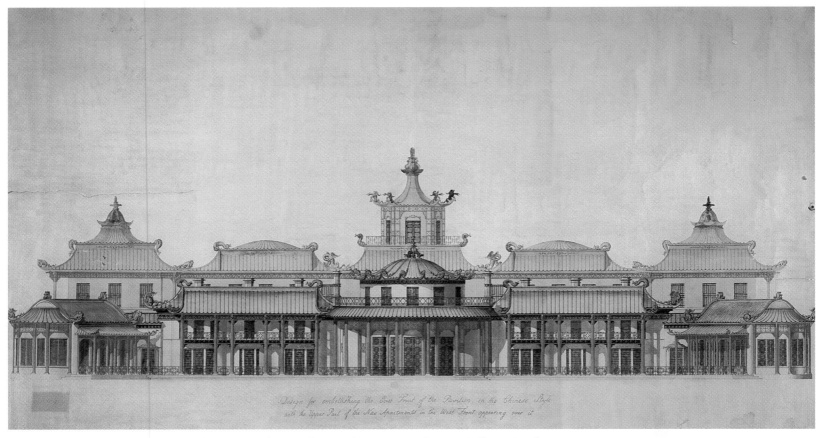

12 Design for the Pavilion in chinoiserie style. By William Porden, c. 1805. CAT. NO. 8.

13 The Stables; the Rotunda. By Augustus Pugin, c. 1820. CAT. NO. 12.

14   The Stables; the Rotunda. By Augustus Pugin, c. *1820.* CAT. NO. 13.

1806 Porden wrote respectfully to inform him that 'the delay in the building of
the Riding House has risen solely from the impossibility of procuring timber of
sufficient size for a Roof of such Width. When the Prussian Ports were blockaded,
Timber rose to an enormous price, and the Merchants would not part with large
timber at any price. . . . Mr. Porden was under the necessity of delaying the alteration of the offices because his Funds were not sufficient . . . it (The Works) could
not be (compleated) without involving himself and many Tradesmen in ruin'.[35]
In January 1807 he wrote, 'The distress of many of these Creditors is I believe
very great and the clamour against His Royal Highness will be in proportion . . .
the naked timbers of the roof of the Riding House stand exposed to all weathers,
a monument of disgrace to His Royal Highness and all concerned.'[36] By May 1808
he was protesting, 'I can only defend myself from ruin by proving openly that
the debts are not mine; but the Prince's.'[37]

It is likely that the forcing of the Prince's credit beyond its limits, as revealed
in the correspondence concerning the Stables, sufficiently alarmed the Prince's
advisers, and perhaps even the Prince himself, to inhibit further work on the
Pavilion itself until 1813 – despite all the evidence afforded by the designs that
he was more than prepared to embark on further stylistic experiment.

15 The Riding House. From John Nash, Views of the Royal Pavilion, Brighton
(1826). CAT. NO. 14.

Humphry Repton's
'Designs for the Pavillon at Brighton'

Any account of the relationship between Humphry Repton (1752–1818) and John Nash makes a curious tale, a tale that acquires subtle ironies when one takes into account the probable influence of Repton's designs on the Pavilion as completed after 1815 by Nash.

Repton has told the story of how they first met:

'I one day listened to my friend the Honble. Edward Foley, when he said in his peculiar manner – "that he wanted to bring me acquainted with a very talented Architect adding – "If you two, whom I consider the cleverest men in England, could agree to *act together* you "might carry the whole world before you." Now this was a bait exactly suited to my aspiring vanity! So I consented to the introduction to Mr. Nash! – and *We Met* – We were charmed with each other at the very first interview! Two such congenial minds were never brought together since the days of David and Jonathan! Or Pylades and Orestes! We acted as with one joint Soul! Our homes were alternately visited . . . our Offices (in which my sons assisted) were as the property of both – We jointly design'd and built houses at places where I or he had previously been concerned, and I felt that my income was *certain* to increase greatly, from the *percentage*, which it was *agreed* we should share between us. . . .'[38]

Alas, David and Jonathan had not attempted to deal in percentages, and within five years the Repton/Nash partnership ended in bitterness. One recognises in Repton's complaints the authentic note of betrayed confidence; he spoke of 'the most painful time of my life – which had power to shatter my brightest hopes, to shake my nervous system – and to humble if not intirely [sic] to smother my ambitious vanity'.[39] He did not cease to recognise Nash's ability, nor to lament the lost partnership; '. . . I never can forget the delight and satisfaction which I enjoyed (and lost!) in a ['friend' – deleted] companion possessing one of the most able heads I have ever known . . . powers of *fascination* beyond any one I have ever met with.'[40]   It is strange to reflect that had that partnership continued, Nash might well have provided the architectural designs for the garden designs produced for the Pavilion by Repton in 1805, and described below. As it was, it appears possible that he did produce a design for a conservatory at Brighton as a consequence of Repton's first invitation, from the Prince of Wales, to Brighton in the summer of 1795 – at a time when alterations were in the air. The partnership would explain the exhibition in the Royal Academy of 1798 of 'A Conservatory for his Royal Highness the Prince of Wales' by John Nash. This Nash conservatory has been identified as [16],[41] but the structure appears extremely large for such a modest building as the Marine Pavilion. The style of the watercolour itself is, on the other hand, not typical of Repton. It seems to the author that it could be of a later date than 1798.

The design [16] is for a spacious, utilitarian structure of cast iron and glass; it is of a different genre from the poetic designs produced later by Repton, and

16   Design for a Conservatory. CAT. NO. 15.

is hardly likely to have found favour with the Prince. It is not, as far as the author knows, shown on any contemporary plans, and there seems to be no evidence that it was ever built. It did not prejudice Repton being called in at a later date, in 1805, after the extension of the Marine Pavilion and the building of the Stables.

The result of that latter summons was Repton's 'Designs for the Pavillon at Brighton', presented to the Prince of Wales as a combination of manuscript text and illustrative watercolours (now in the Royal Library) and published in book form in 1808. It is the most thoroughgoing celebration of the Indian style in architecture of the early nineteenth century – more so than the Nash realisation of a decade later.

Repton's autobiography vividly illustrates the course of events at Brighton, from the feverish joys of his first hopes to the sickening frustrations of final failure. It casts a good deal of light on manuscript and book; it is also most interesting for its account of the Prince of Wales. In his 'Prefatory Observations' to the book, Repton pays tribute to the Prince's help in evolving expedients appropriate to Brighton: '. . . I am indebted to the elegance and facility of the Prince's own invention, joined to a rapidity of conception, and correctness of taste, which I had never before witnessed.' This remark has been dismissed as flattery, and indeed it may well contain such an element; but with such a patron it cannot be rejected out of hand, and the phrase 'rapidity of conception' rings true.

The autobiography reveals, as well as an understanding between the two men, yet another instance of the influence of Walsh Porter on the Prince.[42] Repton recounts how the Prince

mentioned several concerns of mine, with which he had been much pleased, and particularly one 'in which' he said 'you *dared* to make a perfectly straight gravel walk. The moment I saw it, I was determined to see you before I proceeded farther with this small spot –' We then walked out and for nearly an hour he talked as if he had never thought on any other subject than gardens, Parks and Landscapes – but with such justice in his remarks as I have seldom heard from any admirer of Nature. Having heard that the Prince had commended the taste of Mr Walsh Porter in a place near Fulham, I had been to see that spot, . . . and there I had seen many things done out of the common way with good effect – and others so whimsical and absurd that I dreaded the sort of taste I might have to encounter at Brighton – But . . . the Prince said there was doubtless much to approve in the ingenuity with which so confined a spot had been treated. . . . But he added 'I hope you do not give me credit for admiring his sofa Camel, or his miniature Gothic, and his flaming Chimney piece!' The three things that had appeared to me the most extravagant. This proof of our similarity of tastes gave me confidence, and I begged him to explain his own ideas on the gardens of the Pavillon. He replied 'I confess I have never satisfied myself – nobody understands that the importance of a thing does not depend on its real but its apparent extent – in short I wish you to consider the subject well, and to give me your opinion unbiassed by any thing you may have heard to be mine, or by any prevailing taste or fashion, by which the World is apt to be led.'[43]

On the day following this conversation, Repton measured out the ground by lines at right angles, dividing the whole into fifty-foot squares; at each intersection was placed a stake on which was written how many feet and inches the ground was to be raised or sunk, together with a corresponding diagram. The Prince 'followed all these lines and anticipated my explanations – Indeed I had never before met with a person so remarkably quick in conceiving all I proposed, or who was so judicious in deciding to adopt – or to reject or correct the plans. . . .'[44]

It behoves one now to bring into consideration the manuscript and book, since textual variations, together with information contained in the autobiography, enable one to attempt to reconstruct the course of events.

The task that Repton was summoned to perform has long been taken to be to 'deliver his opinion concerning what Style of Architecture would be most suitable for the Pavillon'.[45] It seems that, on the contrary, he was first asked to deliver his opinion not on the house, but on the gardens.

After a few preliminary skirmishes, a letter of November 17 1805 to Repton declared that the Prince would be 'glad to have your opinion upon the Gardens of the Pavillon. . . .'[46] On November 24 they met, and the conversation concerning Walsh Porter described above took place; on November 25 they together did the measuring out. On December 13 the drawings, together with the slides (superimposed flaps that allowed 'before' and 'after' views to be shown), were presented to the Prince; Repton included in the occasion his three sons, who were received by the Prince 'individually with that flattering attention so peculiar to himself'. The drawings were greatly admired, and after an hour 'HRH told me that I must now proceed further – I *must give him* my *opinion about the style* of an *entirely new house*, which might best assimilate with the large dome of the Stables, already built –.'[47] No sooner had the exultant Repton, made giddy by 'such puffs of Royal praise', left the presence, than he was called back to the Prince, by then in the company of Mrs Fitzherbert in her house on the Steine; in a sumptuous drawing room, darkened by a quantity of muslin and silk draperies drawn across the windows, and in the presence of a coldly disapproving – and uncomprehending – Mrs Fitzherbert, whose 'person was large, and loaded with lace and drapery', Repton had again to explain his plans: the Prince, however, took out his pencil and himself proceeded to demonstrate. It was on this occasion that the Prince told Repton to include the site of the Duke of Marlborough's house (see [36] and p. 61) in his plans, and said also, 'Recollect it is not a mere Marino, or Summer retreat I want, but such a Residence as I may *hereafter live in*,' by which Repton understood 'that it was a Royal Palace for a King, that I was now commanded to design – and I received the most particular instructions respecting his wishes. . . .'[48]

Repton goes on to say, 'when in due time I had the satisfaction of delivering my book at Carleton House . . . the Prince said – "Mr. Repton I consider the whole of this book as perfect! I *will have every part of it carried into immediate execution*. Not a tittle shall be altered – even you yourself shall not attempt any improvement –"'[49]

It seems from the above account that the Prince's initial ecstasies were the result of his seeing the proposals for the gardens; one does not know whether he saw on December 13 the text that described the gardens, although internal evidence leads one to believe that he did, or at least part of it.

This evidence is provided by the graceful and misleading obfuscations in the manuscript whereby Repton ingeniously sought to widen the scope of the inquiry to include the house. It is obvious that it was in his interest to exceed the instructions of his royal employer; this he did, but in such a manner that offence was neither given nor taken. There are small but significant differences between manuscript and book; in both, ingenious sophisms confuse the argument and enlarge the subject.

At times one has the feeling that both manuscript and book convey impressions that are to some extent implicitly contradicted by the sequence of events as given in Repton's autobiography: his recollection was perhaps imperfect. One inconsistency with the facts is that of the Prince's remark (quoted above as made to Repton when he delivered his book, in manuscript form, at Carlton House) to the effect that 'not a tittle shall be altered'. For the published designs for the building itself *do* differ significantly from the original versions in watercolour and far more than a 'tittle' was altered. The new buildings were made substantially more extensive in the printed book than in the manuscript, and certain of the elevations and domes were enriched (discussed below). The Prince's prohibition must have been fictitious or rhetorical, for it is hardly to be conceived that Repton would have altered designs that had been given the seal of royal approval. It is more likely that he and the Prince discussed them, and that he incorporated in the printed book changes that had been the subject of their discussions. It is also possible that the Prince did not like the design for the interior of the dining room; had he shown enthusiasm for it, is it not likely that Repton would have been encouraged to produce designs for other interiors? It was the Prince's practice to have a multitude of designs produced, each approaching nearer to his ideal, and there is no indication that this process was ever followed with Repton.

The dedication to the Prince in both volumes reads: 'The Approbation YOUR ROYAL HIGHNESS was pleased to express of the general Outline of an Opinion I had the honour to deliver concerning the GARDENS OF THE PAVILION, induces me to hope that this WORK will meet with the same GRACIOUS RECEPTION, as it contains the Reasons on which that Opinion was founded.' It is quite clear from this dedication that the 'GARDENS' were the subject of the 'Opinion'; the last reference, to the 'Reasons' on which that opinion was founded, is to the discussion of architectural styles that expanded the printed book. Already, therefore, the confusion begins, since the 'Reasons', which hardly affect the gardens at all as *gardens*, are architectural. Nonetheless, it is a long step from this to redesigning the Pavilion itself.

On page 11 of the printed 'Prefatory Observations' Repton slides easily from an observation on gardens to a paragraph on architecture before (page 111) declaring that 'Having long regretted the prevalence of this mistaken fashion' – which could refer to gardens, or houses, or both, since both had previously been mentioned – 'I was rejoiced to receive his Royal Highness's commands to deliver my opinion concerning a place which was deemed by every body too small to admit of any improvements; and indeed such it actually was, according to the modern system, which required UNCONFINED EXTENT WITHIN ITSELF, AND ABSOLUTE EXCLUSION FROM ALL WITHOUT.' The word 'place' used here is ambiguous, but the expression 'too small' would be insulting if applied to anything but the garden – although the Prince might mentally have extended it. Repton then proceeds to speak of the garden.

So far, Repton has made it clear, or clear enough, to the Prince, that he was called in to advise on the gardens. But in the discussion in the manuscript on 'Garden Entrances' (and it should be said that the manuscript betrays signs of haste) he alludes to the idea that 'as in some places architectural ornaments must be called in aid of vegetation, it becomes necessary to decide what style such orna-ments should assume'; to the printed text is then added an abrupt conclusion, absent in the manuscript, that at a bound justifies the whole of the architectural plans that follow: 'especially as these buildings must have a reference to the style of the mansion, as well as that of the stables; this naturally leads to the following enquiry concerning the various styles of architecture which have been, at different times, introduced into England.'

That 'naturally' is a quibble, given that the 'Enquiry' that follows refers to the style of a hypothetical future mansion, not the one that the Prince actually had! But it seems that Repton had been encouraged by his patron. And a sentence in the manuscript on the 'Interior', which clearly reflects Repton's uneasy sense of exceeding his brief, is significantly excluded from the printed book: 'Lest I should exceed the limits of my instruction, the plan represents only the supposed dining room, which may be varied to suit any internal arrangement required: without here going into such detail, I shall take the liberty of introducing some general hints respecting the interior of houses.' It was no doubt this sense of con-straint that led him to justify the design by utilitarian reasoning (see below). After all, as he says in another context, 'I have frequently given designs for furniture to the upholsterer, for monuments to the statuary, and to the goldsmith . . .';[50] he did not doubt his own abilities for interior decoration.

In his text Repton elaborates again on his familiar dictum that the character of a garden should not be confused with that of a park; he emphasises the import-ance of 'the utmost artificial neatness', and of extending the short summer season of flowers by artificial means. His concept of 'the artificial Garden, richly clothed with flowers, and decorated with seats and works of art, [where] we saunter or repose ourselves without regretting the want of extent, any more than while we are in the saloon, the library, or the gallery of the mansion' has the happy attractions of beauty, control, and domesticity. It lacks aspiration.

The 'Prefatory Observations' dilate on the style to be chosen for the new Pavilion. The Indian style is justified in the following famous and often quoted terms: 'When therefore I was commanded to deliver my opinion concerning the style of Architecture best adapted to the Additions and Garden Front for the Pavil-lon,' (note how circumscribed the terms of this command were) 'I could not hesitate in agreeing that neither the Grecian nor the Gothic style could be made to assimi-late with what had so much the character of an Eastern building. I considered all the different styles of different countries, from a conviction of the danger of attempting to invent any thing entirely new. The Turkish was objectionable, as being a corruption of the Grecian; the Moorish, as a bad model of the Gothic; the Egyptian was too cumbrous for the character of a villa; the Chinese too light and trifling for the outside, however it may be applied to the interior; and the specimens from Ava were still more trifling and extravagant. Thus, if any known style were to be adopted, no alternative remained, but to combine from the Archi-tecture of Hindustan such forms as might be rendered applicable for the purpose.'

The method followed by the author below, in discussing the Repton designs, will be to cite, wherever possible, the watercolours in the manuscript, and to refer to the published aquatints only where significant differences exist between the two versions.

The ground plans [17, 18] delineate both garden and Pavilion. The utilitarian and ornamental parts of the garden are separated by a corridor. The differences between unpublished and published plans are, as far as the gardens are concerned, minor; in the latter more trees are shown to the west of the Pavilion. It is obvious from the printed text that Repton put much emphasis on bedding out; 'To accomplish the great object of a perpetual garden, it will be necessary to provide for a regular succession of plants; and the means of removing and transplanting.' (It is ironic that the modern municipal garden that now exists in these spaces is maintained by much the same methods, albeit with different results.)

The variations in the Pavilion itself are more important. The Hall or Music Room becomes decisively the Music Room, and is extended to the north and south; the north wing, facing the Outer Court, becomes the Entrance Hall and is made much more substantial. The result of these expansions would have been to have created an uncomfortably small Inner Court.

The 'View of the Stable Front' [21, 24] shows the square pool (square because Repton says it will appear larger than a round pool 'of the same dimensions', whatever that may mean) after the trees have been removed; the pool itself is placed in a 'dell'. The gilding on the apex of the Stable dome may be clearly seen.

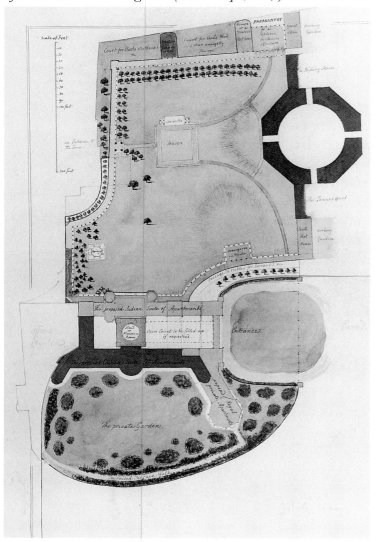

17 Ground plan of the Pavilion. From Humphry Repton, 'Designs for the Pavillon at Brighton' (manuscript, 1805). CAT. NO. 16.

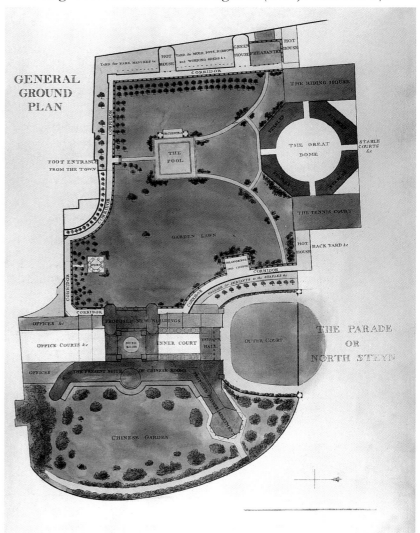

18 Ground plan of the Pavilion. From Humphry Repton, Designs for the Pavillon at Brighton (1808). CAT. NO. 17.

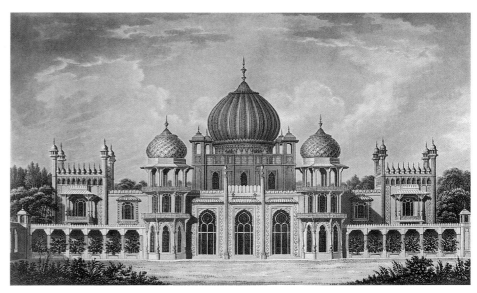

20 *West Front of the Pavilion. From Humphry Repton,* Designs for the Pavillon at Brighton *(1808).* CAT. NO. 23.

19 *West Front of the Pavilion. From Humphry Repton, 'Designs for the Pavillon at Brighton' (manuscript, 1805).* CAT. NO. 22.

Repton proposed to unify the dome with its surroundings by enriching the gardens with smaller buildings in the same style, stating however that the dome 'will always form the leading feature of the scenery'. Nash might almost be thought to have followed this precept, save that he showed his greater flair by concentrating the 'multiplicity of buildings' advocated by Repton actually on the *roof* of his Pavilion; his solution means that the dome does not form 'the leading feature of the scenery'.

The 'View from the Dome' [22, 25] shows the view south from the Stable yard, looking on to the square pool, beside which is an 'Orchestra or platform for a band of music'. Repton regrets the incongruity in his Eastern scene of the chapel cupola on the right, but concludes that it is fortunately not so correct a specimen of Grecian architecture as to intrude.

The discussion that follows on styles of architecture is a piece of special pleading on behalf of the Indian style; Repton shows an awareness that Gothic, Indian, and Grecian have similarities and could be ambiguous. Another writer who saw these similarities, and who, like Repton, derived them from the common influence of stalactites and caves, was William Hodges; his *Select Views in India* was published between 1785 and 1788, and in December 1786 he was given by Reynolds the honour of mention in a Discourse, 'The Barbaric Splendour of those Asiatic Buildings which are now publishing. . . .' In the circumstances, it is strange that whereas in the manuscript Repton gave credit to the 'accurate designs of Hodges and Daniels, and other artists', in the printed book the name of Hodges is omitted. Perhaps, for some reason, Repton feared too direct a reference.

The two designs for the 'West Front of the Pavilion' (incidentally, Repton tends to use the term 'Pavilion' in the manuscript, and the more Frenchified or formal 'Pavillon' in the printed book) have expressive differences [19, 20]. The manuscript

21 *View of the Stable Front, seen from the garden. From Humphry Repton, 'Designs for the Pavillon at Brighton' (manuscript, 1805). Shown with flap closed.* CAT. NO. 18.

22 *View from the Dome. From Humphry Repton, 'Designs for the Pavillon at Brighton' (manuscript, 1805). Shown with flap closed.* CAT. NO. 20.

23 *General view from the Pavilion. From Humphry Repton, 'Designs for the Pavillon at Brighton' (manuscript, 1805). Shown with flaps closed.* CAT. NO. 25.

24 View of the Stable Front, seen from the garden. From Humphry Repton, 'Designs for the Pavillon at Brighton' (manuscript, 1805). Shown with flap open. CAT. NO. 19.

25 View from the Dome. From Humphry Repton, 'Designs for the Pavillon at Brighton' (manuscript, 1805). Shown with flap open. CAT. NO. 21.

26 General view from the Pavilion. From Humphry Repton, 'Designs for the Pavillon at Brighton' (manuscript, 1805). Shown with flaps open. CAT. NO. 26.

shows the ground plan of the Dining Room with an elaborate floor pattern. The book shows more decorative work on the window surrounds, with added canopies; pierced trellises in place of solid screens; a much more elaborate treatment of the small domes, which has the effect of making them appear less squat; an enriched treatment of the base of the large dome, and the addition on the last of a zig-zag pattern somewhat resembling that later used in the interior decoration of the Music Room. The arcades differ in the two designs; that in the printed book has a more vertical emphasis. It can hardly be doubted that these variations are the result of observations by the Prince.

The Prince's known prejudices may be flattered in the text on the 'Interior' that follows, in that Repton refers disparagingly to the 'rage for what is called SIMPLICITY'; he includes also a fascinating paragraph on 'ENFILADE'. In the manuscript, Repton writes, 'The position of doors and windows may be varied and improved in many respects, but I doubt whether the entrance of any room should be in the centre of its length'; in both manuscript and book, he says, 'The modern fashion of laying two or three rooms into one, by very large folding doors, is magnificent and convenient where the rooms can be used together: but as great effect of Enfilade (north and south) is preserved in the Chinese suite of rooms at the Pavilion, and may also be created in the attached Corridors; and as magnificence of extent may be produced by INTRICACY and variety, as well as by CONTINUITY, perhaps the Enfilade from east to west may be not so desirable, the distance being comparatively shorter'. These old-fashioned opinions seem precisely to have suited the archaistic prejudices of George IV. Both at Carlton House[51] and in the Marine Pavilion, as altered by Holland, the effect of enfilade was important: in the latter it was preserved and intensified by Nash – there seems never to have been any question of, for example, centralising the doors to the Saloon, as those in the State Rooms at Buckingham Palace (where the rooms were used together) are centralised. A glance at Plan H will show how thoroughly the principles of enfilade are followed.

The design for the Dining Room [27] is, as has been said, the only design for an interior in the printed book. However, in the manuscript is a passage (not published) which makes it clear that originally included in the manuscript material was a drawing illustrating a comment recommending the use of coloured glass, together, it seems, with drawings of alternative treatments for the ceiling. None now exist with the manuscript material; had it been decided not to print them, as apparently was the case, since the relevant passage had been omitted, a sufficient explanation of their disappearance is given by the long residence of the manuscript with the printer. As Repton wrote on December 13 1815, in a letter now enclosed with the manuscript book, 'I have the honor to send you a Book which I was very much surprized and mortified at receiving from the hands of an Engraver, to whom (with His Royal highness the prince's gracious permission) it had been committed – but I fully supposed that it had long ago been returned, as I had directed. . . .'

Extracts from the omitted passage are given below. Not only are they of interest in themselves, but white ground glass, together with stained and painted glass, is used in the upper windows of the Nash Music and Banqueting Rooms in something of the way advocated by Repton. We know from the Crace accounts (see p. 110) of the Prince's interest in experimenting with coloured glass. Repton's theories of light were influenced by the work of Dr Milner, President of Queen's College, Cambridge.

27　The Dining Room. From Humphry Repton, 'Designs for the Pavillon at Brighton'
(manuscript, 1805). CAT. NO. 24.

In large modern rooms which are very lofty, the management of the windows has been attended with great difficulty . . . this suggests the idea, that perhaps more general use may be made of coloured glass in adorning our rooms: by this, I do not mean the modern windows painted by Jervis, etc, which are only transparent copies of pictures . . . but there is a charming effect of transparency which depends on colour and combination, without the aid of design; and also of design without the aid of colour; and . . . the gaudy colours of glass . . . may be kept separate and relieve each other by introducing the most beautiful outlines in clair obscure on white ground glass, and adding the enrichment of the colouring in the frame which surrounds it; of this also a hint is given in the annexed drawing [not present]. . . .

There is a curious effect from purple glass. . . . All green objects seen through purple glass appear white and thus a beautiful landscape illumined by the midday sun of Summer would appear a perfect Winter scene covered with snow. . . .

In this sketch some ornaments are introduced to enrich the ceiling, which from their novelty may appear extravagant; but the difficulty of reconciling the mind to new forms will operate at first against every attempt to introduce them. For this reason the decorations are varied in the following different drawings [not present] of the same ornaments, or buildings: observing as a general rule, that they be kept equally distinct from those of the Gothic or Grecian style, and that they bear some reference to the origin and construction of the Indian style. . . .

Repton's design for the Dining Room has been condemned as graceless and ugly. It is possible that, combined with strong colour, as it would have been, it may have been acceptable. The bulbous and inflated forms seem a curious anticipation of late Regency taste.

A short passage on 'Ornament' contains a specious piece of reasoning, to the effect that Gothic ornament is derived from the 'BUD OR GERM', Grecian from the 'LEAF', and Indian from the 'FLOWER' – 'a singular coincidence, which seems to mark, that these three styles are, and ought to be, kept perfectly distinct'. To which one might retort that all three are found frequently on one plant.

The 'General View from the Pavillon' is virtually identical in watercolour [23, 26] and aquatint, although the latter shows a small flower bed with a green iron border added to the extreme left foreground. The view faces due west, with the Aviary on the left and the Stables on the right. It may be remarked that the decussated motif of the foreground screen is almost identical to that used in wallpapers in the Royal Pavilion which are now commonly referred to as 'Gothick' – an adequate comment, perhaps, on Repton's remark quoted in the preceding paragraph.

The leafy perspective [28], through the windows of which are seen the bare boughs of wintry trees ('I deferred seeing the spot, till all the leaves being off the trees, I might not form an erroneous opinion of what they now concealed'),[52] 'represents the perspective of the West Corridor . . . although in reality this conservatory can be only fifty feet long, the ENFILADE' – again the insistence on enfilade – 'is increased to an indefinite length, by a Mirror so placed as to reflect the whole of the North Corridor, which goes off at a right angle'. In a work published in 1816 and dedicated to the Prince Regent, Repton ingenuously explains the origin of this device: 'A circumstance occurring by accident has led me to avail myself, in many cases, of a similar expedient. Having directed a conservatory to be built along a south wall, in a house near Bristol, I was surprised to find that its whole length appeared from the end of the passage, in a very different position to that I had proposed: but, on examination, I found that a large looking glass, intended for the saloon . . . had been accidentally placed in the greenhouse, at an angle of forty-five degrees, showing the conservatory in this manner: and I have since made occasional use of mirrors so placed, to introduce views of scenery which could not otherwise be visible from a particular point of view.'[53]

In making the charming watercolours for the 'Orangerie' in summer [32] and winter [29], Repton made an error indicative of haste. The horizontally arranged flaps that should depict 'Winter', opening in the middle to reveal the attractions of 'Summer', are in fact, one Winter, one Summer, so that the watercolour beneath had to be conjoined Winter and Summer. This error has been corrected in the present illustrations by photography. The columns appear in the watercolour as if meant to be gilded; the more opaque method of aquatint gives the impression of paint.

The wonderful and strange 'Pheasantry' [35] – with the cupola and overhanging roof, meant to shield from tropic suns – is identical in watercolour and aquatint. Repton refers in the published book to 'cast iron . . . which is peculiarly adapted to some light parts of the Indian style', and the slender columns, topped by vases, would no doubt have been made of that material. The juxtaposition of lotus capital and base displays a less than sure taste.

The East Front [30, 33] is shown as it would have appeared looking south from the proposed new private apartments (extreme left [37]); the latter were to have floors elevated to give a good view of the sea. The perimeter wall and ground were to be raised to furnish a Terrace Walk. One odd feature is that Holland's Conservatory appears to have disappeared; does that mean that the Prince was thinking of getting rid of it, little used as it was? If so, he changed his mind, for it was later repaired. Even odder is the proposal of a Chinese design for the

*28 The West Corridor. From Humphry Repton, 'Designs for
the Pavillon at Brighton' (manuscript, 1805).* CAT. NO. 27.

East Front, screened with trees; the anomaly is caused by the restricted brief given by the Prince. Such a proposal can hardly have been meant seriously; however latitudinarian contemporary taste may have been, the idea of a Chinese East Front dwarfed by the orotund forms of Repton's Indian design behind and to the north is grotesque beyond endurance. Wisely, he did not attempt to depict it. The attitude of the Prince of Wales to the proposed hybrid is hard to fathom.

The 'View of the West Front' [31, 34] shows in the aquatint, not illustrated here, the more elaborate domes and pierced gallery seen in [20]. A few extra beds have appeared in the lawn, which the lofty windows of the Dining Room face. The humble aspect of Holland's West Front is in striking contrast.

The 'View of the North Front' [36, 37] is full of interest, showing as it does Holland's Marine Pavilion and its added Conservatory huddled unpretentiously amongst its neighbours, with the large block of Marlborough House to its north (not, incidentally, purchased by the Prince until 1812). It was in Repton's interest to emphasise the 'unworthy' appearance of the Pavilion, but one feels nonetheless that this impression is nearer the truth than the more 'official' views of some of the topographers. The flap opens to reveal the full range of Repton's north front, on which was the main entrance (in 1818 the Prince Regent briefly returned to this idea, which tends to confirm the view that it was he who suggested the extension northwards.) The gilded glories of the private apartments are seen on the left. It is not clear how Repton intended the walls of the octagonal end of these to be treated, but the watercolour suggests a surface uncommonly like stucco, studded with flint or some other material. It sounds an unlikely material, but Repton himself had added a very vernacular flint and brick wall to accommodate his Terrace Walk and circumscribe the grounds. Or it might, perhaps, be some form of tile.

The smaller domes in this design are plain, on both watercolour and aquatint; the main dome, with an open balcony beneath it, is quite different from any other

29 The Orangery: winter.
From Humphry Repton,
'Designs for the Pavillon at
Brighton' (manuscript, 1805).
CAT. NO. 28.

30 The East Front. From
Humphry Repton, 'Designs
for the Pavillon at Brighton'
(manuscript, 1805). Shown
with flap closed. CAT. NO. 31.

31 View of the West Front.
From Humphry Repton,
'Designs for the Pavillon at
Brighton' (manuscript, 1805).
Shown with flap closed.
CAT. NO. 33.

32 The Orangery: summer. From Humphry Repton, 'Designs for the Pavillon at Brighton' (manuscript, 1805). CAT. NO. 29.

33 The East Front. From Humphry Repton, 'Designs for the Pavillon at Brighton' (manuscript, 1805). Shown with flap open. CAT. NO. 32.

34 View of the West Front. From Humphry Repton, 'Designs for the Pavillon at Brighton' (manuscript, 1805). Shown with flap open. CAT. NO. 34.

*35 The Pheasantry. From Humphry Repton, 'Designs for the Pavillon at Brighton'
(manuscript, 1805).* CAT. NO. 30.

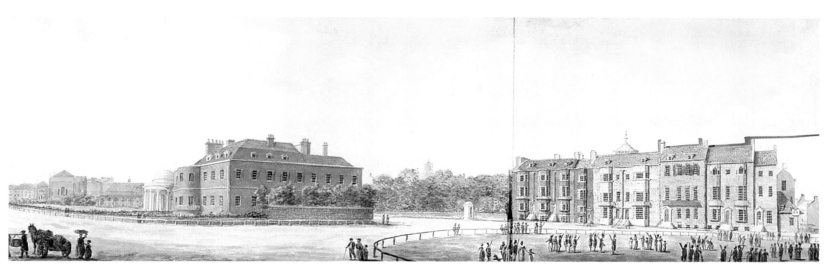

36 View of the North Front. From Humphry Repton, 'Designs for the Pavillon at Brighton' (manuscript, 1805). Shown with flap closed. CAT. NO. 35.

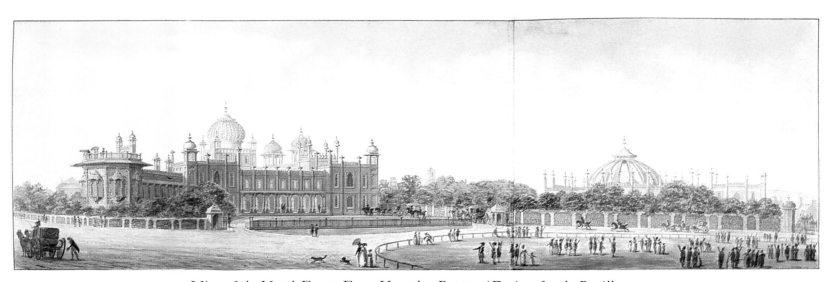

37 View of the North Front. From Humphry Repton, 'Designs for the Pavillon at Brighton' (manuscript, 1805). Shown with flap open. CAT. NO. 36.

depicted and, especially in the watercolour, it looks as if the ribs that run to its summit might be filled with glass, somewhat in the manner of Porden's Stable dome. There is no comment in the text of any kind on this design, and therefore no elucidation. One might recall in this context that Hopper's Gothick Conservatory at Carlton House was to have the vaulting between its ribs filled in with glass.

Taken as a whole, Repton's designs for the Garden are ravishingly pretty, and those for the Pavilion are full of interest, and even beauty. And yet one feels that the Prince was right not to make use of them, even had he been in a position to do so. The designs for the building are correct even to pedantry, much inferior to the unforgettable image provided by Nash; they lack flair. The gardens, charming though they are, and studded with enchanting conceits, consort oddly with the basically serious aspect of Repton's Pavilion. As a combination, they are not convincing. Nevertheless, had Repton's designs never been produced, it is conceivable that the form of Nash's Pavilion would have been substantially different. Repton himself, by reprinting his Pavilion designs in the early 1820s, must have intended a mute comment at the hour of his rival's triumph.

38   The West Front, the Pavilion. From John Nash, Views of the Royal Pavilion,
Brighton *(1826)*. CAT. NO. 42.

39   The East Front, the Pavilion. From John Nash, Views of the Royal Pavilion,
Brighton *(1826)*. CAT. NO. 43.

John Nash and the Rebuilding of the Pavilion

It was through John Nash (1752–1835) that George IV achieved his most spectacular and extensive architectural triumphs.

Nash was by no means a perfect architect. He has never been popular with those whose perceptions are too nice to appreciate his virtues, but 'although poor Mr Nash . . . has fared so ill at the hands of connoisseurs – and it cannot but be denied that his buildings are a jumble of every sort of style, the result of which is rather "baroque" than original – yet the country is . . . much indebted to him.'[54] Just so. His greatest strength lay in a powerful rhetoric that carried all before it, and that causes one to suspend judgment on matters of detail: he was at times capable of fastidious understatement. One of his faults was an insensitivity to texture, which in the case of works undertaken for George IV was controlled by the latter's interest in fine materials.

A natural courtier, Nash was easy, confidential, and bustling. His relations with George IV became intimate (a privilege never attained by Holland); he had indeed attained something of the status of confidential servant before building anything for the Prince. Interestingly enough, he had also, by 1812, a close relationship with Lord Yarmouth, the Prince's intimate friend and another collector of French furniture.[55] By the 1820s king and architect were, despite occasional storms, cordial friends; the former had been entertained at Nash's Castle on the Isle of Wight. The King was foiled in his attempts to give Nash a baronetcy, but was frequent in expressions of esteem; after his death Nash expressed anxiety – there is no need to doubt his sincerity, despite self-interest – that those things in which 'our dear King' was most interested should be carried into effect.[56]

The Prince Regent's first choice for new work at Brighton was not Nash; despite the latter having begun work upon Marylebone Park in 1811, and upon the Cottage in 1812, it was James Wyatt who came in 1812 to advise upon alterations. An estimate of £200,000 was made; of this a moiety was spent, a total of £2373 16s 0½d.[57] The recently acquired Marlborough House (plan G) was to be connected with the Pavilion; according to a somewhat decayed bill of 1814, a scheme was made to 'convert the two Drawing Rooms at Marlborough House into one Drawing Room . . . put up Ionic Columns with Niches or Circular Recesses for side boards. . . etc.' at a cost of £1127 14s 0d.[58] It was proposed also to repair dry rot in the Conservatory. Nothing in this indicated plans for a speedy rebuilding; it seems probable that grandiose plans were made, but died, in September 1813, with their architect, and that the schemes concerning Marlborough House were stop gaps. Nash was at this time extremely busy, at Carlton House and elsewhere.

However, on January 24 1815, he went to Brighton, and the pantomime arrived at the point of the transformation scene. Regent and architect went hand in hand into realms of unabashed fantasy [39], and into precisely that mixture of styles so deplored by Repton; the perils of archaeological pedantry had been observed. In an unpublished preface to *Views of the Royal Pavilion* Nash made quite clear – after the event – the principles that had guided the Prince Regent and himself. As here set out, all sounds logical, clear, and coherent; there seems every reason to believe that the long period of cogitation had led to a considered solution to the problem set by the impulsive building of the Stables. There is, incidentally, no reason to doubt Nash's attribution of aesthetic decision to the King, and the reference to the latter's dislike of the ubiquity of Greek revival simplicity is illuminating:

H.M. in fixing upon this [Eastern] character was induced by a strong dislike to the absurd and perverted taste which universally prevailed of introducing the simplicity which is the charm of the Greek Temples into every structure whether suited or not to the purpose of the building, and even into the interior of our houses and to the furniture itself – H.M. knew also that the forms of which the Eastern structures are composed were susceptible more than any other (the Gothic perhaps excepted) of rich and picturesque combinations. [The reference to Gothic *may* possibly have been an echo of the King's earlier discussions with Wyatt, and indicates the similarity of his intentions, albeit using differing styles, at Brighton and at Windsor.] H.M. was . . . offended with the incongruity of character between the Stables and the Pavillion and with the comparatively mean appearance of the latter . . . The Nature of the soil and the great height of the Stables rendered the planting them out . . . perhaps wholly impracticable, and if the Character of the Stable buildings had been changed still their enormous size would have depressed and rendered mean the [Pavilion]. . . . It was therefore determined by H.M. that the Pavillion should assume an Eastern character, and the Hindoo style of Architecture was adopted in the expectation that the turban domes and lofty pinnacles might from their glittering and picturesque effect, attract and fix the attention of the Spectator. . . .[59]

The 'attention of the Spectator' is indeed fixed by the glittering and picturesque effect of the domes and pinnacles. The use of the Gothic term 'pinnacle' in that passage, rather than 'minaret', may just possibly be the result of an unconscious recollection of that influential manual, Uvedale Price on the Picturesque. Price, explaining that lack of symmetry makes for picturesqueness, comments that the 'splendid confusion and irregularity' of Gothic often make it *appear* unsymmetrical and picturesque.[60] That remark is true of the Pavilion – had it been completed to plan it would have been, with the exception of the clock tower and the overhanging balcony of the King's Apartments, almost entirely symmetrical (plan H).

The King's expectation was justified by its realisation. The exterior of Nash's Pavilion [38, 39, 42–47] is as arresting and as unforgettable as the Sagrada Familia in Barcelona; with the latter, it is one of the great eccentric buildings of the world. Very rarely is eccentric art great art, and the Pavilion certainly is not: the building has provoked tedious humour; yet it has its own magical charm, and whilst we smile we applaud.

Holland's building had been greatly extended in size (compare plans G and H). The two large State Rooms, the Music Room and Banqueting Room, the latter followed in sequence (but not in enfilade) by the Great Kitchen and domestic offices, had all been added, as had the King's Apartments and the new wing to the north. Taken together, these had enabled Nash to produce a building extremely long in proportion to its breadth, a device that increases apparent size almost as well as do the extended curved wings of a Palladian house. Not that it had not been widened also; to the west the Entrance Hall had been enlarged and the Octagon Hall added; to the east the ground-floor drawing rooms had been considerably widened, a device that embedded the bow of the Saloon more securely in the East Front as a whole, and robbed it of a pre-eminence that would have been an anomaly in the extended east facade. Despite the immense skill of these changes,

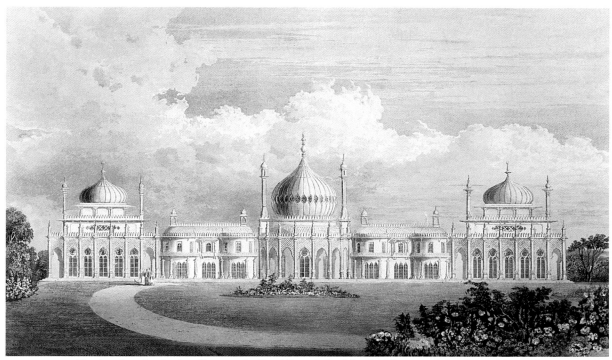

40 Design for the Steine Front, the Pavilion. John Nash, Views of the Royal Pavilion, Brighton *(1826).* CAT. NO. 38.

41 Plan and section of the Pavilion. 1815. CAT. NO. 39.

a comparison of the earliest Holland building [2] with the Nash façade [39] shows the Marine Pavilion clearly encapsulated within the Royal Pavilion, in a way that demonstrates the dazzling virtuosity of the architect. His success is such that one is led almost to doubt the indubitable truth of his self-deprecating assertion that with this building he fell into 'the trap which every one falls into who is led to add to old Houses . . . they are led on from one desirable object to another until not infrequently it would have been cheaper and generally wiser to have rebuilt the whole.'[61]

The apparently effortless solution of the problems posed by the Holland Pavilion and the Porden Stables had at last arrived, although the question of style was at first open; according to Nash 'it became a subject of serious consideration

42 The West Front, the Pavilion. By Augustus Pugin. C. *1822.* CAT. NO. 40.

whether the intended alteration of the Pavillion should assume an Eastern character in conformity with that of the Stables or retain its modern character and the Stables be planted out [screened with trees] or its Eastern character obliterated. . . .' Nash declared also that 'it was not intended at that time to do more than rebuild the Eating Room and Conservatory placing them on an even line with the Center of the Building. . . . H.M. also widened the passage of communication forming the present Gallery, and added a Hall of Entrance.'[62]

These intermediate intentions are fascinatingly present in a sketch now in the Crace collection at the Cooper–Hewitt Museum [41]. A comparison of this with the disposition of the building as Nash found it (plan G) reveals that it was proposed to retain the two wings either side of the old 'Principal Entrance' on the west. The new Music Room to the north and the Banqueting Room to the south of the Marine Pavilion end in rooms of decreasing sizes; these were built much as drawn, but were encased in the North Front and in the kitchen range respectively, of which no trace (or only an outline trace of the latter) is seen in the sketch. The Corridor was apparently to be entirely sacrificed, for in the sketch it is subdivided into rooms corresponding exactly with those – the Red Drawing Room, two 'Apartmts for private Secretary, a Waiting Room' – later built either side of the new Entrance Hall on the west side of the Corridor (plan H).

The elevation of the East Front seen in the sketch displays the choice of pagoda or dome hovering over the Music Room; as shown, the building would have as yet possessed only three domes altogether (or one dome and two pagodas). Nash may have been influenced in the choice of pagoda by the success of the ballroom built in 1814 to house the celebrants of victory; this had a pagoda roof of similar form (now rebuilt at Woolwich). Nash's *Views* shows an alternative design [40] for the East Front which has elements in common with the sketch, but 'H.M. chose the latter. . .', a more elaborate design than either. The differences between the two are clear enough, but carry also a significant difference in attitude perhaps not so immediately apparent. The Prince, in rejecting [40] in favour of [39], rejected a design that, felicitous as it was in largely keeping within the restraints of a Moghul style, bore no comparison with the wild originality of the edifice that arose. In place of three domes, two of which were of the flattened shape seen often in Indian architecture, appeared six, all of the same voluptuous and swelling contour, together with two sweeping tent roofs of Chinese concavity. The minarets became taller and more numerous; the bows of Holland's wings

43 The West Front, the Pavilion. By Augustus Pugin. c. *1822.* CAT. NO. 41.

disappeared behind stately ranges of stone-surrounded windows. The lacy screen on Saloon, Banqueting Room, and Music Room, was a brilliant invention that helped to unify the façade below the roof level. The whole building displays an insistent repetition of exotic motifs that, taken with the opposed curves of Chinese pagoda roofs and Moghul domes, succeeds in instantly impressing itself upon the mind.

The chosen material was brick covered with stucco, incised and painted in slightly differing hues to imitate stone; this method of trompe l'œil can be seen clearly in the aquatints, although not in the watercolours. The 'Hindoo' detail of domes, porticos, pillars, minarets, and other decorative detail was executed in Bath stone from the Combe Down quarry. Divorced from its context, some of the detail looks Gothick – for instance, the battlements, the diaper pattern of the screen [39] – and the giant chimney behind the central dome [46] is supported by no other than two ogee flying buttresses, stucco on timber, alas invisible from the ground, and is flanked by battlemented turrets. Also largely invisible from the ground is the fish-scale slate roof.

The longitudinal section [1] shows the use of iron in the building; especially noteworthy are the huge cast-iron cores of the minarets. These cores were covered with bitumen; over them huge single pieces of stone were slipped like a collar – an expensive process, but necessary, if the effortless ease of the minaret was not to be marred by vertical joins.

The upper sections of the towers that carry the smaller cupolas and that surround the horizontal diamond shaped windows [46, 47] are constructed entirely of timber, faced by iron plates to which the stucco is attached. These have lasted amazingly well. Iron plates exist also on the cupolas themselves, beneath the surface of the stucco.

One vexatious problem, that badly strained relations between Nash and the King, concerned the roofs and the permeability of Nash's famous 'mastic'. On November 21 1822 Knighton, Private Secretary to the King and Keeper of the Privy Purse, wrote in a letter of which the importance is indicated by the rare presence of the King's signature, that 'It has been represented to His Majesty that the covering of the Magnificent Dining Room, the interior of which, has cost so large a sum, is now in that State, that to secure it from injury, Pans are obliged to be placed over the Surface, to guard the Interior from the Influence of the Rain . . . and that when it rains . . . two Men are under the necessity of

44 The North Front, the Pavilion. By Augustus Pugin. c. 1822. CAT. NO. 47.

watching . . . Night and Morning . . . the whole proceeding, in employing this Mastic, was considered an Experiment, which His Majesty feels most inconsiderate Conduct. . . .'[63] This message was transmitted at one remove to Nash, an action in itself a snub, and he hastened to reply in terms that indicate some fright: '. . . I should go to the Pavilion in the first instance, but reflecting on the terms on which I have been received there [presumably affable] and ignorant of H.M. present disposition I am fearful of giving offence by appearing there without H.M. permission. . . . I beg to state that *I know* the Mastic in a *perfect* State to be *impervious to wet*. . . . I adopted the Mastic because I know I know [sic] of no other Material in which such *ornamental Roofs* could be executed. . . . I have since had very great experience in it . . . and thence arises my confidence that the defects at the Pavilion may be remedied.'[64]

Other complaints followed, and in 1827 the pagoda roofs of the two State Rooms, which in [39, 44, 45, 47] may be seen in mastic imitating stone, were sheathed in copper, the bright green of which is so familiar a feature of the building today. It is possible that the mastic may partly survive on the smaller domes, or that the material used may have been Stanhope's composition, also employed on the Pavilion roofs.[65] (Extensive later repairs have removed much of the evidence). Given these troubles, one is astounded to see Nash in 1831 unblushingly assert to a Parliamentary Committee that he had used this mastic (made, incidentally, of a first coat of tar and chalk, and a second coat with coarse sand added) for thirty-five years, that all the houses with flat roofs built by him had it 'still sound' and that 'at the Pavilion in Brighton, where the work has been done twelve years, and the composition is laid upon timber (much more likely to shrink . . .) the water has never penetrated'.[66]

The use of copper on the pagoda roofs was something of a solecism. There is no doubt that the exterior of the building was treated to convey the impression

45 The East Front, the Pavilion. By Augustus Pugin. c. 1823. CAT. NO. 44.

46 The Entrance Portico and West Front, the Pavilion. By Augustus Pugin. c. 1822. CAT. NO. 45.

47 The King's Apartments, the Pavilion. By Charles Moore. c. 1822. CAT. NO. 46.

48 Design for a conservatory. c. 1824. CAT. NO. 48.

that it was built entirely of Bath stone, and this uniformity of hue was an important constituent of its ethereality of effect (an effect that must have been lessened by the removal in 1921–3 of the flint wall from before the East Front,[67] beyond which the Pavilion must have risen as the towers of All Souls rise beyond the Hawksmoor screen). However, the use of copper was later extended to other parts of the Royal Pavilion estate, and its application during the reign of George IV renders it sacrosanct. Not so the various pistachio colours applied during the present century. Uvedale Price gives wise advice, which fits the situation and will have been known to Nash: 'No person, I believe, has any doubt that stone – such as Bath or Portland . . . – is the most beautiful material for building. . . . The true object of imitation [on stucco] seems therefore to be the tint of a beautiful stone; and if those who whiten their buildings would pique themselves on matching exactly the colour of Bath, or Portland stone, so as to be neither whiter nor yellow, the general neatness and gaiety might prevail, without crudeness or glare.'[68]

The freshness of stucco and stone would have been maintained by regular renewals in 'fresco' and ferruginous washes. The style of the building, inside and out, is of a nature that does not age with grace, and the pristine insubstantiality of the exterior is marvellously held in the Pugin watercolours [42–45].

The whole length of the West Front, including part of the service range with the clock tower (a water tower) to the south, is given in [38] and [42]; the tower was considered important, and considerable expense was incurred in making it higher than originally planned.[69] Its demolition in the middle of the nineteenth century was unfortunate; its great gilded weather vane, in the form of a dragon, alone survives. Perhaps one day the dragon may have the good fortune to top a reconstructed tower.

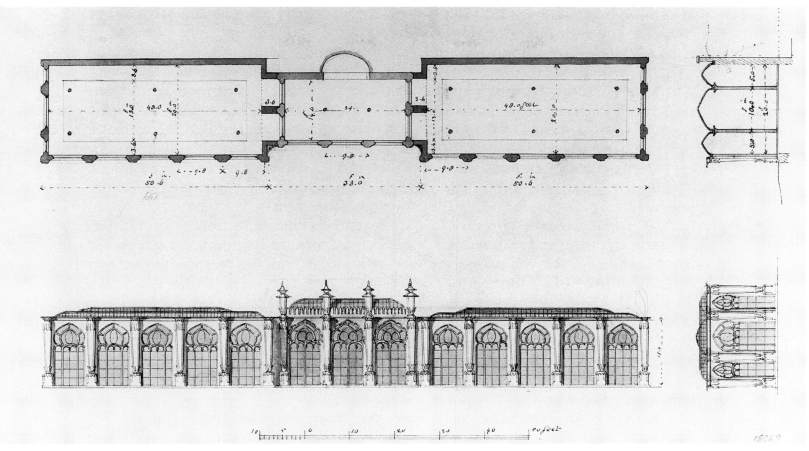

49 Design for a conservatory. c. *1824.* CAT. NO. 49.

The watercolour [46] shows the entrance portico, containing the Octagon Hall (see pp. 235–6) that was added in 1819. The windows to its right are those of the Red Drawing Room (see pp. 229–31); on the lower stuccoed surface of the cupola tower beyond can be clearly seen the deliberate variations in hue of the simulated stone. The two towers on either side of the central dome are perhaps the most overtly Gothick features of the building; that on the right contains a magnificent wooden spiral staircase with an elliptical curve that, it has been remarked,[70] could have been designed only by an architect who began life as a carpenter. The drive, with its circle for the easy manoeuvre of carriages, is of gravel that harmonises with the building (unlike the tarmac that now disfigures it, as it disfigures also, with a far more serious result, the grand environs of another creation, or part-creation, of George IV). The northern wing [44, 47] was also added in 1819; on the ground floor, beneath the overhanging balcony to the west [47], lie the three rooms that make up the King's Apartments (see pp. 223–8); the windows show the continuing use of the half-curtain. To the left of the Apartments is the room that served as George IV's bathroom; above it is a small room amongst the varied uses of which was, at a later date, that of nursery for Queen Victoria's children (the bars then inserted on the windows are still there today). The range of apartments above the King's Apartments was used by ladies as various as Lady Conyngham and Queen Adelaide.

The masterly plan given by Nash (plan H) for the gardens was never carried out in its entirety, although its inclusion may well mean that it had received royal approval. Its serpentine paths and picturesque massing of trees, designed with the utmost skill to give the Pavilion the impression of lying in lawns and embedded in greenery, are utterly different from the prosaic modern style, which has taken the grounds as they were left 'unimproved' by George IV, widened them for motor vehicles, and added municipal bedding out.*

Nash himself would not have supplied the original planting lists; these would have come from W.T.Aiton, 'Gardener to His Majesty', who worked at Kew with Sir Joseph Banks, from where the plants were probably sent to Brighton. At St James's Park and at Buckingham Palace it appears that the system was for Aiton to give a list of shrubs to the Office of Woods; this was then submitted to Nash, who advised whether the shrubs were suitable for his projected landscape. For St James's Park, Nash had sent up his own gardener from Cowes to superintend the planting and to discriminate between the trees. The lists supplied by Aiton include many exotics, including those arriving from India and China.

It is probable that George IV lost interest; the chinoiserie charms of Virginia Water, paradisical and secluded, took the place of those of Brighton. He last visited the Pavilion in 1827. But two designs survive [48, 49], by Nash or emanating from his office, for a Conservatory or Orangery in the grounds. This is not shown in plan H; the presumption seems therefore to be that it was an afterthought. They are stately designs, showing a structure with a total length of something over a hundred and twenty feet. It may be that the Conservatory was meant to close the view from the west gardens to New Road, which is concealed in plan H by a thick belt of trees, and which was the site of Repton's small 'Western Conservatory'. What a pity it was never built!

Apart from other reasons, it is likely that money was lacking for what must have been by then a project marginal to the King's main preoccupations – Windsor Castle and Buckingham Palace. Otherwise, his eager appetite would surely have seen it erected.

The estimates and bills for the Royal Pavilion show clearly at what a cost this glittering whim was realised, and in what a sickening manner the enterprise lurched from financial crisis to financial crisis. Tradesmen were accustomed to an intermittent and unsystematic payment of bills, but the complete disregard of sense or caution, and the lack of any sign of having learned the lessons that experience would surely have taught both Prince and architect, seem in retrospect heartless and prodigal. As far as Nash was concerned it was also foolish, since he himself advanced large sums. Estimates were not only exceeded: they contained such items as 'The Alterations of the 2 Iron staircases [those in the Corridor] 00.0.0' – completely unpriced![71] The King's frequent vacillations played havoc with them even as they were; it was recognised that Nash 'laboured under peculiar disadvantages in the conduct of these concerns . . . much excess expenditure must be attributed to the alterations that have taken place after the Works have been nearly completed.'[72] Serious attempts were made to control the situation; in 1821 Knighton was writing in a letter marked 'secret' that he would 'leave no stone unturned to sell every thing that I can lay hands on, to bring The King out of his present disgraceful Position; – for to be in Debt is a disgrace –.'[73]

A hundred and fifty years later, in an age when much greater sums are spent far less innocently, all this is forgotten; the view of the Pavilion across the western lawns, or from the traffic-congested roads of the Old Steine, continues to lift humdrum existence on to a more vivid plane. But the gasps of the multitude are reserved for the prodigalities of the interior; conjured up as they were by a constitutional king, they give, in a way given by no other building in these islands, a sense of the unbridled luxuries of despotism.

* Since these words were written the Sussex Garden History Society has sponsored an installation that should result in the grounds looking eventually as Nash designed them.

THE INTERIOR

The Crace Firm

Any attempt to elucidate the history of the interior of the Royal Pavilion, or to place in context the wonderful designs, executed and unexecuted, that survive, must rely heavily on the ledger entries of the Crace family. These were acquired by a successor firm in 1899; typed copies were given to the Royal Pavilion in 1932.[1] The originals were apparently destroyed in the blitz. The ledgers record works done on interior decoration between 1802 and 1804, 1815 and 1819, and 1820 and 1822.

The Crace firm had a long and honourable history.[2] Its fortunes were founded by Edward Crace (1725–99) who, beginning as a painter of coaches, had by 1773 sufficiently extended his practice to be engaged upon decorating Wyatt's Pantheon. In 1781 a royal connexion was formed, in that he was put in charge of the King's pictures, an appointment he retained until his death; in 1826 his catalogue of the collection was given by his grandson Frederick to George IV. Edward's son, John (1754–1819), good looking and of good address, obtained important commissions as a decorator, working for Taylor, Wyatt, Stuart, Holland, and Soane; he 'did much to improve the style of decoration of that period, being materially assisted by able French artists who came to England owing to the disorders of the French Revolution'. He worked for the Prince of Wales at Carlton House and at Brighton, where his services are recorded in the abstracted account of the building and decorating of the first Pavilion.[3] He retired in 1812.

It was John Crace's son, Frederick (1779–1859), who was the most talented member of the family to work at Brighton, and who, as a result of that talent, enjoyed the signal favour of George IV. He began his career in December 1793, by an apprenticeship with 'Mr. Richard Holland, eminent builder'; in 1794 he was sent to superintend work done at Carlton House, and the story is that he was 'first noticed by the Prince and Mrs. Fitzherbert when he was at work upon gilding the iron railing of the staircase'; he is recorded at Brighton in 1795. Unsatisfied with the allowance of £300 a year that he received from his father, he went into business on his own account in 1806, at the age of twenty-seven.

Elated, perhaps, by early success, he seems to have acquired a tinge of pomposity. John Crace used to relate an episode that happened 'when they were working at Brighton. Frederick *was responsible for the work* [my italics] but on one occasion [John] came down to Brighton to inspect. He was conducted round with so much solemnity by his son that it was too much for him, and during the dinner-hour he stepped out to a neighbouring toyshop. When Frederick returned with his father to finish the inspection he was greeted with squeals from the penny whistles with which his workmen were armed.' Obviously his workmen were not above ragging him; could his self-importance perhaps have accounted for the tone of the subscription to [140]? And could [179], which is obviously a caricature, be of Frederick, who was 'a remarkably tall, stout, hearty man'?

There are indications of an interest in things Chinese in both John and

Frederick; according to the story, young John Crace came into favour with Queen Charlotte by expeditiously saving a China vase that she upset. John's house in High Row, where he lived after his retirement, had 'many Chinese curiosities in it and several Chinese paintings were hung on the walls'; a painting by Dighton showed him displaying a piece of oriental china to the Prince. Frederick 'made many studies of Chinese art'; he was also 'clever in the imitation of woods and marbles, and his father employed him much at this, which was then a novelty and much in vogue' (referring to the 1790s).

Frederick Crace was a decorator and designer of great ability and virtuosity, but was rivalled by another man who worked extensively on the Pavilion from 1815 onwards – Robert Jones. The latter appears to have worked independently of the Craces in the sense that he was not a member of the Crace firm; perhaps the Prince played off one against the other. Jones' designs are more *spirituelle* than Frederick Crace's; they have spontaneity and fire. The man appears as anonymous as his name, but it is just possible that a hint of his training is preserved in a chance allusion. In February 1839 John Gregory Crace delivered two lectures on the history of paperhangings to the Royal Institute of British Architects; he mentioned a 'very superior Chelsea Manufactory', established in 1786 by George and Frederick Eckhardt, of which the wallpapers were 'finished' (painted) by 'Artists constantly retained by the Manufacturer among whom were Boileau, Feuglet, Joinot and Jones'. The evidence might well be dismissed as too slight, but the fact that it was a Crace who mentioned this particular 'Jones', together with the individual style and the occupation of Robert Jones himself, is perfectly consistent with such previous work, and makes the identification possible. Certainly, Robert Jones' verve and dash are of a type that might well have been acquired as the result of being the only Englishman working amongst foreign artists.

Although Frederick Crace and Robert Jones appear to have worked as independent agents, this does not mean that they did not collaborate. A letter from Watier, who appears to have occupied the position of Clerk of Works, sent on December 23 1817, makes the situation clear: 'Upon receipt of this which is sent to you by express, you will lose no time in attending the Prince Regent's commands to be here imidiatley [sic] to make some arrangts. respecting the Rooms which is to be divided between You & Mr. Jones to whom I have written by the same Messinger [sic] to come down imidiatley. . . .'[4]

This close collaboration, which included the architect, is confirmed by a study of the accounts. On the same page, for instance, of Messrs Bailey and Saunders' accounts for the Music Room in 1817[5] one reads such items as the following:

To a Canopy made to Mr. Nash's design formed into an octagn. with Ropes up each rib. . . .

To makg. a Model for a chimney Piece to Mr. Crace's design. . . .

To 100 Carved Ornamts. to Mr. Crace's design. . . .

To 6 Pedestals for the Orleans Vases made to Mr. Jones' design. . . .

To makg. a model for the Pagoda Stands to Mr. Craces design. . . .

The Music Room was a complicated undertaking that probably needed all available forces; one finds that in less complex areas – for example the Red Drawing Room or the King's Apartments – one artist (in this case Jones) appears to have been employed.

Many hands appear to be discernible in the surviving designs, and attempts to distinguish them are attended by frustrating ambiguities. Those executed at any one period – for instance, the designs made possibly for the Glass Passage and adjacent areas [82, 84–100] – have general similarities, but may be from different hands; in this group it appears possible that [82, 87, 93, 94] came from the same hand, and that [89, 95–99], which appear similar but have a lighter, not so 'barbaric' palette, and a different idiom for the rock-work, are by another artist. Again, the designs for the Entrance Hall [148–150, 154–156, 160] could all be from the same hand, but it seems more likely that several artists were involved, all working in the same idiom. The inscription 'For Mr. Crace' on one of the less skilful drawings [148] is perhaps significant; it indicates that this design, at least, is not from the hand of one of the Craces.

These early designs have in common the 'barbaric' element remarked by observers; they display a thorough-going but at times somewhat old-fashioned use of the Chinese idiom. One is tempted to conjecture that John Crace was the guiding spirit, and that he was perhaps assisted by the gifted and very young Frederick; it would have been as natural for Frederick's style at this stage to reflect that of his father as it would have been for it to develop into something rather different. It did so develop, for nothing could be more different from John's style than some of the later, very sophisticated designs that may be attributed to Frederick [246, 250]. An inscription by John Gregory Crace on the flyleaf of a book of designs records that it contains 'Scraps from Chinese drawings drawn by Frederick Crace 1800–1820 – this book was often looked over by King George the 4th'.[6] If this is accurate, and one may perhaps assume that it is, it may confirm the theory of a development of style, for at one end of the book are designs in the style of 1802–4; the others, very different, many of which may be related to the later Corridor, are in the style of 1815 and afterwards.

Especially perplexing is the relationship between the hands of Frederick Crace and Robert Jones. At times the styles appear sharply differentiated; Jones' designs for the Saloon and Banqueting Room [51, 230] are different from anything attributable to Frederick Crace. One is on equally firm ground with the later Crace designs for the Music Room. After that, one begins to wonder. For instance, the two 'marbled' designs for the Entrance Hall [161, 162] appear more likely to be by Crace than by Jones, despite the fact that the accounts firmly place the wall paintings as from Jones' hand (see p. 159). And the drawing of dragons [231], which seems to be by Jones, may provide the clue to the identification of other designs. But what is one to make of the early designs for the Music Room [237–239, 245], which appear to have some of the characteristics of both artists? Or of [254] and [255] on the one hand, and [256] on the other? If the account quoted above refers to these designs, the first two are by Frederick Crace, the second by Robert Jones. It probably does not; some of the 'clues' may be misleading.

One factor may have influenced the situation. Placed as they were, it is hardly possible that the two artists were not conscious of some rivalry; indeed, the King's purposes may not have been served without the introduction of the desire to surpass. Even without that element, they were working in a fashion that may well have encouraged one to assimilate aspects of the other's style, a process seen at work in much greater artists, and one that may have been at times necessary, given the context, to produce an integrated result. It seems possible that this rivalry, if rivalry it were, continued as work proceeded and spurred the artists on to search for greater originality. The change, for instance, in Crace's own style in the later Music Room designs – painted in much more opaque pigments, reinforced with Chinese white (a return in some ways to the style of 1802–4) – is extraordinarily striking; the heavy, rich colour and congested decoration produced an effect that was quite new (did it, incidentally, owe some of its hallucinatory

50 The Saloon. c. *1815.* CAT. NO. 53.

intensity to the effect on his mind of the opiates consumed in large quantities by George IV, who used laudanum to dull the pain of his growing infirmities? The stately pleasure domes of Kubla Khan and of the Prince Regent may have had a common origin). Quite new, again, was Jones' Indian riposte in the Saloon, for which, unfortunately, so few designs survive.

Before a detailed description of the designs is embarked upon, it may be useful for the reader to be given a general idea of the conclusions reached, and of the broad developments of style between 1802 and 1822.

It has become clear that more of these designs were certainly or probably executed than has previously been thought, and that more belong to the 1802–4 period. The appearance, or aspects of the appearance, of the 1802–4 Saloon, Entrance Hall, Conservatory, Glass Passage, Dining Room, Ante Room to the Dining Room, and possibly Boudoir may be recovered. The period of experiment that began in 1815, or possibly slightly earlier, is amply documented; one knows how the Entrance Hall and Ante Room to the Dining Room looked in their brief 'marbled' phase, the appearance of the first versions of the Corridor, of the Blue and Yellow Drawing Rooms, and of the elaborated version of the Saloon that disappeared in 1822.

The chinoiserie styles seen in the designs for the interiors at Brighton vary considerably in character. The appearance of the 1802 Saloon, for example, as preserved in the 1815 drawing [50], is in a manner distinct from that of the 1802 Entrance Hall [150], or from that of the design for the Glass Passage [82] from the same period. One very interesting style [161, 241] relied much upon decorative marbling; it was an original idea to combine this technique with chinoiserie, and one supposes that it may have been the result of a fusion of the decorative marbling and graining used so extensively at Carlton House with the oriental style. The result of this combination of marbling and chinoiserie with the deep and brilliant palette of high 'Regency' taste was amazingly successful, and one regrets the disappearance of these decorations.

Another vein of decoration is seen in combinations of marbling with the unorthodox use of sky motifs (the latter, again, perhaps drawn from the vocabulary of classical decoration), Chinese arcades, fretwork, and occidental rustication [147, 151, 154, 156]. The last achieves an almost surrealist poetry, which reaches its zenith in the strange designs for the Entrance Hall [148, 155].

Another category, that of the 'Chinese rococo' designs for the reworked Saloon [67], the first version of the Corridor [181], and the Yellow [116] and Blue [105] Drawing Rooms, appeared in 1815 and was on its way out by 1818–19; its advent may have been influenced by the peculiar talents of Robert Jones. The style is characterised by elaboration, bright colour, unforced gaiety, and a chic lightheartedness of spirit. Its ingredients survive today in certain details of the Corridor and Red Drawing Room, and may possibly blossom again in the South Galleries, of which enough remains recorded and in store to permit an accurate reconstruction.

The final style seen in the Pavilion, that most in evidence today, was perhaps conjured forth by the construction of the two great State Apartments of Music Room and Banqueting Room; their large and solemn forms demanded a treatment adapted to a scale hitherto unknown, either to the building or to the chinoiserie style itself. An added opportunity was given by the use in the interior, as on the exterior, of the Indian style, seized perhaps most whole-heartedly in some of the early designs for the Entrance Hall [153] and, of course, in the resplendent later Saloon [81]. It has been thought that the increased sense of regality of the Prince Regent may have played its part in the assumption of this new pomp and splendour – as, indeed, it may possibly have played its part in the use of Indian motifs. The intense romanticism of the dedication by Denon to Bonaparte of his Egyptian volume,[7] of which several copies were in the Prince's library and of which a copy was sent down to Brighton in September 1804,[8] must have appealed to the Prince's temperament, and was applicable equally to his relationship with the subcontinent of India and his recreation of its monuments: 'Joindre l'éclat de votre nom à la splendeur des monuments d'Egypte, c'est rattacher les fastes glorieux de notre siècle au temps fabuleux d'histoire; c'est rechauffer les cendres des Sesostris et des Menès, comme vous conquerants, comme vous bienfaiteurs.' A British monarch who could place in his bedchamber at Brighton a boulle cabinet bearing a depiction of 'Pharaoh's Dream' must have been capable of an equal self-identification with the great Mughal Emperors of more recent history.

Whatever the reason, the magnificence of the new State Apartments influenced the smaller rooms, sometimes in a role as foil (the two white and gold Drawing Rooms, next to overpowering crescendi of colour), sometimes, no doubt, in an attempt to weld the building into an harmonious whole. Richness cannot be said to have subdued fantasy, but it did to a degree restrain it. Moreover one most significant element, absent earlier, and absent from the retained Corridor, was at this time added. George IV had always been extremely fond of gold; he was no doubt in agreement with Burke that 'all colours are blended well by Gold. Gold is the colour of light, and produces the effect of sunshine.'[9] His palaces glittered with gold; Carlton House was described as 'the palace of Aladdin, and the ideas of him who desired "nothing but gilding, nothing but what looks glittering" are outvied. . . .'[10] Gold was now seen everywhere in the Pavilion, in the utmost profusion; it would have been inconsistent with the playfulness of the earlier style, but was perfectly in accord with the new grandeur.

The early decorations employed Chinese wallpapers and furniture, in association with multitudinous Chinese and oriental 'curiosities'. It is noticeable that as time went on these became progressively less important. The most breathtaking of the later 'Chinese' wallpapers, that in the Corridor, is English, as is the magnificent 'damask' dragon wallpaper; it is as if the fused, eclectic style evolved eventually for the Pavilion could less and less accommodate anything not especially created. In place of the 'curiosities' appeared large quantities of porcelain, oriental and chinoiserie, often mounted in gilt bronze of the grandest and most sumptuous order. The Chinese export furniture was pushed into the background by the elaborate confections of Robert Jones, and Bailey and Saunders, and by exotic spoils from France. The original type of interior can perhaps best be seen in the South Galleries [274], where two 'curiosities' survive on the bamboo tables. It would probably have been difficult to retain the earlier objects. Apart from lacquer, which has the strength of combined black and gold, many Chinese objects have a delicacy that is not flattered by the bold colours and strong forms of Regency taste; this is especially true of the wallpapers. The 'historical' and other Chinese wallpapers that were such a feature of the 1802–4 decorations would have been difficult to place in the new surroundings.

The techniques used in the decorations altered also. Surviving examples lead one to believe that the early work may have been done using a comparatively simple range of techniques; there was no great attempt at refinement of finish. It is clear also that most of the decoration consisted of flat painting; there seems to have been little three-dimensional ornament, save in the Saloon. The methods employed from 1815 onwards were very different. The old, witty illusionistic painting, in which every conceivable existing and non-existing wood was imitated and invented, continued; to it was added the most intricate and highly wrought carving, finished resplendently in regular or green gold, oil or water gilt, burnished and matt – or in silver leaf, glazed in colours to give every metallic iridescence (the last technique, when applied to snakes or dragons, can impart an uncanny life). Mirrors appeared everywhere; on the walls, in door panels, and in recesses. The effect was brilliant, sophisticated, and grand.

Below is given an exposition of the designs, room by room where possible; this method seems the clearest way of explaining the changing situation in a building where frequent changes of area and nomenclature can induce a sense of vertigo.

51 Design for the Saloon. By Robert Jones. C. *1816–22.* CAT. NO. 76.

The Saloon

It seems appropriate to begin with the Saloon, the only interior in the building that, as the principal room of Holland's Pavilion, and as an important room of Nash's Pavilion, has preserved its basic shape unchanged since 1787; its decoration chronicles the King's changes in taste over that long period.

That basic shape has a harmony that never fails to please; it is circular, with chimneypiece on the west wall facing windows on the east, and semi-domed alcoves to the north and south, as delineated in plan A. Two early unexecuted designs survive [52, 53], in the Etruscan or Pompeian style; the inscription 'This Design for the Great Saloon was received from M. Lignereux' refers to an artist who was paid, in association with Dominique Daguerre, for work at Carlton House.[11] The designs show alternative treatments for each side of the fireplace, and are not without some amatory references. Is it too fanciful to see perhaps a concealed 'M' (Maria Fitzherbert) in the somewhat peculiar drooping leaves towards the top of the alcove designs (where they would have been not immediately apparent)?

The only depiction of the Saloon in its earliest phase is, from the point of view of an assessment of the decoration, unsatisfactorily imprecise, however charming it may be in other respects [54]. Rowlandson's watercolour is also unsuccessful in reproducing accurately the proportions of the room, although a chimneypiece in Holland style is apparent, and the playful garlands and ovals of the wall decorations are typical of the artist mentioned by Wigstead as responsible: the 'Grand Saloon' is 'beautifully decorated with Paintings by Rebecca, executed in his best manner'.[12] For this work Biagio Rebecca received a total of £360, of which £160 was 'paid by Mr. Holland for the Ceiling only';[13] the artist had to wait until January 1793 before his account for the work was finally settled.[14]

The Saloon remained unchanged for fourteen years; the Crace ledgers then document a burst of activity between Midsummer 1802 and Midsummer 1804, at which latter time the customary signal for completion was given by the process of 'high Varnishing the whole of the Ornamental Works twice with Copal'.[15] It is highly probable that [53], hitherto thought to depict alterations of more than a decade later, and certainly dating from more than a decade later, at a time when further changes were in view (see p. 90), substantially presents much of the appearance of the 1802–4 scheme. This is suggested both by a circumstantial account published in 1809, in Attree's *Topography of Brighton*, and by the Crace ledgers. The former needs full quotation:

This room forms an oblong of fifty-five feet. The ceiling is admirably contrived and executed, and represents a clouded sky, from which are suspended, by flying dragons, three immense lanthorns, exquisitely embellished with paintings, among which is seen the *Faum*, or bird of royalty, in all its rich and variegated plumage, and such as in China is only permitted to ornament the palace of the Emperor. The cornice and frieze of this elegant apartment are scarlet, blue and yellow, before which hangs a yellow silk net, with tassels and bells, splendid in effect,

52 Design for the Saloon. 1787. CAT. NO. 50.

53 Design for the Saloon. 1787. CAT. NO. 51.

and perfectly unique. The cornice is supported by four columns, and eight pilasters, with dragons twisting round them, and a light corridor or charmingly painted gallery passes round the dome, from the open work of which eight dragons appear in the act of flying through, and each suspending by an elegant chain a painted lanthorn, though of much smaller dimensions than the three former. In the various lanthorns are upwards of thirty organd burners, which diffuse a brilliance more easily conceived than expressed and display the panneled sides of the room, and a beautiful paper of a blue ground, the ornaments of which are white etched with silver, interspersed with birds of the richest plumage, and which, literally appear animated, and fascinate the beholder, to the most enchanting advantage.

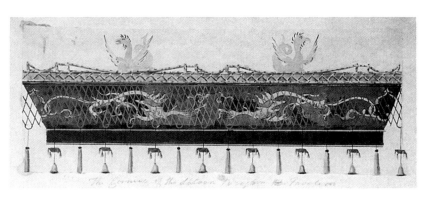

54 The Saloon. By Thomas Rowlandson. C. *1790.* CAT. NO. 52.

55 Design for the Saloon. 1802–4. CAT. NO. 54.

It may easily be seen that the above account reproduces many of the features of [53]. The Crace ledgers emphasise the connexion, as do other related designs.

For example, the ledger accounts for Midsummer to Christmas 1802 mention '7228.0 ft. Run of Bamboo Shadowed spotted and varnished' at a cost of £90 7s od; this decoration seems likely to be the frieze above the cornice in [53].[16] Beneath it may be discerned the 'Bamboo railing projecting on face of cornice. 3 times painted etc. and spotted', and beneath again is a 'Bamboo zig zag on cornice' and 'Wood netting three times scarlet'.[17] The nature of this design, with its three-dimensional elements, may perhaps be seen more clearly in [55], with its wood netting and dragons; it seems likely that this design belongs to the 1802–4 period, or, just possibly, it may date from a later refurbishment described below. A charming cornice design showing dragons chasing a fabulous beast that appears to be looking apprehensively back over its shoulder [56] shows something of the same idea, and may possibly have been associated with the Saloon (attached to the same sheet, probably after 1815, is a dado design probably connected with the Conservatory/Music Room, not illustrated). The bamboo motifs of [53] and [55], seen again in [57], of a type constantly used at the Pavilion and last displayed in their full glory in the 1815 Corridor, are derived from Chinese export rattan furniture; they constitute a hugely enlarged and witty use of the panels seen in chairs and tables, and of the very fragile detached panels that were inserted by Marsh and Tatham into their simulated bamboo furniture.

The Saloon was given a sky ceiling. The Crace ledgers mention 'Three times fine Sky colour distemper £7. 14s. 6d';[18] this, one coat more than usual, was a preparation for 'clouding'; the main account for sky ceilings painted by Louis Barzago[19] does not mention the Saloon, but it is highly probable that he painted that also. Other items in the ledgers include '3 Canopys with bells, birds, dragons, etc. in proper colors';[20] one may be seen to the right in [53], as yet without the decussated netting and elaborate 'Carlton House' type window draperies that were

and heightened – £40. o. o', and 'Painting 4 Pilasters scarlet ground, very fully enriched yellow ornaments on Do. heightened and shadowed. £25. 4s. od'.[26]

Four fascinating designs exist that do not appear to have been intended for the 1802–4 Saloon, but yet have affiliations with it. Certain motifs seen prominently in [53] are repeated in [62–64]; the first two display three Gothic arches, with a window on the extreme left, followed by a chimneypiece or, more likely, a console table, in the centre, and a sketchily indicated door on the extreme right. Despite their obvious connexions with the decoration of the 1802–4 Saloon, by no stretch of the imagination could their proportions have been fitted within that room, nor, indeed, within any room that ever existed in the Pavilion. Yet the connexion is inescapable; they seem, moreover, to be by the same hand as do other designs from the 1802–4 period and to share details with yet other designs; for example, the Chinese fretwork in blue seen above the windows in [53] is identical with that seen in certain designs for the Entrance Hall [148, 154, 155]; the pilaster fretwork in pink and yellow that borders the blue and silver wallpaper seen in [64] is virtually identical with the blue and white pilaster decoration seen in [141] and [142]. Incidentally, the wall on which the decoration of [64] is placed appears too small for the 1802 Saloon; perversely, the related overdoor decoration [58] – related by the yellow bamboo motif and by the border above in blue, yellow, and pink – is for a larger room.

There is one possible explanation for all these consistencies and inconsistencies, here offered very tentatively. It has been said above that [62] and [63] could be accommodated in no room that ever existed in the Pavilion; is it possible that they are designs made for one of the two wings added by Holland in 1801 *before* these had taken their final shape? This, if true, would mean an earlier date for the decision to insert Chinese decorations than has hitherto been supposed. The plan (plan G) made by Nash of the Pavilion 'as before 1815' shows a configuration of door (or window?), chimneypiece, and alcove in the Holland Dining Room added in 1801 that may, just possibly, relate to these designs. The overdoor design [58] could possibly have been meant to be contiguous with the wall design [64], perhaps a larger room leading into a smaller; the interpretation may seem forced, but no more unlikely than that the resemblances were fortuitous.

After 1804 nothing much appears to have been done to the Saloon until 1815. The Crace ledgers for the quarter ending October 10 1815 then first mention the Saloon in connexion with 'cleaning and repairing 8 large frames to India papers etc. £40. o. o', 'clouding 3 large ceilings £40. o. o', 'repairing and cleaning India paper', and cleaning dragons, canopies, columns, etc.[27] The work on the ceilings would have been necessitated by damage from smoke from lanterns and candles over eleven years; the rest was presumably wear and tear.

It is at this time, probably early in 1815, that [53] appears to have been painted. The artist seems to have sat in the Saloon and drawn the old room as he saw it, with windows and alcove (the pole alone remains) stripped of their drapery. The chandelier, drawn on a separate piece of paper and in line, has been attached to the coloured drawing – presumably in order to demonstrate how the new chandelier would look. An identical coloured drawing of the chandelier exists separately, on a piece of paper watermarked 1814 [60]. Other, rejected designs exist for the Saloon chandelier [65]. The two slight pencil sketches [61, 71] appear to have been destined for this room, as do others [66, 73–75]; the last group has the decussated fringe that was a motif of the Saloon.

One drawing [76] is of interest for an ancillary reason. A slight, but lively and accomplished drawing of a lantern is surmounted by a most crudely drawn bird, obviously meant to retain the lantern in its claws. The bird looks as if it had been added to the existing sketch as a suggestion, and the hand is that of an amateur – who would have been the most likely person to do this? Is it possible that this crude sketch is the idea in rehearsal not only of the bird that eventually was to fly, accompanied by serpents, above the central lustre of the Saloon in its final form [81] (replacing a dragon from the intermediate scheme [67]), but is the fore-runner also of the much greater dragon that was to perform a similar office for the Banqueting Room gasolier? One has to admit that there is no evidence either way other than the absence of verifiable earlier examples.

Pugin's drawings meticulously recorded what was before his eyes; he does not show a patterned carpet in his depictions of the revivified Saloon that came into being in 1815 [67]. A design exists that may, from its circular shape and general colour, have been meant for the Saloon [68]. The design, of naturalistic chinoiserie flowers and foliage, is of a similar nature to that seen in a drawing from the Crace book – not necessarily for a carpet – [70], and to the carpet installed in the South Galleries [274]; the former dates probably from 1815 or afterwards, whilst the date of the South Galleries carpet is probably, but not certainly, also after 1815. However, this does not mean that [68] may not be earlier; it has affinities with the designs of 1802, both in technique and in the mannered juxtaposition of the Venetian red line with the blue infill of the 'star' shape, seen also in the surrounds of the pointed windows in [63].

The Crace accounts indicate that work in the Saloon had finished, or virtually finished, by Christmas 1816.[28] The result is seen in Pugin's pencil drawing and watercolour [67, 69], which display the gaiety and splendour of the Saloon in its new guise. The blue and silver wallpaper has disappeared, to be replaced, according to the watercolour, by what appears to be a Chinese wallpaper with a grey/cream ground. The Crace ledgers refer to 'Chinese' and 'India' paper, terms not used of the blue and silver wallpaper,[29] and contain also an account that appears to refer to the wallpaper of the Saloon, unfortunately in another colour – green. There is some ambiguity, as may be seen:[30]

PAPER PROVIDED BY ORDER OF HIS ROYAL HIGHNESS FOR ROBSON & HALE

To 1 very fine set of India Paper, green ground coloured flowers, birds, etc. containing 24 sheets	£63. 0. 0
. . . 7 sheets of India Paper green ground and colored flowers and birds	£7. 7. 0
Painting by order the rail work and marble base to India paper and painting the representation of water with reflecting shadows in 8 pannels to paper in Saloon, including 5 Chinese Drawings of Ducks	£21. 0. 0
Providing 7 sheets of India paper with birds, cut up for Saloon	£10. 10. 0
Mr Crace and his men attending His Royal Highness in arranging the hanging of the India Paper and birds in Saloon, Prince Regent's bedroom and other rooms.	£2. 2. 0

The circumstantial account of the 'rail work' and water, with '5 Chinese Drawings of Ducks' (one may be seen on the left in [67]), is corroborated by the details of Pugin's pencil drawing; a green background would have made sense in the progression from blue (the Blue Drawing Room; see [105]), to green (the Saloon), to yellow (the Yellow Drawing Room; see [116]).

From Pugin's drawing, it seems almost as if the Prince were here beginning to create a chinoiserie version of the Carlton House style. Perhaps it is the weightier

62 Design for a wall with three Gothic arches. ?1801. CAT. NO. 57.

elements that contribute to this impression – the central chandelier, now firmly in place, and the voluminous new yellow draperies hung from the old window canopies, which themselves have been given the 'Chinese net work' at their tops. The upholstered wall seats, again with netting, and the large circular ottoman – the latter soon to be moved into the centre of the room, a yet more formal and weighty arrangement – give unity to the floor area, despite the elegant clutter of furniture near the windows, which includes two 'Japan black cabinets'[31] and two types of chair in simulated bamboo.

One can see in Pugin's watercolour drawing the '4 new square Chinese lanthorns red and striped yellow with dragons at the corners varnished £6. o. o';[32] the square and octagonal lanterns shown are similar to two pencil designs [71, 76]. Also visible are some of the '52 bells and ornaments yellow, red and varnished' which had been added to the cornice, of which the 'Chinese net work' had been coloured 'brighter yellow'.[33] No mirrors (although they may have been removed for the renovations) are shown between the windows in [53]; now, however, they are placed in those positions, their frames 'red ground with 3 bamboos round'.[34]

The white marble chimneypiece seen on the right in Pugin's drawing is still in the Royal Pavilion, although not in the Saloon; it is in a delicate and beautiful chinoiserie manner very much like that of Holland – it probably survived from the 1802 redecorations. On it, for the first time in this room, stands the famous 'Kylin' clock. In gilt bronze and Chinese porcelain, it exhibits the base added by Vulliamy, but as yet appears to be without the gilt sunflowers that were later to tie the clock in more closely with the sunflowers that were to blaze forth in Jones' decorations.

The 1815–16 Saloon was to enjoy only a short life. In 1819 a small sum – £28 – was paid for 'Cleaning and repairing the whole of the ornamental painting, being very much injured by smoke of lamps'.[35] A temporary stay of execution only; indeed, it seems within the bounds of possibility that as early as 1816 or 1817

63 *Design for a wall with three Gothic arches and Chinese lantern.* *?1801.* CAT. NO. 58.

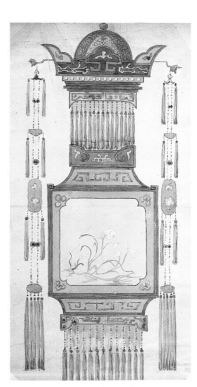

65 *Design for a lantern.*
Probably 1802–4.
CAT. NO. 62.

64 *Design for a blue and silver wall decoration.* *1802 or earlier.* CAT. NO. 60.

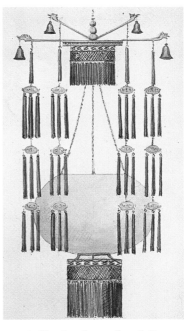

66 *Design for a chandelier,*
probably for the Saloon. *1815*
or earlier. CAT. NO. 68.

67 The Saloon, 1817. By Augustus Pugin. CAT. NO. 73.

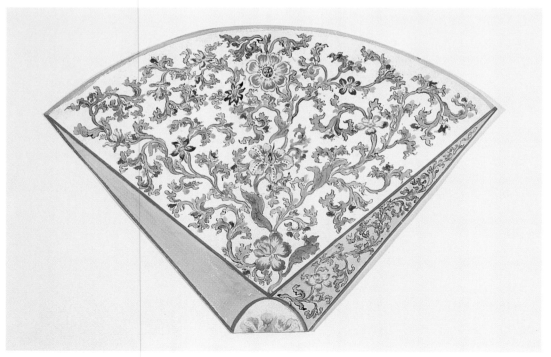

68 Design for a carpet, probably for the Saloon. Possibly by Frederick Grace. C. *1815.* CAT. NO. 74.

69 The Saloon, 1817. By Augustus Pugin. CAT. NO. 72.

70 Design of naturalistic flowers and foliage. C. *1815.* CAT. NO. 75.

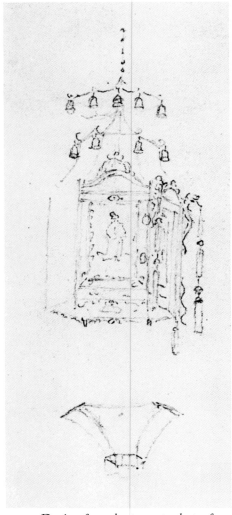

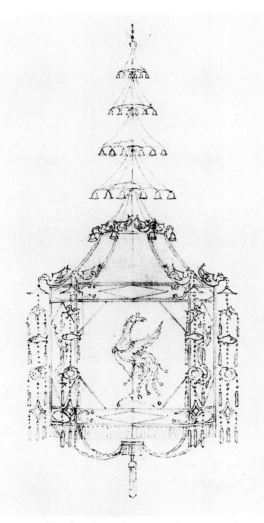

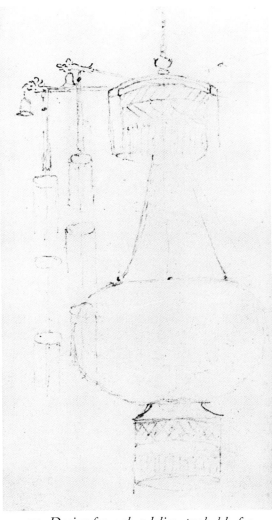

71 Design for a lantern, perhaps for the Saloon. 1815 or earlier. CAT. NO. 65.

72 Design for a lantern. 1815 or earlier. CAT. NO. 66.

73 Design for a chandelier, probably for the Saloon. 1815 or earlier. CAT. NO. 67.

the desire completely to redecorate the Saloon may have existed, but that the work had been delayed by the need to complete and decorate the new Banqueting and Music Rooms, before plunging yet another part of the building into chaos. The clue may be given by the ravishing watercolour, inscribed 'design for the door recess at each end of the Saloon', that exhibits in its full virtuosity the free and painterly style of Robert Jones [51]. For this design, whilst containing motifs that were to be used in the Saloon, contains also motifs (rehearsed in the Entrance Hall [153, 162]) that appear in the Banqueting Room (the wall paintings, the over-door) and in the Music Room (the palm-tree pilasters). Unless it were the intention to echo the style of the Banqueting Room within the Saloon, which seems unlikely – but not impossible, since the two Drawing Rooms on each side of the Saloon do, in their final form, balance each other stylistically, and the baroque principle of complementary colours in adjacent rooms is followed throughout the palace; the two great State Rooms, the Music Room and Banqueting Room, do have elements in common and it may have seemed logical to extend the idiom to the Saloon – unless this were the intention, [51] may be the first extant design to herald a new style within the Pavilion, and one unique to it.

The most obvious innovation is the introduction of Indian motifs; they are,

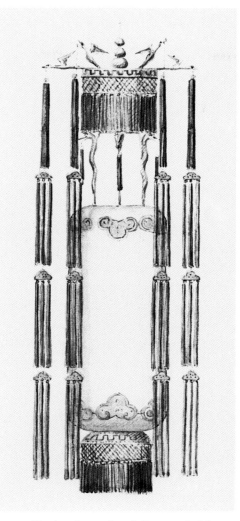

74 Design for a chandelier, probably for the Saloon. 1815 or earlier. CAT. NO. 69.

75 Design for a chandelier, probably for the Saloon. 1815 or earlier. CAT. NO. 70.

76 Design for a lantern surmounted by a bird. 1815 or earlier. CAT. NO. 71.

moreover, used in a manner that, without copying exactly the form given by the rays of the sun or the petals of a sunflower, manages to convey the impression of a burst of light or of movement outwards from an epicentre, an effect of splendour and festivity. The same movement can be seen elsewhere in the building; in the extraordinary opening-up of petals at the apex of the Music Room gasolier, in the plantain leaves of the Banqueting Room dome, in the strange explosions of light in the paintings on the tent roofs of the Banqueting Room, and in the star-shaped mirror motifs above the Banqueting Room gasoliers. One remarkable feature, in this Indian room, is the extraordinary use of the Egyptian winged solar disk, which appears, fully fledged, capping the serpent-wreathed pilasters in the two apses.

The colour of [51] is highly developed; much more 'high Regency' than what it was meant to replace.

The Indian motif of window and mirror canopies may be seen in its fully worked out form in a 'Design for the Curtain Cornice etc – from the Saloon – approved by His Majesty 3 July 1823 – R. Jones' [77]. The curtains as made are seen in context in a beautifully worked pencil drawing by Pugin [78]; they are seen also in an aquatint from Nash's Views [79] and in a Pugin watercolour at Windsor

[81]. For purposes of comparison, the etching in Nash's book is also reproduced [80].

The reason for this multiplicity of images will emerge below. Perhaps one should first comment on the obvious difference between the Saloon of 1815–16, and that of 1822–23. Gone are the rococo gaiety, the high and bright colours, the light and brittle forms. In their place is a sumptuous grandeur, characterised by lavish gilding and a rich but restrained colour scheme of crimson, gold, and silver. The enormous central lustre has a stately pre-eminence, unaccompanied by the host of lesser lights that clustered about its predecessor; the furniture is arranged in a strictly symmetrical manner, with the ottoman moved into the centre of an elaborate but strongly designed carpet, the last decorated with serpents and sunflowers around a radiating centre – another example of movement outwards. Most persuasive of all is the extremely high quality of the finished work, the wood-work splendidly carved and water gilt, the bronzes superbly chased and thickly gilded; no hint of the gimcrack or the impermanent.

A letter from the Lord Chamberlain's office, dated June 24 1823, contains estimates for 'Furniture etc. to complete the fitting up of the Saloon';[36] it gives the names of the principal craftsmen and firms employed. A large sum (£2724) was to be paid to Robert Jones, 'Artist Decorator'; the largest (£2757) was to go to Bailey and Saunders, cabinet makers (who were responsible also for the Axminster carpet). Others mentioned were Ashlin and Collins (plate glassmen), Henderson (carver and gilder), Parker (ormolu manufacturer), Perry (lamp- and lustre-maker), Westmacott (the statuary chimneypiece), Rundell, Bridge & Co. (goldsmiths). The total estimate amounts to £11,529 16s 10d; the letter includes an ominous statement that 'notwithstanding the allowance to this Department is reduced in the Present Year to *£36,000* . . . his Grace [the Duke of Wellington] does not contemplate that the proposed Expenditure for the Pavilion will occasion any exceeding whatever at the expiration of the Year 1823'.

Some interesting points emerge from a comparative study of the Pugin drawing [78], the aquatint [79], the Pugin watercolour [81] and the etching [80]. These are of more than academic interest in view of the present unrestored and bastardised style of the Saloon, beautiful though it is even in its mutilated state. In restoring the interiors of the Royal Pavilion, the *terminus ad quem* has been always taken to be the last state of any particular room during the occupation of King George IV. For the purposes of restoration, Queen Victoria and the Corporation of Brighton do not exist.*

One point concerns the cabinets. All four views show, between the windows, a somewhat eccentric form of cabinet. They appear to have been of a dark reddish-brown, perhaps rosewood, with gilded curlicues and a grey, or perhaps white, marble top; they were previously placed in the Yellow Drawing Room (see p. 134). Unlike almost all the other furniture shown in the Nash aquatint, they appear entirely to have disappeared. They are not the cabinets designed for this room by Jones, of which six at least are still in existence; these, ivory and gold in colour, are perhaps the most splendid and luxurious pieces ever made for the Pavilion; their elaborate motifs, in carved and gilded wood and the most superb gilt bronze, which echo the Indian motifs on chimneypiece and mirror crests, are largely repeated *on the back* of the cabinet fronts – since the mirrored backs occasionally send a glancing reflection back to the spectator. These would certainly have been depicted had they been completed, and indeed they are depicted, albeit miniscule,

* Since these words were written, an exception has been made in favour of Queen Victoria.

on the aquatint that shows the Pavilion in section [1]. There is evidence that the Jones cabinets were being made whilst the aquatints for Nash's book were being printed.

The drawing [78] shows a column in the alcove, bearing a Chinese vase with gilt bronze mounts; there were obviously four of these in the Saloon, since the etching [80] shows one in the opposite alcove. The latter column has, in the aquatint [79], been cunningly converted into a white cabinet resembling in shape those by Jones, but lacking any ornament. The column in the watercolour [81] has undergone the same transformation, this time with a rudimentary but essentially accurate indication of ornament.

This is interesting because it establishes a sequence that has a bearing on the upholstery and wall panels. The drawing, engraving, and aquatint all show fluted crimson silk in the panels, and plain crimson upholstery on the benches and otto-man (the surface around the panels, incidentally, is a wallpaper in brown and silver). The watercolour, the last in the series, is quite different. Here the panels display a flat crimson surface heavily decorated with palm and other motifs in gold; the upholstery is also covered with gold decoration. The curtains are made of 'His Majesty's Geranium and Gold Colour Silk . . . decorated and fringed to Mr. Jone's design'. As always, George IV's second thoughts had resulted in greater elaboration and richness.

The Pugin drawing [78] shows the lustre with one of the serpents that were to accompany the central bird and that are shown in later illustrations; the whole, a particularly successful union of dignity and fantasy by Robert Jones,[38] has entirely disappeared. The decorative top consisted of 'a gorgeous bird, in full relief, with wings of flowered gold and silver, enwreathed by serpents resplendently col-oured crimson and green'. The bird and serpents were fully three-dimensional; from their appearance in the aquatint [79] it seems likely that they were covered in silver leaf glazed in colour, a technique used elsewhere on similar details in the Pavilion. The bird's wings, however, appear to belong to a different idiom; they are, so to speak, flatly curved, and the drawing, aquatint, and engraving all show that they seem to have a thin 'spine'. Is it possible that this thin spine was of metal, and were the wings of glass? They are painted in a style similar to that used on glass, not on wood, and are different in nature from the realistically carved wings of, for example, the dragon above the gasolier in the Banqueting Room. Both top and lustre came from Perry, who specialised in glass; 'Articles delivered by Mr. Perry for Brighton without an order' included 'Lustre for the Saloon £950. Decorative top for Do. £145'.[39] The case is by no means proven.

One feature, the extraordinary white marble chimneypiece, with entwined serpents and Indian style canopies in gilt bronze executed by Samuel Parker, was the subject of a little drama recorded in the Royal Archives: 'the introduction of Mr. Parker was in consequence of an Estimate having been given by Mr. Vul-liamy which was thought too high'. Nash gives Vulliamy's estimate at £1,500, whereas Parker's estimate was 800 guineas; the episode appears to have caused some bad blood. Parker's undertaking clearly demonstrates Jones' deep involve-ment in the processes of manufacture: 'I hereby undertake that the chimneypiece . . . designed by Mr Jones and delivered by him to me [that is, Westmacott's mar-ble] to be executed in Ormolue burnished and finished under Mr. Jones' directions . . . that the Modelling Moulding finishing and burnishing should be of the most perfect kind and executed from the drawing to be delivered from time to time by Mr. Jones – and that the whole shall be done under his inspection and to his entire approbation.'[40]

77 Design for the curtains, the Saloon. By Robert Jones. 1823. CAT. NO. 77.

On this chimneypiece stands, as before, the Kylin clock, now in the glass case that was to cover all the clocks in the Pavilion; its sunflower motif is repeated in the sunflowers over the door recesses (a giant central sunflower is hidden by the lustre) and in the huge sunflowers of the carpet. Standing before the candelabra on the chimneypiece are two somewhat out-of-scale Chinese figures. Nowhere in the room can be seen any bell ropes; is it possible that these figures were hand bells?

The figures survey a scene of a rich and sophisticated exoticism, that seems strangely to transcend national frontiers.

78 The Saloon. By Augustus Pugin. C. *1823.* CAT. NO. 78.

79 *The Saloon. From John Nash,* Views of the Royal Pavilion, Brighton (1826). CAT. NO. 79.

80 *The Saloon. From John Nash,* Views of the Royal Pavilion, Brighton *(1826)*. CAT. NO. 81.

81 The Saloon. By Augustus Pugin. C. *1823–4.* CAT. NO. 80.

82 *Designs for a passage with a canopy, probably an unexecuted design for the Glass Passage.*
1803 or earlier. CAT. NO. 83.

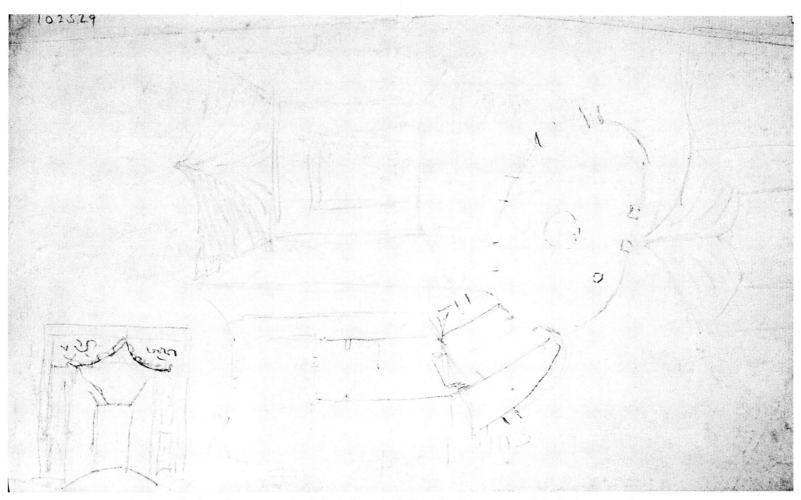

83 Rough plan of rooms south of the Saloon, including the Conservatory/Music Room, and designs for a passage with a canopy. By ?King George IV. 1803 or earlier. CAT. NO. 82.

ject.[50] Moreover, a wine cooler in the Egyptian style, with the Pavilion brand on it, exists in a private collection.[51] If Robinson did design an Egyptian Gallery at the Pavilion, it is possible that it was not very successful; it attracted no attention beyond Attree's terse note.

This cannot be said of a feature that, installed in 1803,[52] was the subject of general approbation, and of which the fame persisted long after it had been destroyed by Nash – the Glass Passage. Holland's alterations of 1801 had included not only a 'large new Eating Room and Conservatory' but also 'the communications to them'.[53] It was the communication between the Library/Breakfast/Small Drawing Room (made by Holland from the Breakfast Room and staircase combined), and the new Conservatory/Music Room, that became the Glass Passage. Attree describes it as 'perhaps the most strikingly beautiful of all that the most exquisite art and refined taste have hitherto invented of a similar description, to fascinate the eye, in this country. It is entirely formed of stained glass, exhibiting the insects, fruit, flowers, etc. etc. of the Chinese country; and when you are within it, it has the appearance of, and literally is, a magnificently painted CHINESE LANTHORN, twelve feet long, and eight feet wide, and which on all particular occasions, is brilliantly illuminated on the exterior, which shews its transparency, and produces an effect too exquisite to be described'. This description was repeated, in its essentials, by succeeding writers, including Brayley.

Amongst the Crace drawings preserved in the Royal Pavilion is a fascinating sheet [83] of very rough scrawls that appear to relate to this area; they are on

84 Designs of chinoiserie motifs. 1803 or earlier. CAT. NO. 84.

the back of drawings of chinoiserie details [84]. A comparison with plan E makes
it plain that, despite incorrect proportions and faulty drawing, the plan in the
centre right of the sheet is of the oval of the Conservatory/Music Room, with
the 'Glass Passage' leading from it to the Breakfast Room. The irregularly shaped
area may be identified from the accounts as a water closet.

The sheet shows also a projection that appears to jut from the Glass Passage
into the Breakfast Room; the pilasters on either side of the east and west walls
of the latter are roughly indicated, showing that the staircase had been demolished
by the time this plan was made. Most interestingly, there are on the same sheet
three small and rough drawings of what appears to be a lobby with a pagoda
shaped roof and a door at the far end. These sketches share their essential features
with a very elaborate and highly worked design from the Cooper–Hewitt collection [82]. This design is in the 'early' Pavilion chinoiserie style, perhaps by John
Crace, or by Frederick in extreme youth. It seems possible that the projection
into the Breakfast Room seen in [83] could well be the canopy of [82], and that
[82] itself is a design for the area occupied by the Glass Passage.

This conjecture is confirmed by an examination of the obverse of [83, 84]. Not
only, on the left, is there a sketch for the centre finial of the canopy, in the colours
actually followed in [82], but at the upper right is a silhouette of the dragon that
slithers down the edge of the canopy. The almost abstract treatment of this dragon
has some affinity with the abstract treatment of the serpents that form the scrolling
pattern at the base of [85], a device that is seen quite often in this period and
afterwards (see also [142]); it is apparent in the scrolling patterns seen on the
walls and in the carpet of [82]; the pattern in the centre of [84] appears to be
for that carpet.

The question that forces itself on the attention here, as occasionally elsewhere,
is – who drew the plan and designs of [83]? Perspective and proportion are

85 Designs for scrolling patterns in lilac, yellow, and two shades of pink. 1801–4. CAT. NO. 85.

hopelessly awry, in a way not seen in the roughest scrawls of more practised draughtsmen.

Does this then mean that [82] is a design, executed or unexecuted, for the Glass Passage? It seems certain that it was meant for the area occupied by the Glass Passage, and to some extent it fits the extant descriptions. It does not, alas, fit the accounts in the Crace ledgers, as will appear below.

However, two other drawings exist that appear also to have the necessary ingredients for a Glass Passage [91, 92]. The proportions of this design are somewhat different from those of [82], but that is not an impediment to the possibility of its having been meant to occupy the area of the Glass Passage; by the very nature of the site a certain degree of latitude was likely, and it is clear from [82] that the ceiling has been artificially lowered. The designs in stained and painted glass would, of course, have appeared within the framework of Chinese lattice.

Oddly enough, [91] also seems to have its scribbled precursor [90], in a rudimentary but somehow unmistakeable form. It has on the obverse designs for pillars and pilasters and is, again, in what appears to be an amateur hand. It is a coincidence that two such rough sketches should survive amidst a mass of material that, although itself rough, none the less constitutes working drawings of a professional standard. The survival might be explicable had the rough sketches been produced by an eminent hand.

The Crace ledgers document what actually was installed. From Midsummer to Christmas 1803 they include mention for the 'GLASS PASSAGE between Breakfast and Music Rooms' of '12 pair folding doors Chinese fret for squares both sides', 'extra grained Tea wood on ceiling to imitate boards', 'Rose wood two colours and shadowed', 'white ornaments on blue ground two shadows', 'Red fillets cut on edge of blue margins'. There is enough in the accounts that correlates with details in [91, 92] to make it probable that these designs are close to what was

86 Designs for glass panels and framework. Probably 1802–4. CAT. NO. 89.

actually executed; there are incompatabilities, and it is difficult to reconcile the number of 'folding sashes' and 'folding doors' given in the ledgers with the designs, but an account under 'Glass Passage' for 'making patterns and alterations' testifies that the Prince's usual habit of changing his mind operated.[54]

The accounts make much of the glazing and give a vivid sense of its effect: 'to glazing in coloured glass 12 Chinese sash doors in fret work of purple, yellow, green and blue glass' (one knows from surviving examples how brilliant and deeply suffused these colours in flashed and stained glass would have been), 'to painting flowers and insects of Chinese pattern on 56 squares of glass'. The Prince, active as ever in his role of interior decorator, was making technical suggestions: 'making patterns and painting ornaments on glass to try effects with burnt glass by order of the Prince'.[55] A 'Chinese lanthorn' and ornaments, with 'Chinese tassells and decorations compleat', is also recorded as having been made for the 'Lanthorn Passage'.[56] Finally, the whole of the Glass Passage was 'high varnished' twice with copal varnish, which dries very hard and glossy.

The Glass Passage is mentioned thereafter occasionally as repairs were effected; the water closet and lobby each side of it are also mentioned: 'graining the wood-work of water closet cedar wood and varnished'.[57] The last note, from October 1816 to Ladyday 1817, mentions '1 square repainted with flowers etc for the Glass Passage adjoining Blue Drawing Room';[58] by that time the Breakfast Room had joined the vast majority of its fellows in the limbo of vanished rooms, and the beautiful and famous Glass Passage, as fragile as its name may suggest, was soon to follow it. It is possible that the Prince regretted its disappearance, for the second scheme for the Corridor [172] was to see installed two painted and stained screens at either end that do, in an attenuated manner, echo the theme of the Glass Passage.

There now follows a group of designs concerning which one may make only conjectures in the void; none appear to have been used, even bearing in mind that it seems possible that certain rooms were decorated in several different schemes in quick succession. Two considerations might perhaps be borne in mind. The first is the possibility that ideas for chinoiserie interior decorations may have been in circulation, and designs consequently made, before the forms of the rooms for which they were destined had been finally settled; designs may therefore exist for rooms which themselves never existed, and a comparison of existing plans with existing designs makes this more than possible. The second possibility results from a curious accidental consequence of the changes – that the 'Eating Room' of before 1801 (plan A) north of the Saloon, with its chimneypiece on the west wall, a bow window, a flat window, and, at its north end, an alcove separated from the main room by pillars, exactly duplicated the configuration of the post-1801 'Library' (plan E) created by the removal of the staircase to the Prince's bedroom. In such circumstances, the possibility of confusion between the two areas always exists.

87 Design for a window alcove. 1802 or earlier. CAT. NO. 92.

The design in [93] appears to be from the same hand as [82] and shares with it a carpet so similar as to be virtually identical (but on a slightly different scale). An archway is faintly indicated on the left; given the common carpet, one is tempted to see in this an archway to the Glass Passage area. However, that would make the mirrored fireplace wall in the design the west wall of the Breakfast Room, and a glance at the plans will show that at no time does that room appear actually to have had a fireplace and doors in that particular order (although one has to remember that false doors are not uncommon).

It is possible that associated designs may provide a clue. A sky ceiling may be seen faintly indicated in [93]; the ceiling in [94] is not visible, but [93] appears to be by the same hand as [94] and shares with it the cornice rockwork, an identical skirting board and small dado above with blue marbling; a similar Chinese wall-paper may be glimpsed beneath the curtains, which are a similar brownish-red in colour. Both designs are somewhat naive and old-fashioned, especially when compared with the Saloon. Another design [87] is merely [94] without the curtains, and with clear glass substituted for what appears to be the blue and green stained glass of [94]. [87] also has buff teawood indicated in the right window recess as an alternative, very like that on the doors of [93]. Both alcoves have teawood on their ceilings.

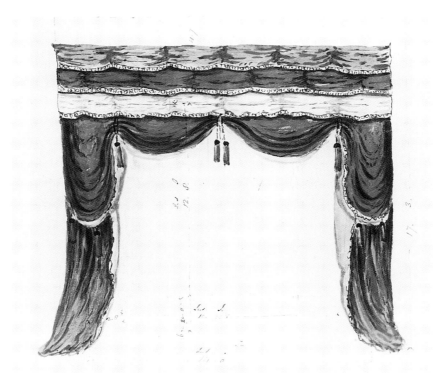

88 Design for curtains. 1802 or earlier. CAT. NO. 93.

The presence of the window alcoves indicates that all three designs are very likely to have been made for one of the series of rooms along the East Front of the building; their form may mean that they were made at an early stage of the rebuilding. The abrupt termination of the Chinese wallpaper, and the curious change of the dado where it reaches the fireplace wall, are puzzling; consistency is not a virtue appreciated in these early, rather crude designs, but is it possible that the decorators knew there was not enough wallpaper to cover all the walls? If so, was the Prince indeed given the wallpaper, as Brayley records in his account of the Chinese Gallery, and are these rather primitive designs the earliest, tentative records of an attempt at chinoiserie decoration in the building? All is speculation.

Another design [88] from the same hand and period depicts drapery for a window. Associated generally with the preceding designs, it is possible that it is associated with the same areas also.

The next four designs [89, 95–97] appear to be closely associated with each other, and again to be from the one hand. They share many features in common: the same rockwork cornice is seen [89, 95, 97]; the same shape of panel with Chinese scenes [95, 96] or with books [97]; the red Chinese trellis on a sky background [95–97]; the panels of blue marbling [95, 97]. Just as obviously, they have links with [98] and [99], which were intended for the one wall. The former shares with [89, 95, 97] the rockwork cornice, and with [96] a very similar scheme of compartmentation in blue, buff, and two shades of pink; the latter also shares the rockwork cornice, and with [95] and [96] the red Chinese fret on a sky background, the blue marbling, and blue skirting board, whilst its doors are closely related to the doors in [97].

It seems possible that [89, 95–97] may be reconstructed into a design for one room, and that room the 'Library' depicted on Holland's plan (plan E). The wall with the fireplace, at the extreme right of which is seen a pillar, may be the wall facing the window, with the pillar beginning an alcove within which is a wall of books [97]. The door is not centred in the plan, but an alteration may have

89 Design for an aperture and curtains, possibly for the Library. 1802. CAT. NO. 97.

been intended. It seems possible that [98] and [99] may be designs for that same wall without an alteration in the door, although the proportions appear different, perhaps due to a difference of scale of the door. The pillar seen in [95] is seen also in [89] where the central space is spanned by curtains, lacking the central supports seen in plan E. The same type of pillar is seen on the window wall [96], where the curved bow and the flat window have the same relationship as they have in plan E.

The wall with books encourages identification with Holland's Library, although it should not be forgotten that the configuration of that room was, as has been said above, identical with that of the 'Eating Room' north of the Saloon before the alterations (plan A). And the 1795 plan (C) shows a proposal to open up the rooms north of the Saloon into one large Library. In any event, the term 'Library' does not appear in the Crace ledgers. But the decorations, as described in the Crace ledgers, are most interesting. From 'Christmas to Midsummer 1803' the Breakfast Room[59] was decorated, at a cost of £174 1s 3¼d.[60] Difficult as it is to relate accounts to a design, there are certain correspondences that do not contradict the possibility that the designs discussed above, or some like them, were actually installed. The main colours used appear to have been grey, fawn, blue, and red; Chinese fret railing, 'fret work cut on pilasters white and shaded red', 'Chinese scroll ornament on fawn stiles white and 3 shadows' are amongst the items mentioned. One would not, perhaps, take so much notice of these very vague correspondences were it not that from Midsummer to Christmas 1803 an entirely different scheme of decoration was recorded,[61] this time at a cost of £136 4s 11d. The emphasis this time was on a scheme predominantly yellow: '334 ft Sup. of Yellow Pannels 3 times done', 'frame round pictures Yellow ground Chinese fret on Do. very rich etc', and 'Painting in two Pannels on Yellow ground, – 2 pedestals, Stands and Incense pots proper colors and shadows', 'Three Trophies and ornaments to the six pictures, very fully enriched colors and shadows'. In the ledgers these descriptions appear under the heading 'Small Drawing Room',

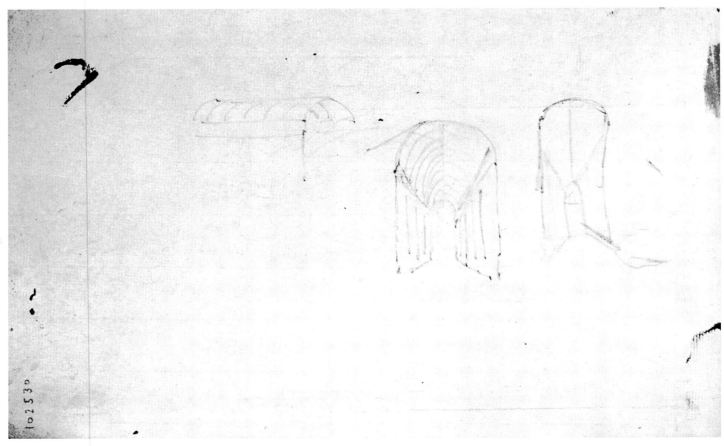

90 Designs for a passageway, perhaps the Glass Passage. By ?King George IV. 1803 or earlier. CAT. NO. 88.

but that this room was the same as that called the Breakfast Room is confirmed by its position as described by Attree in 1809, next to the Ante Room and Glass Passage; Attree spoke of it as a room 'the ground of which is bright yellow. On the walls are six paintings . . . the tops of them are ornamented with Chinese embellishments, articles of dress, musical instruments, incense pots etc etc.'

Attree describes the Ante Room in 1809 as 'decorated with nine very fine paintings, (done in China) exhibiting the manners of the people. The frames of the pictures are novel and striking, the tops being ornamented with trophies of war, and military arms of the Chinese nation. The ground of this room is scarlet, and displays the paintings to the most agreeable advantage.' The execution of this work is described in the Crace ledgers; from Midsummer to Christmas 1802 the ceiling was skied, an eighty foot 'run of Cove Grey' with 'Chinese Fret and fillets on each side' was installed, together with a '297 ft. Sup. of Scarlet 5 times and varnished', a 'Run of Architrave round Pannels', a 'Run of Skirting Marble', 'No. 5 labels over doors and side of chimney Buff ground bordered Scarlet and black shadowed', and 'Sup of Satin Wood two colors'.[62] All of these features may be seen in [100], which probably represents the first stage of decoration as seen on the west wall, facing the window, of the Ante Room (plan E). At a slightly later date, from Midsummer to Christmas 1803, the work was completed, including, 'Fixing and pasting 9 pictures on wall', '3 large trophies to pictures consisting of implements of War in colors and shadowed', and '26 Pannels in doors etc. cut in red Chinese fret work and shadowed' (no doubt to match the red Chinese fret work on the cove in [100]).[63] The 'trophies of war' may well be seen in [101]; the theme was not, to one's knowledge, used in later decorations. One can never,

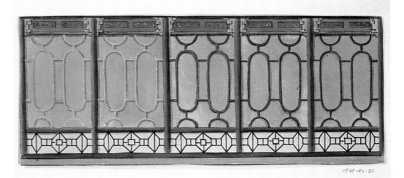

92 *Design for fretwork, perhaps for the Glass Passage. 1803 or earlier.* CAT. NO. 87.

91 *Design for a passageway, possibly the Glass Passage. 1803 or earlier.* CAT. NO. 86.

93 *Design for a room with Chinese wallpaper. 1802 or earlier.* CAT. NO. 90.

94 Design for a window alcove with curtains. 1802 or earlier. CAT. NO. 91.

95 Design for a chimneypiece wall with chinoiserie landscapes, possibly for the Library. 1802.
CAT. NO. 94.

96 Design for a window wall, possibly for the Library. 1802. CAT. NO. 95.

97 Design for a doorway and bookcase, possibly for the Library. 1802. CAT. NO. 96.

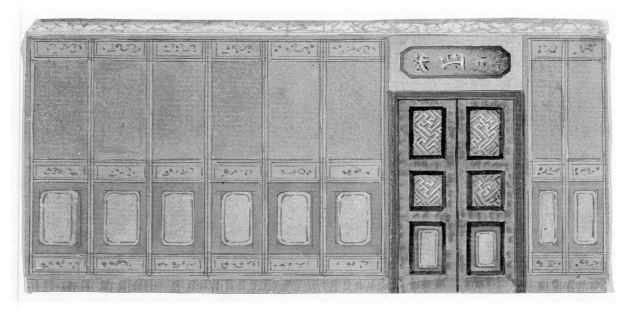

98 Design for a wall with doorway, possibly for the Library. 1802. CAT. NO. 98.

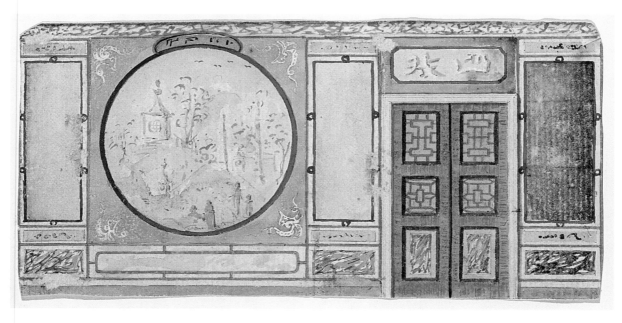

99 Design for a wall with doorway, possibly for the Library. 1802. CAT. NO. 99.

*100 Design (incomplete) for a wall with doorway, probably for the Ante Room. 1802 or
earlier.* CAT. NO. 100.

however, rely on the Prince's consistency, for included in the very accounts just quoted is an item, 'Painting the ground of 3 Pictures over doors 4 times as altered by the Prince'.

The designs described above all date from 1801–4. Those that follow are designs for the new decorations installed in and after 1815, and the context becomes somewhat clearer. For the sake of clarity the apartments north and south of the Saloon will now be dealt with separately. The area south of the Saloon became known as the 'Blue Drawing Room', and, after the building of the Nash extensions, as the 'Green' or 'South' Drawing Room; sometimes, in the Crace ledgers, it is referred to as the 'Banqueting Room Gallery'. The area north of the Saloon was known as the 'Yellow' or 'North' Drawing Room, and sometimes as the 'Music Room Gallery'.

101a, 101b, 101c Designs for implements of war. Probably 1801–4.
(a) 'A Chinese Battle-axe and Helmet'. (b) A shield. (c) A flag. CAT. NO. 101.

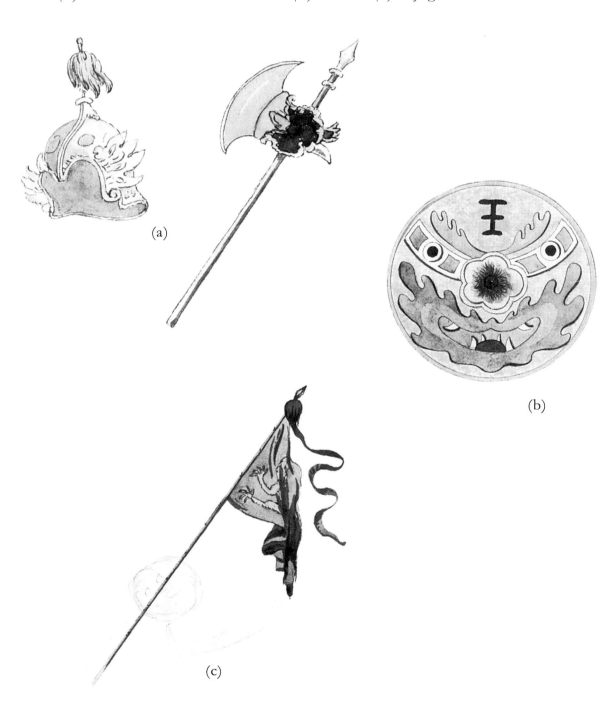

(a)

(b)

(c)

The Blue/South Drawing Room

It will be remembered that the alterations of 1801–2 had swept away the staircase between Breakfast and Ante Room (plan A), and had incorporated the staircase area into a new Library/Breakfast/Small Drawing Room; the Ante Room remained (plan E). By the period October to Christmas 1815 the area had been opened up into one large room, as a reference to the 'three compartments' of the ceiling makes clear.[64] It is possible that this conversion had been accomplished by Wyatt before his untimely death, since the Pugin/Nash plan of the Pavilion 'previous to the alterations' (plan G) shows one large room occupying the area. This room, however, was disposed in an irregular fashion in the matter of fireplaces and doors, and lacked the balanced fashioning of the completed Blue Drawing Room [102, 105] as shown in the watercolours and engravings: at this earlier date a centrally placed door at the south end led still to the Glass Passage; a chimneypiece faced the window at the south end of the apartment but was not balanced by a chimney at the north end – a door gave into the Corridor. A chimneypiece on the north wall of the room faced down its length to the door into the Glass Passage.

Work began on the Small Gallery/Blue Drawing Room in 1815. The accounts for the period October 1816 to Ladyday 1817 are the first to use the term 'Blue Drawing Room',[65] and their details make it obvious that a scheme had by then been installed closely resembling that seen in [102] and [105]. Not entirely, however; the Glass Passage was still in existence, and its removal necessitated alterations which are recorded as having taken place during the course of 1817. The Prince's mercurial character is perfectly shown in the changes that scudded over the surfaces of the Small Gallery/Blue Drawing Room during the course of 1815. In July Frederick Crace attended 'His Royal Highness with 8 assistants putting in patterns of sundry works in the Small Drawing Room and Gallery'; on August 15 he again attended with nine assistants.[66] The decorations first installed included a sky ceiling in all three 'compartments', with flat ornaments on blue, yellow, and red grounds; already blue appears predominant. There is then an alteration, and pink assumes an importance, often in conjunction with blue. This is the period when the Corridor was being given its marvellously beautiful pink and blue scheme (see p. 167), and the Prince may have felt he was unwise to compete with it. In any case, the '2nd Alteration and as now finished' saw blue return, and many of the details are recognisable in the details of [102] and [105].[67] It is at times easier to pick them out in the etching than in the watercolour.

Thus we have 'Ornamenting 2 pannels over doors with Chinese enrichments of dogs, essence vases etc';[68] 'ornamenting the cove round the three compartments blue ground . . . and Chinese scroll ornament'[69] (scroll replaces fret in quite a few instances, and pencil sketches of frets exist that may have been made for this room); 'ornamenting the skirting board etc. yellow blue and highly varnished'.[70] The ceiling in 1815 was clouded.[71]

102 The Blue Drawing Room, c. *1820. From John Nash,* Views of the Royal Pavilion, Brighton *(1826).* CAT. NO. 103.

There is an interesting item in the 1815 '2nd Alteration and as now finished': 'Preparing and ornamenting a pair of glass folding doors, blue ground with sunk pannels and a Chinese blue fret ornament . . . yellow and blue shadows and fret to glass work painted and varnished'.[72] It is probable that these were remodelled doors installed at the south end of the Blue Drawing Room, leading to the Glass Passage. These doors seem to have been faced at the north end of the room by a mirror, which later in 1815 was given a canopy: 'To Painting a Canopy over glass – red, yellow and blue ornaments, bells gilt and blue scroll, and 2 large columns supporting Do. red with Dragons, silvered, scaled and varnished.'[73] By October 1817, work on the new Banqueting Room and the consequent disappearance of the Glass Passage had led to the rearrangement seen in [102] and [105], which in effect is a duplication of that facing it from the north end. The cove and ceiling, 'damaged by alteration', were repaired (the latter was coloured grey; the sky ceiling had disappeared);[74] a floor-to-ceiling mirror was installed, and given a canopy in the quarter ending April 1818 with '2 enriched columns with various Chinese Devices, gilding the dragons, bells, etc and high varnishing the whole

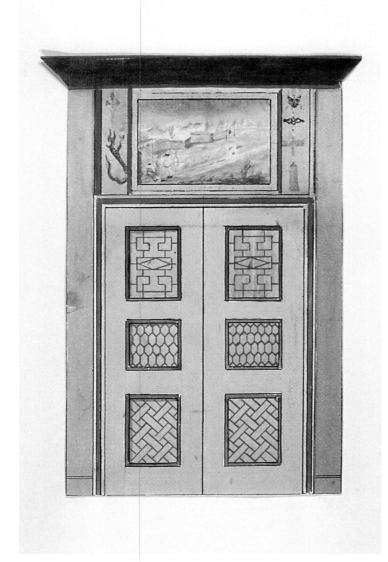

103 Design for a door and overdoor. CAT. NO. 105.   *104 Design for a wall decoration.* CAT. NO. 106

to correspond with one that is already done'.[75] Later in the same year the ceilings were again painted sky colour, and other details were again altered.[76]

Throughout all these later changes the prevailing hue of blue was not altered. It is that hue that has led to the next four designs [103, 104, 108, 109] being attributed in the past to the Blue Drawing Room. The evidence is equivocal. The designs for the doors [103, 108] appear not to have the same proportions as the doors in the Blue Drawing Room; the character of their decoration is reminiscent of the earlier rather than the later period (as a glance at [93] and [99] will show), although it must be admitted that this is not altogether true of the painting technique they display. The wall panels [104, 109] are equally problematical; the stiffly composed frames around the pasted-on Chinese paintings are, again, somewhat in the 1802–4 manner, and do not have the hint of the Pompeian that one sees in the trompe l'œil decorations around the applied paintings in the Blue Drawing Room; the free and transparent technique smacks, however, of a later date. (To

105   The Blue Drawing Room. By Augustus Pugin. Before 1821. CAT. NO. 102.

some extent, the problems presented by these drawings are of the same order as those presented by [234, 235 and 241] (see p. 199.)

The Blue Drawing Room itself displays, after all the dizzying changes of mind and frantic activity, an aspect that is, despite the vivacity of the decoration, tranquil and harmonious [105] – even, where it is unreached by the long rays of the sun, somewhat aqueous. Its beauty is not impaired, but is given an added strangeness, by the buttressing of the ceiling where the staircase used to ascend. The Chinese paintings, applied directly to the wall in something of the way that occidental prints were occasionally used to decorate rooms, are displayed as Attree describes their use in the old Ante and Breakfast Rooms although, as remarked above, in a more sophisticated and even rococo idiom. The decorations around them appear to refer to hunting rather than to war. The Chinese rattan armchair, and sofas and chairs in beech simulating bamboo, add to the fragile and brittle feeling given by the room; in contrast is the solidity of the white marble and gilt bronze

Gallery next the dining room color Yellow pannel to be raised & a dado the same as the other Gallery

106 Design for a wall decoration. C. *1820.* CAT. NO. 108.

chimneypieces, which were in the event to survive when all else had been swept away. By 1821 the Blue Drawing Room had disappeared, to be replaced by a scheme of great, if eccentric, charm.

Before looking at that replacement, a drawing inscribed 'Gallery next the Dining Room color Yellow Pannel to be raised & a dado the same as the other Gallery' claims attention [106]. This charming design was obviously produced at the same time and is allied stylistically with a design for the drawing room north of the Saloon [121]. These are quite different in effect from the more controlled and 'hard-edge' schemes eventually adopted, but it is evident that, as with the later schemes,

107 Design for a wall decoration. c. 1820. CAT. NO. 109.

the intention was to balance the two Drawing Rooms by giving them a decorative unity. The connexion would have been reinforced by giving [106] the same dado as that in [121]. Incidentally, the draped curtain seen in [106] may have been inspired by the Weisweiler pier tables eventually placed in the North Drawing Room; as will be seen below, other details came from the same source.

Yet another drawing [107] may possibly have some connexion with the North or South Drawing Rooms; it appears to be for panels on either side of a fireplace, with perhaps a mirror placed in the centre. It does not fit any wall in the Entrance Hall, with which it has been associated.

108 Design for a door and overdoor.
CAT. NO. 104.

109 Design for a wall decoration. CAT. NO. 107.

Two designs for mirror frames in the Crace Collection in the Victoria and Albert Museum appear to be associated with this room [110, 111]; one is prompted to ask whether the somewhat Gothick top in [110] was so designed to key with the Gothick cornice of Nash's South Drawing Room? The uprights of both are related to the gilt bronze details designed by Jones for the Saloon, and also with the South Drawing Room wall decorations – this is especially noticeable in [111].

110 Design for a mirror frame. c. *1820.* CAT. NO. 110.

111 Design for a mirror frame. c. *1820.* CAT. NO. 111.

112 The South Drawing Room. By Augustus Pugin. 1821 or later. CAT. NO. 112.

The disappearance of the Blue Drawing Room was inevitable, since the re-modelling of the eastern front of the Pavilion by Nash had included the extension outwards of the whole window area; the 'Palm Tree' pillars [112–115] mark the old limits of the window wall, and they support the wall of the upper storey – beneath their fantastic carved and gilded wooden exterior stands a cast-iron core. The main eccentricity is in the proportions of the room, which had altered radically. In the time of the Breakfast and Ante Rooms the height of the ceilings had been proportionate to the comparatively small rooms; the subsequent enlargement into the area occupied by the Blue Drawing Room had created a long, low room. The new alterations produced a room fifty-two feet long, and thirty-three feet broad; the proportions thus engendered appeared extraordinary to contemporaries – much more so than to us, accustomed in modern buildings to mean and eccentric proportions. In the early nineteenth century, a low ceiling in a palace was a paradox.

Through the open door at the south end of the room may be seen the gas torchères, if such a term is permissible, of the Banqueting Room, of which the height and gilded splendours are in dramatic contrast with the august simplicity of the South Drawing Room; the latter's predominant white and gold, with a light-pink ceiling and green upholstery, are simple, however, only in contrast.

The walls were covered in flake white, a lead paint with a slightly striated surface, due to which the pattern overlaid in gold leaf was textured in a way that caught the light. The pattern of this flat gilded decoration is interesting, and in this context a diversion must be made, since the related gilded decorations of the North Drawing Room must be brought into the discussion [126]. Both rooms were influenced in various ways by the furniture and objects that had stood first in the Chinese Drawing Room at Carlton House, subsequently in the Rose Satin Drawing Room, and were now to be brought to Brighton. These included: two types of pier table, both probably designed by Weisweiler, and copied by Bailey and Saunders in 1819 to make up two pairs; a French clock, the 'Drummer Boy Clock'; and a set of six candelabra, also probably French.[77] The decoration of these pieces displays Chinese fret motifs that almost at times resemble a Greek key pattern, plus bamboo, canopies, scaled palms, dragons, and a fish. It may be that it was intended at first to make more than two copies of the tables, for the mirror frames in the South Drawing Room exactly copy, in carved and gilded wood and in flat gold, the front legs of one of the pier tables, with its gilt bronze designs edged with gilt bronze bamboo. The wall decoration of the South Drawing Room, ambiguously Chinese or Greek, does not quote directly from the furniture and objects mentioned above, but it does reproduce, enormously enlarged, round shapes that look suspiciously reminiscent of the gilt bronze knobs that often held the screws attaching ormolu galleries to the tops of tables and other objects.

There are mirrors everywhere in this room, in the door panels as well as on the walls. Those on the curved walls that lead into the enlarged bay window are oddly conceived in that they stand proud of the walls (a curved mirror would give a distorted reflection); one does not, in practice, notice this anomaly, but it may be seen in [112]; incidentally, the sofa in this drawing is covered still with its protective holland cover. The delicately gilded cornice of the room is based on a Gothic fan vault; there are similarities here to details of the ceiling of the Nash Dining Room at Carlton House,[78] as there are also in the King's Apartments [265]. One is led into speculation on the architect's, as opposed to the decorator's, part in the ensemble; this seems to be an instance where Nash provided the detail – unless the decorator provided the same detail in Carlton House also!

A change was made in the recess; an account of 1821 mentions 'Preparing and gilding the Palm Trees of the Looking Glass in recess'.[79] By the time Pugin recorded the room for the engraving (published on July 26 1823) the looking glass had been replaced by a sun-ray motif in green pleated silk; the curtains were in green embroidered silk. The carpet, wall to wall and in a pattern of ultimately Turkish derivation, is of a type that has become more common since, but would in the early 1820s have been the last thing in exotic sophistication.

The furniture continues the note of dignified splendour. Gone is the bamboo, although the sofa tables from the Blue Drawing Room, which are inlaid with rattan ornament, remain. In its place are rosewood tables, the delicate and beautiful

113 The South Drawing Room, 1823. From John Nash, Views of the Royal Pavilion,
Brighton (1826). CAT. NO. 115.

OPPOSITE

114 The South Drawing Room. By Augustus Pugin. 1821 or later. CAT. NO. 113.
115 The South Drawing Room. By Augustus Pugin. 1821 or later. CAT. NO. 114.

giltwood chairs supplied in 1789 by Hervé for Carlton House, the large giltwood
sofas adapted by Tatham in 1811 to match the Hervé chairs from the Chinese
Drawing Room, and now taken from the Rose Satin Drawing Room at Carlton
House, and four most magnificent Japanese lacquer cabinets with white marble
tops and gilt bronze feet. It will be noticed that the pier table in the drawing [112]
is replaced in later illustrations by a lacquer cabinet mounted in gilt bronze. Also
mounted in gilt bronze are the many candelabra, as are the two pairs of superb
Chinese ewers and vases in the window embrasure. It is these latter objects (alas,
missing today) that add a note of profusion that seals the sense of discreet luxury.

116 The Yellow Drawing Room. By Augustus Pugin. Before 1821. CAT. NO. 117.

The Yellow/North Drawing Room

It will be remembered that the ground floor of the north wing of Henry Holland's original Marine Pavilion had been opened up by October 1802 into one large room with a fireplace in the centre. Here was installed the 'Egyptian Gallery' mentioned, but not described, by Attree in 1809.

Between October and Christmas 1815 the room was redecorated; the Prince had been attended by nine, six, and eight assistants on three occasions spanning August, September, and October, in considering patterns for the room.[80] The Crace ledgers record a sky ceiling, and a scheme of at least twenty-six 'Chinese pictures on walls with enrichments of Dragons, birds and various other decorations', all in the colours of yellow and lilac.[81] The cove was bright yellow, with a 'purple Chinese enrichment', and to it were added 243 Chinese drop ornaments in various colours. The agonies of indecision that attended the genesis of the Blue Drawing Room seem to have been replaced in the Yellow Drawing Room by a straightforward progress to completion.

The result is seen in a pencil drawing, and in a watercolour, by Pugin [117, 116]. Colour and decoration alike are splendid and festive; we here see 'rococo' chinoiserie at its height, leaving far behind the comparatively strait-laced and 'academic' chinoiserie of some of the earlier rooms. It is possible that Robert Jones was employed more in this room than in the more sober Blue Drawing Room, and this may be a reason for the difference.

One superb feature is the extraordinary columns supporting a kind of banner; they appear next to windows and chimneypiece. The accounts give a vivid idea of their appearance: 'Painting a canopy over glass – red, yellow and blue ornaments, bells gilt and blue scroll, and 2 large columns supporting Do. red with Dragons, silvered, scaled and varnished'.[82] Also to be seen, especially above the dado on the right, are some of the '16 Chinese dogs' – 'lilac and shadowed'.[83] Another Chinese dog [119], which is quite large, is obviously not a design; it may well be a working drawing, in the size it might have appeared on the dado. The accounts give details that cannot be discerned in the illustrations of the room. Most interesting is 'ornamenting the centre window in 12 compartments with various Chinese ornaments in colors'; perhaps this idea was short-lived. On the doors were painted birds, fish, and elephants; bats 'silvered and varnished green and purple' were employed on the draperies; pineapples were placed on the tops of the columns adjacent to the doors.[84]

Two designs, obviously for this room, appear to be one a development of the other [118, 122]; the first is an uncertain rehearsal of the second. Another [124] is for the same scheme, as is yet another (unillustrated) in the Victoria and Albert Museum. The enchanting birds appear fleetingly in other designs; there appears to be no pictorial record of their use elsewhere in the Royal Pavilion, but there are allusions to them at various times. An extract from the *Morning Chronicle* of

117 The Yellow Drawing Room. By Augustus Pugin. Before 1821. CAT. NO. 116.

February 8 1816, preserved in the Crace papers in the Victoria and Albert Museum, may well refer to their use in the Yellow Drawing Room; a verse on 'Fum and Hum the two Birds of Royalty' says that,

> When Fum first did light on
> The floor of that Grand China warehouse at Brighton
> The lanterns and dragons and things round the dome
> Were so like what he left 'gad' says Fum 'I'm at home'.

A series of sketches for 'The Royal Bird Call'd Foo hum' remains; the birds appear to be based on some species of Chinese pheasant, highly fantasticated. The line drawing [120] may have been used for the same purpose as the dog [119]; a bird with outspread tail [127] is in a less accomplished hand than a very free drawing [123] and a splendidly haughty bird with tail feathers resembling those of a peacock [129]. These last appear to have been inscribed by the same hand. Several other drawings that employ these birds are discussed below.

The furniture was a mixture of simulated bamboo and Regency 'boulle' with what appears to be a pair of 'Louis Seize' occasional tables. The cabinet at the north end of the room later migrated to the Saloon (see p. 98). The piano may have entered because of the room's use as a Music Room whilst work went on elsewhere; henceforth it was to remain.

118 Design for a wall decoration, the Yellow Drawing Room. C. *1815.* CAT. NO. 118.

120 Design for an exotic bird. C. *1815.* CAT. NO. 122.

119 Chinese dog. CAT. NO. 121.

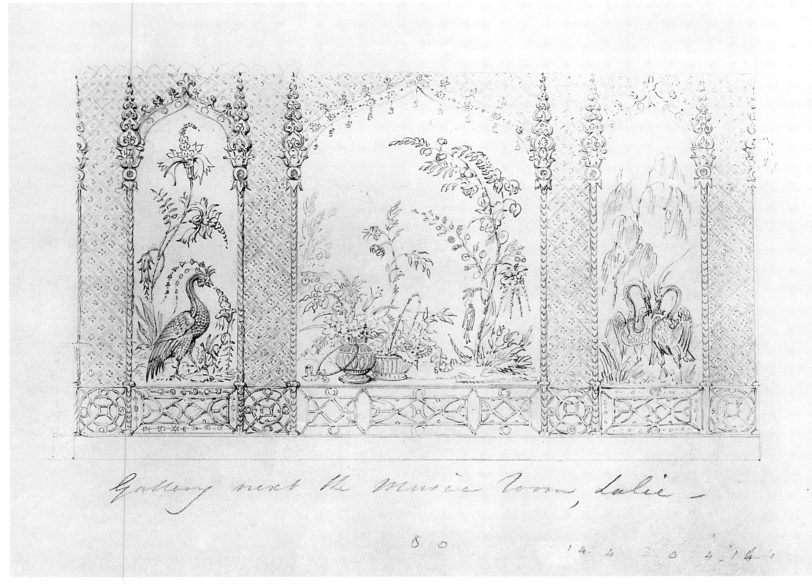

121 Design for a wall decoration, the Yellow Drawing Room. c. 1820. CAT. NO. 126.

Between October 1816 and Ladyday 1817 some mysterious holes were cut to 'ventilate' the Yellow Drawing Room and other rooms;[85] these may have been ventilators fitted in the floor near the windows, and the intention may have been to discourage rot; in any event, the damage occasioned had to be repaired. In 1819 the Prince Regent continued to tinker with the room, as recorded in the ledgers;[86] they are then silent until in 1821 the complete redecoration of the 'Music Room Gallery' was begun.[87]

It was towards this latter date that a very pretty design [121] was produced; it is perhaps from the hand of Robert Jones, and is inscribed, 'Gallery next the Music Room, Lalic'. It seems possible that the strange last word contains transposed letters, and is meant to read 'Lilac' (or perhaps the spelling was phonetic, and reflected contemporary pronunciation). The likelihood is increased by the fact that the related design reads, 'Gallery next the dining Room color Yellow'.

It is to be remarked that the ogee arches and pillars have both Gothic and Indian references; the background diaper has also a Gothic and Indian flavour; it would probably have been a block-printed wallpaper of the type actually used in Saloon and Banqueting Room, to which its design is very similar. Or it may have been hand-painted; both occur. The dado, without in reality being in any way similar,

122 Design for a wall decoration, the Yellow Drawing Room. c. *1815.* CAT. NO. 119.

124 Design for a wall decoration surmounted by an exotic bird, and for a wall decoration of frames for pictures. c. *1815.* CAT. NO. 120.

123 Design for an exotic bird. c. *1815.* CAT. NO. 124.

125 The North Drawing Room. By Augustus Pugin. 1821 or later. CAT. NO. 127.

gives an effect reminiscent of, and in harmony with, the famous chimneypiece from the Chinese Drawing Room in Carlton House that by now had been installed in this room. A payment in October 1820 to Westmacott recorded 'Marble and materials Repairing and repolishg. the red Bersn [sic] Marble Chimney Piece from Carlton Palace & now fixed in the Yellow Room at Brighton'. It had perhaps been installed and been found to have pinched proportions, for a note of January 5 earlier in the same year had mentioned 'Addl. Marble to widen the Chimney Piece in Yellow Room'.[88]

The room was redecorated in 1821 at a cost of £1,208 10s 0d; the ceilings were coloured 'light pink', and the walls ornamented with 'Chinese trellis in Gold' on a background of stretched linen.[89] The decoration may be seen in the pencil drawing and in the watercolour by Pugin [125, 128], and in the aquatint [126]. Again, Nash's extension of the façade has allowed the construction of two amazing pillars; this time pagoda topp'd and wreathed with serpents. The wall decoration is richer and more elaborate than that in the South Drawing Room, with more than a hint of the Indian, and perhaps even the Turkish, in its details. The carpet [126] is identical with that in the South Drawing Room, another attempt to unify. Yellow remained the principal colour in upholstery and curtains.

The drawing reveals the giltwood chairs by Marsh and Tatham ranged two-deep in the window, perhaps as the result of some assembly. The small console table

126 The North Drawing Room, c. 1823. From John Nash, Views of the Royal
Pavilion, Brighton *(1826).* CAT. NO. 129.

with griffin heads on the wall flanking the windows appears to have been replaced
by a different piece in the aquatint. The furnishings are as eclectic – and as
harmonious – as any in the palace. Two 'Louis Quatorze' 'mazarin' desks (made
by Louis Legaigneur in London), what appear to be two 'Louis Seize' tables, a
Regency piano, and the beautiful gilt bronze candelabra set on columns of Orientalising English stoneware, accompany all the other beloved and exquisitely refined
objects that had enhanced the Drawing Room at Carlton House – the Weisweiler
cabinets (and the Bailey and Saunders copies), seen most clearly on the extreme
right of [125], with their tasselled ormolu curtains and front legs composed of
Chinamen as terminal figures, themselves echoed in the chimneypiece. On the
furniture now stand the Drummer Boy Clock and the set of candelabra upheld
by enamelled Chinese maidens, much of the enamelling on both objects having
been renewed by Robert Jones for the occasion.[90] Finally, there is the set of gilded
seat furniture by Hervé, with serpents wreathed around the legs, as on the pillars,
and Chinamen seated cross-legged on the top rail; it seems probable that they
had been re-covered in 1819 with the very same yellow silk supplied for them
in 1790 and taken off in 1811.[91] George IV was conservative, and knew a good
thing when he saw it; these aspects of his character, together with perhaps more
than a dash of sentiment, had influenced the transmogrified rebirth in the Pavilion
of one of the most beautiful and successful rooms of his youth.

The Conservatory/Music Room
and the Dining Room

The interiors of the two large rooms added in 1801 by Holland to the original Marine Pavilion (plan E) have been something of a mystery. The most circumstantial account of that at the south end of the building, the conservatory, appears to be given by Attree, who describes '"THE CONSERVATORY", though it is more often distinguished as the Music Room. It is fifty-five feet long, thirty feet wide, and twenty feet high. The roof is painted in imitation of the tea and rose wood, and is supported by twenty columns of a scarlet colour, with the five-clawed dragons twisting round them. The sides are covered with a Chinese historical paper, superb in appearance, and indescribably brilliant in effect.'

A design exists that appears to fit part of this description. It is for a large room, it has the scarlet columns and five-clawed dragons, and it has also the 'Chinese historical paper'; one may perhaps remark that of all the genuine Chinese papers seen in the drawings this seems the most splendid – such a paper might well have been thought a gift worthy of a Prince [131]. This design is linked with a ceiling design by an identical detail: the red Chinese fret [132] is the same as that around the 'Chinese historical paper'. And the shape of the ceiling design means that it must have been intended for either the Conservatory/Music Room or for the Dining Room at the north end of the building. Attree, in the extract quoted above, says that the 'roof is painted in imitation of the tea and rose wood', as indeed it is in this design.

The Crace ledgers provide more information. Amongst other items are included 'Clouding the ceiling', 'Margins round fret on ceiling, blue red and shadowed', 'Fret on ceiling, red and shadowed', 'Tea Wood on Cove grained and varnished, Rosewood shadowed as reeds and varnished'; these features may be seen in [132]. The ledgers also mention 'Fret ornament on pilasters, blue border, red fret', 'full enriched Blue frieze, shaded white etc', 'Dado imitation to represent pannels and Stiles shaded', 'Blue reeded ball Stone capping and shadowed', '36 Ornaments in Pannels of imitation Dado shadowed', '10 Columns highly finished Scarlet ground to Shafts . . . Dragons highly finished on Do. . . . the bases stone colour . . . 10 Plinths under bases of Columns in imitation of Marble. . . .'[92] This work was done between Christmas 1802 and Midsummer 1803; the evidence is circumstantial. There are details in the accounts missing from the designs, or unidentifiable, but they are minor.

For which wall of the Conservatory/Music Room was [131] intended? The most suitable is shown in plan E to have a fireplace in its centre. However, plan E shows a fireplace also in the Entrance Hall, where we know that there was instead a stove [150]. The scrawled plan [83] shows a circle in the centre of the Conservatory; is this possibly the site of a central stove? Plan E is given the early date of July 1801, and could easily have been altered in execution.

130 Design for a ceiling (detail), probably for the Conservatory/Music Room, or perhaps for the Dining Room. 1802 or earlier. CAT. NO. 133.

One is enabled to add to the picture of the 1802 Conservatory a design for 'A Lanthorn for the Old Music Room', which is inscribed also 'and Fel down on Mr F.Crace on the night of the first Grand entertainment' [140]. The design painted on the central panel of this lantern exists in the Royal Pavilion collections painted on a piece of glass from a much smaller lantern; the painting in this latter case is Chinese (genuine Chinese script clears doubts caused by clever Occidental imitations) but such original oriental work was often copied by native artists. The lanterns for the Music Room were made between Christmas 1803 and Midsummer 1804; '. . . with ground glass squares. Painting on squares various Chinese Mandarine Figures and caracters [sic], glazing with coloured glass a frame to Do. . . . tassells and decorations compleat.'[93]

Two other designs exist [130, 133] for a ceiling of the same shape as that for which [132] was intended; one might be tempted to see them as designs for the Dining Room. However, they have no obvious connexion with the Dining Room designs, and are more likely to be another choice for the Conservatory/Music

131 *Design for a wall decoration, probably for the Conservatory/Music Room. 1802 or*
earlier. CAT. NO. 130.
132 *Design for a ceiling, probably for the Conservatory/Music Room. 1802 or earlier.* CAT. NO. 131.

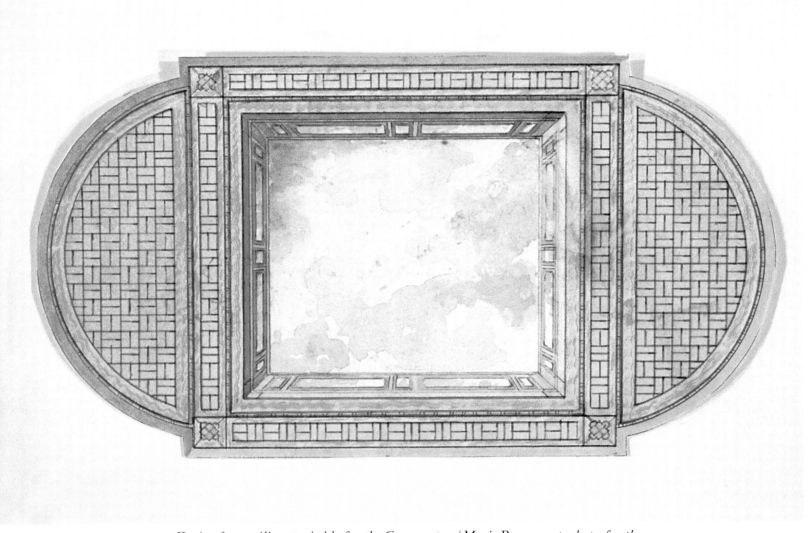

*133 Design for a ceiling, probably for the Conservatory/Music Room, or perhaps for the
Dining Room. 1802 or earlier.* CAT. NO. 134.

Room. Other designs for sky ceilings [134, 139] appear to contain balustrades
related to those in the preceding drawings. On the other hand, both display motifs
– dragons of a later type; moths; serpents not unlike those on the 1815 Corridor
staircase – that seem to hint at a date later than the 1802–4 period; moreover,
the handling of the drawings is more accomplished. One's suspicions are confirmed
by the fact that one of these two designs [139] is on paper of which the watermark,
'J. Whatman', is exactly the same as that on a design for the Entrance Hall [152],
which is undoubtedly from the later period.

Another sky ceiling design [135] strikes, with its treillage, urns, climbing plants,
and what seems a witty hybrid between perfume burners and Prince of Wales'
feathers, a different note. The design, eminently Conservatoryish, may represent
a very early essay; the treillage may link it with [141] (see below).

Sky ceilings, incidentally, were always amongst the favourite decorative devices
of George IV. They existed at old Buckingham House; they were used plentifully
at Carlton House and the Pavilion. One was even installed in a stand constructed
for him at the Curragh Races![94] They seem never to have been widely used in
England, but were a favourite motif on the Continent during the Biedermeier

134 Design for a ceiling. C. *1820.* CAT. NO. 136.

period. The three remaining sky ceiling designs [136–138] all belong to the pre-chinoiserie period; the first two, with their amatory references, have an indefinably bedroom air, and the trailing garlands resemble motifs used by Holland at Carlton House. The author is unable to identify their location.

Attree's description of the 'Banqueting' Room at the north end of the Pavilion is cursory: 'This apartment is of the same dimensions as the Conservatory at the extremity of the South, but the ceiling is clouded.' (Obviously the Conservatory's clouded ceiling had been altered in the intervening period.) Unfortunately, the Crace ledgers are just as uninformative; it seems that the accounts for the Dining Room have not been preserved. However, an interesting group of designs may be thought possibly to have something to do with this area [141–145]. In the past [141] has been considered to be an early design for the Nash Banqueting Room; this seems most unlikely, both on general grounds of style and handling – it appears to date from the 1802–4 period rather than after 1815 – and because the proportions are not those of the Nash Banqueting Room. The design is, indeed, somewhat uncertain – the inclusion of the shell motif, surrounded by treillage, is an odd touch; it hints at a period of transition, and hints also at a possible connexion with 135. The design would in that case probably date from 1802, or possibly earlier.

[141] is linked with [142] by the pilaster and dado motifs, and by the motif running above the pilasters, virtually identical in both; it is linked with [143] by the general colour scheme, and by the fact that [142] shares its pink scrolling decoration with [143], just glimpsed above the door in the latter. Obvious identical features are shared by [143, 144] and [145].

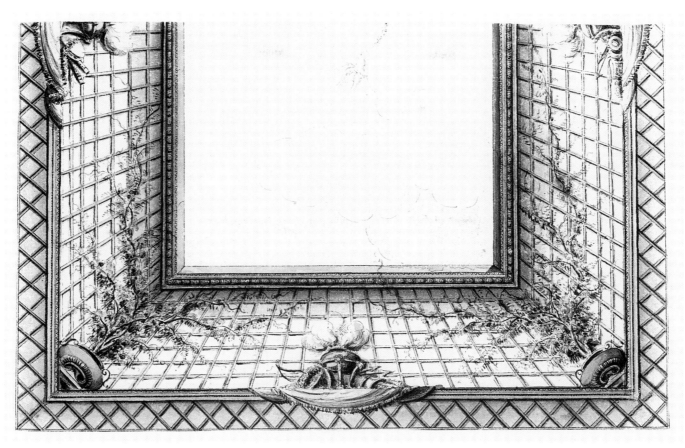

135 Design for a ceiling (detail), perhaps for the Conservatory/Music Room or Dining Room. 1802 or earlier. CAT. NO. 137.

136 Design for a ceiling. 1801 or earlier. CAT. NO. 138.

137 Design for a ceiling. 1801 or earlier. CAT. NO. 139.

*138 Alternative designs for
a ceiling. 1801 or earlier.*
CAT. NO. 140.

139 Design for a ceiling. C. *1820.* CAT. NO. 135.

140 Design for a lantern.
1803–4. CAT. NO. 132.

141 Design for a wall with chimneypiece, probably for the Dining Room. 1802. CAT. NO. 141.

142 Design for a window, probably for the Dining Room. 1802 or earlier. CAT. NO. 142.

143 Design for a doorway, possibly for the lobby or its vicinity south of the Dining Room. 1802 or earlier. CAT. NO. 143.

Is it possible to connect this group of designs with the Dining Room? [141] is certainly in the same general proportions as [131], but with the requisite chimneypiece; [142], if in proportion, as it appears to be, is for a large and lofty window, such as would have been found in each of the two Holland wings. The clue is given by [143, 144], which, connected as they are with [141] and [142], yet appear to be on a smaller scale, and for a smaller room. A glance at plan E discloses the possibility that they were meant for the small lobby to the Dining Room just south of it. If so, it is these two last designs that decisively attach [141] and [142] to the 1801 Holland Dining Room, for the ante room to the north of the Conservatory/Music Room always was, and always was meant to be, a quite different shape – that of the Glass Passage.

It seems at the present moment impossible to establish whether these designs were executed. The only account for the Dining Room lobby surviving from 1802 mentions 'Satin wood' and 'black filletts' – and that is all.[95] A little more evidence is available for 1803; the 'Satin wood doors' of the Eating Room are varnished.[96] So far, so good; the doors depicted in [143] are satinwood, not teawood, and one may discern black fillets. However, the decoration recorded for the 'Lobby to Eating Room' in 1803 does not tally with that of [143, 144, 145], since mentioned in that are 'Columns yellow ground and very fully enriched' with bases in 'imitation Marble' etc.[97] The evidence is by no means conclusive, since the Prince often changed designs as they were executed. It does not, however, encourage further speculation.

144 Design for a window, possibly for the lobby or its vicinity south of the Dining Room. 1802 or earlier. CAT. NO. 144.

145 Design for a wall decoration, possibly for the lobby or its vicinity south of the Dining Room. 1802 or earlier. CAT. NO. 145.

The Entrance Hall

The area immediately west of the Saloon, characterised by two niches and a chimney between, was from 1787 part of the Entrance Hall; expanded in size in 1801, it became after the Nash alterations in 1815 part of the Corridor, where niches and chimneypiece remain up to the present day (plans A, E, H). The post 1815 designs for this area are, therefore, dealt with under the heading 'Corridor' (see below).

Attree describes the Entrance Hall as a hall 'the colour of which is of a warm clay, with blue and red mouldings. This hall is thirty-five feet square, and twenty feet high; and is tastefully embellished in the Chinese stile. A light gallery, with an awning, crosses it, beneath which are Mandarine figures, as large as life, each holding a lanthorn glazed with coloured glass, on which are depicted flowers, &c. peculiar to the Eastern world, very nicely executed, and very beautiful in effect.'

There is in existence a large design, comparatively simple, if not crude, that perfectly fits this description [150]; its two niches place it on the east side of the Entrance Hall, and it would have faced the visitor as he entered. The Crace ledgers confirm the identification; those for Christmas 1802 to Midsummer 1803 speak of fawn, red, blue, and buff painting, Chinese fret railings and panels, 'Columns scarlet and varnished', and four 'white marble panels with Chinese caracters [sic]'.[98] Between Midsummer and Christmas 1803 the '2 Chinese Pedestals for Figures 4 oils and flatted and veined in imitation of blue Chinese Marble and varnished' were produced,[99] and from Christmas 1803 to Midsummer 1804 we have 'To making 2 Chinese Lanthorns for Figures in Hall to Entrance, glazing Do. with ground glass squares and painting on Do. Chinese flowers etc. . . . .'[100] The motif of 'Mandarine figures, as large as life' was one of which the Prince was very fond, and they persisted in these niches up to the penultimate scheme for the Corridor (they also, according to the Crace ledgers, briefly occurred in the Yellow Drawing Room). They were, incidentally, clad in real Chinese robes.

There is evidence that the pagoda seen in the Entrance Hall design [150] was a stove; it comes from two designs for the same area [154, 156] of which the central ornament is indubitably a stove, as the cast shadow indicates. Moreover, the pagoda was both beneath a chimneystack and in the situation where a fireplace was indicated (plans A, E). Stoves of this type were in England normally met with only in entrance halls or conservatories. There is much mention in contemporary accounts of the presence of 'stoves' in the Pavilion, and the impression has been created that these were of the type of this pagoda stove. This does not seem probable, especially for the period after the Nash rebuilding, when most elaborate marble chimneypieces were installed. The accounts often mention a 'stove' in relation to these chimneypieces in a context that makes it likely that the term was applied to the container that held the fire, as distinct from fire-irons,

146 Design for a stove. C. *1801–4.* CAT. NO. 149.

fender, and so on. Various stoves are specifically mentioned: 'Rumford Stoves and Copings', 'Hot air cast stoves', 'Register Stove', 'Hot air and brass ventilator'. Most of these appear to have been devices that were, or could be, actually fitted into a fireplace to increase efficiency in one way or another; some could have been used free-standing, but the nature of the Pavilion decorations, especially in the later period, makes it unlikely that they were so used.

Another Pavilion design for a 'stove' [146] may have possibly been meant for the Entrance Hall, or for the Conservatory, which also had five-clawed dragons writhing around columns. However, these particular dragons are much nearer in their general character to those of [62], the columns of which also have the same three-leafed clover effect at their bases.

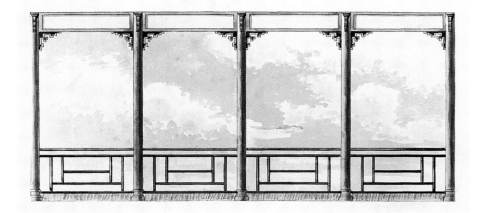

147 *Design for a wall decoration, perhaps for a corridor. 1802.* CAT. NO. 147.

148 *Design for the Entrance Hall, the north wall. Probably 1802 or earlier.*
CAT. NO. 153.

149 *Design for the Entrance Hall, the west wall. Probably 1802 or earlier.*
CAT. NO. 154.

150 Design for the Entrance Hall, the west wall. 1802. CAT. NO. 146.

151 Design for a wall decoration and door, with columns. 1802. CAT. NO. 148.

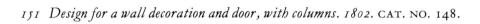

152 Design for the Entrance Hall, the south wall. c. 1820. CAT. NO. 158.

Before leaving the Entrance Hall design [150] to look at other designs for the
same area, one might consider two other designs to which it might be relevant.
Attree says that 'the corridors and staircases are of the same colour as the hall,
but ornamented in the peculiar style of the Chinese covered ways'. Two designs
exist [147, 151] which have the facility of extension to an indeterminate length,
appropriate to a corridor, and which might possibly, given a ceiling in imitation
of a roof, answer the description of a 'Chinese covered way'. We know from the
design for the Glass Passage that something of the same kind had been proposed
in that case, and perhaps executed [91, 92]. This had a blue teawood ceiling and
glazed sides; indeed, the basic structure of columns and capitals is very similar
to that seen in [147] and [151]. It does not need a great leap of the imagination
to see a similar blue teawood ceiling added to [147] and [151]; remove the glazing
and one sees, on either side of one's 'Chinese covered way', the sky! The Crace
accounts mention, from Christmas 1802 to Midsummer 1803, work done on 'Corridors, Passages, Lobby's'; they speak of 'architrave cut in panels on ceilings' and
'Margins cut on ceilings . . . and finished Tulip wood' (the ceilings therefore were
not skied), of 'Imitation of columns Tulip wood and shadowed', of 'Blue railing
cut to form pannels on Walls with 4 shadows' and six 'Ornamented pannel[s]
to imitate sky in centre' (of columns), 'Green Chinese railing on Do'.[101] Given
changes of detail,[102] these accounts are quite compatible with the designs.

There is another shred of evidence, if from a somewhat later source: 'The
entrance to the staircase from the ante room was spacious and truly grand, a strik-

153 Design for the Entrance Hall, the east wall. C. *1820.* CAT. NO. 159.

ing feature being four beautiful pillars in Scagliola marble by Richter'.[103] Presumably the two pillars shown on the right of [151] were repeated opposite, making four in all; however, the author has been unable to relate the design, with its strange projections from the upper part of the walls, to the plans.

The next group of designs for the Entrance Hall is of a curious and aberrant nature [148, 149, 154–156, 160]; the combination of almost Burlingtonian trompe l'œil masonry and a classical architectural framework with chinoiserie scrolls, frets, teawood and rockwork, quasi Indian-Chinese statues, sky ceilings, and Magritte-like sky openings in the walls of [155] and [148] – [149, 160] represent the window wall, the sky in the windows is real, that in the dado is trompe l'œil – all go to make up a quite surrealist ensemble.

The date of these designs is open to question. Indeed, they are not all from the same hand; the style of the cursory rockwork of [148] is different from that of the others; the inscription 'For Mr. Crace' implies that this design was not by a member of the family. The designs must postdate the construction of the enlarged Entrance Hall by Holland in 1801; they must predate the Nash alterations and extensions. The author's guess is that from their general style, and from common motifs shared with [147] and [151] (blue teawood, sky, and Chinese frets as railings) and with [150] (the fret drawn on the left-hand margin of [148], and the frets seen in [154] and [155], are basically the same as that beneath the canopy in [150]), these designs are from the 1801–2 period, and were discarded in favour of the ones used.

154 *Design for the Entrance Hall, the east wall. Probably 1802 or earlier.* CAT. NO. 151.

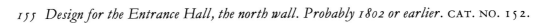

155 *Design for the Entrance Hall, the north wall. Probably 1802 or earlier.* CAT. NO. 152.

It will be seen from plan F that the upper part of the Entrance Hall as extended by Holland gave into the bedchamber storey, and that therefore the canopy and pillars of [150] might well have made yet another 'Chinese covered way'. It seems to have been this feature of the construction that made for the curious arrangement in the upper right of [148] and [155]. There may have been a thought of the same kind as was recorded in 1815, at the time of Nash's alterations: 'At present, this Hall [the Entrance Hall] is in an unfinished state, and plain in appearance; but, it is understood, that a light gallery, with suitable embellishments, are included in the plan of it, and which will occasionally be used by His Royal Highness' band.'[104]

When, in 1815, work started again, the Entrance Hall was amongst the first of the rooms to be redecorated; the work is recorded in the Crace ledgers for the period October to Christmas. It seems to have followed the course so often seen in accounts of the Prince's decorating ventures; he changed his mind half-way through. The ceiling was clouded; the cornice was painted 'in imitation of pink Chinese marble', and the walls were coloured green. Then we have an account for 'Painting and coloring 19 pannels white for Mr. Jones and afterwards repairing and coloring Do. in consequence of Mr. Jone's [sic] paintings being removed';

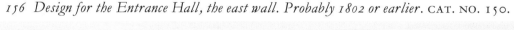

156 Design for the Entrance Hall, the east wall. Probably 1802 or earlier. CAT. NO. 150.

157 Design for the Entrance Hall, the south wall. C. *1820.* CAT. NO. 160.

next came 'Preparing and coloring the walls again – pink stiles and green panels and veining the pannels in imitation of green Chinese marble, the stiles pink marble and the whole high varnished'.[105]

The next two designs [161, 162], which have a beautifully free and painterly handling, appear to be from the hand of Frederick Crace and to relate to the extract given above. In that account we may have that rare occurrence, the story of a rejection as it happened. The Prince can hardly have disapproved of the paintings as such, for they were precursors of those later to be executed by Jones for the Banqueting Room; it may have been that he thought them too exclamatory for an Entrance Hall, for it seems certain that they were replaced by something rather quieter: 'painting in pannels of walls 4 Chinese ornaments green and shadowed marble and 5 Chinese characters over doors'.[106] The doors were grained 'pink wood, mouldings cut in dark pink and blue', similar to that in [161] and [162]; a certain amount of pink marbling was also included.

The ledgers refer also to '1 large Dragon silvered and painted in proper colors'.[107] The fact that only one was made indicates a central part in the decorations; an animal of this description, from whose bosom depended a lantern or chandelier, has existed in the Royal Pavilion stores for many years, and quite possibly is this very Dragon. A late tradition asserts it was then used in the portico.

The succeeding designs for the Entrance Hall [152, 153, 157–159], just possibly by Robert Jones, exhibit an extraordinary talent for fantasy.

First comes a design [152] that is elaborate to the point of incoherence; made for the fireplace (south) wall, it gives the impression of a design worked out impromptu, rather than the beginning of a fully worked out drawing. As elaborate,

158 Design for the Entrance Hall, the east wall. c. *1820.* CAT. NO. 161.

but more convincing, is a design for the east wall, the door of which leads into the Corridor [153]. It is an extraordinary fusion of Indian, Chinese, and Gothick motifs, with the Indian predominating, despite the Chinese paintings. In this dazzling, if congested, design, the style that was to find consummation in the Saloon is rehearsed.

The serpent-wreathed pillars either side of the doorway in the last design are related to the motifs on the Palm Tree and Pagoda pillars in the South and North Drawing Rooms (see [113, 126]) and, more closely, to the huge corner members of the Music Room; the flat vertical decoration immediately adjacent to the doorway is not unlike the Music Room mirror frame, and the upper part of the Music Room corner members. The elaboration of this design is such that it was perhaps never taken seriously, even by the artist; there is no attempt to synchronise the lower part with the scallops of the cornice, here given a greater sophistication than in the preceding two designs.

One feels that the artist must have had some humour – which is perhaps allied to fancy – in his composition; the next design [157] appears as a jocular variation on the armorial decorations, often in stucco, that appear in eighteenth-century entrance halls; Roman *gravitas* is replaced in the trophies by Eastern fancy; dragons sit in the place of eagles, a genial beast grins from a shield, and the spikes of Tartar maces and helmets cluster together. A Tartar chieftain, perhaps reviewing his hordes, appears on the trompe l'œil banner that hangs above the chimneypiece.

A design for the east wall [158] approaches, in the scallops of the cornice and the roundels with dragons, close to the accepted design. The doorway is still in the highly wrought, fused Gothick/Indian/Chinese manner.

159   Design for the Entrance Hall, the south wall. C. *1820.* CAT. NO. 162.

OPPOSITE

160   Design for the Entrance Hall, the west wall. Probably 1802 or earlier. CAT. NO. 155.

161   Design for the Entrance Hall, the south wall. Probably by Frederick Grace. 1815. CAT. NO. 156.

Gains in sobriety and discipline, if these are gains, are seen in the next design [159]; it approaches nearly to the scheme executed, as may be seen by a comparison with Pugin's watercolour drawing [163], where the dado, painted wall panels with dragons, and a slightly less elaborate cornice appear. The overdoor decorations were never installed; the chimneypiece, which strongly resembles those made for the Banqueting Room – and derives ultimately from that placed originally in the Chinese Drawing Room at Carlton House – was rejected when Westmacott came to make it in favour of the design seen in [157].

The final scheme, as seen in the watercolour drawing (made for the engraver, in which all relevant details are picked out in colour) and the aquatint [164], was installed in 1820; the painting cost £730. The woodwork was painted to simulate pollard oak; the separately completed ornamental painting was inserted into the paper on the walls: 'Preparing and painting the walls and rubbing down the edges of paper to receive the ornamental painting in shades of Green'. One item reads, 'Mr. Crace and assistants attending at Brighton to make designs and putting in patterns for the approbation of His Majesty'.[108]

162 Design for the Entrance Hall, the east wall. Probably by Frederick Crace. 1815. CAT. NO. 157.

163 The Entrance Hall. By Augustus Pugin. C. *1820.* CAT. NO. 163.

There may have been a change of mind not shown in the drawing and aquatint. The sky ceiling of 1815 was not reinstated in 1820, when the ceiling was coloured 'light green' with a 'sunk margin around Do. with rosettes in relief'.[109] However, an account from later in the same year refers to 'washing off the coloring and reinstating the painting of the ceiling . . .':[110] this may have been necessary because of the havoc wrought by the lamps, which is frequently recorded elsewhere. Brayley, in Victoria's reign, referred to the ceiling of the Entrance Hall as 'an azure sky, diversified by fleecy clouds';[111] this seems, therefore, to have been the King's final preference.

The furniture in this room, apart from a magnificent grand piano by Tomkinson (dated 1821 and now in a private collection), is comparatively simple. The whole room, understated as it is and in a green complementary to the predominant pink of the Corridor, seems a deliberately modest prelude to the latter's highly coloured fantasy.

164 The Entrance Hall, c. 1820. From John Nash, Views of the Royal Pavilion, Brighton *(1826).* CAT. NO. 164.

165 Design for the Corridor. Probably by Frederick Crace. 1815. CAT. NO. 165.

The Corridor

The Corridor built by Nash was much larger and more important in the scheme of things than its predecessor; it acted both as a dramatic entrance to the two new State Rooms (the Music Room and Banqueting Room) and, with its splendid staircases at either end, as a ready means of communication with the galleries on the upper floors; (it is a great pity that the third large staircase, that adjacent to the King's Apartments, has disappeared, although it could be reconstituted.) The form of these decorative staircases was perhaps contributed by Nash himself; despite the bamboo detail, they are very similar in form to other Nash cast-iron staircases, such as the Gothick staircase at Longner Hall in Shropshire.

Nash opened up and extended the Corridor; the increased length and breadth decreased its apparent height, giving opportunities to the decorators that were triumphantly seized. The effect of length is not lost, but the compartmentalism created by the central skylight, the staircases, and, later, the screens placed at either end, prevented the Corridor from degenerating into the dark tunnel it might easily have become.

From the quarter ending October 1815 the Crace ledgers detail work on the 'New' or 'Long' Gallery. They make clear that by the time work started there were no hesitations over the salient features of the completed decorations — the wonderful wall decorations 'on fine linen blue on pink ground', the chimneypieces ('3 carved and enriched chimneypieces — bamboo and marble'; the 'bamboo' was cast iron), the 'bamboo framing with bells etc across Gallery',[112] and the 'highly varnished 6 niches for Chinese figures' in 'imitation of Chinese pink marble'.[113] The pink and blue decoration is, perhaps, the most daring and exhilarating use of complementary colours to be seen in a building where daring is carried to the extreme and, for some tastes, beyond it; its full effect, together with the ochre of the simulated bamboo, and the gaily coloured lanterns (of which the original somewhat dim lights — a candle — filtered through painted and stained glass, added mystery to the glamour) may be seen most resplendently in the two Pugin watercolours [181, 182]. It may also be seen, prefigured, in a drawing of the area immediately below the central skylight [165].

This drawing is so spontaneous in effect that it might at first glance be thought to depict a room already constructed. However, the simple chimneypiece is very different from the confections actually installed, and the semicircular projections at the bases of the alcoves were in the event made flat, to accommodate cabinets; there are other differences in detail and, most conclusively, the cross-section of the canopy indicates a design and not a drawing. A glance at [150] will demonstrate how the niches from Holland's 1787 entrance hall survived and multiplied in the Nash Corridor. The canopy seen in [165] may have been influenced by that of [150].

166   *Design for a wall decoration below a skylight, the Corridor. By Frederick Crace. 1815.*
CAT. NO. 166.

167   *Design of flowers and leaves in pink and blue, possibly for the Corridor. By Frederick*
Crace. 1815. CAT. NO. 167.

168   *Design derived from Chinese characters in pink and green, probably for the Corridor.*
By Frederick Crace. 1815. CAT. NO. 168.

169 The Corridor. By Augustus Pugin. Before 1820. CAT. NO. 169.

The clearly depicted pattern of stylised foliage bordered with frets, shown in [165] above the canopy, is almost exactly paralleled in a Crace watercolour [166]; it exists also in two finished pencil sketches in the Royal Pavilion collections (not illustrated); one sees how nothing was left to chance. Motifs that may have been considered for this area include scroll motifs in pink and blue [167] and motifs based perhaps on Chinese characters [168]. In the event, the red Chinese fret motif of [166] was, as executed, not in paint but in pink glass, illuminated from outside; subsequent alterations to the outer skylight of the Corridor obliterated this effect, but current restorations of the roofs should ultimately restore the illumination. The design in [165] is close to that followed, as may be seen from Pugin's drawing [169], watercolour [181], and aquatint [170]; all belong to the first phase of the Corridor decoration. In 1822 various changes were made, illustrated again in a Pugin drawing [171], watercolour [182], and aquatint [172]. (The 'tidying-up' process that makes the aquatints less interesting is amusingly shown in the alignment of the rug; displaced in [181], it is put straight in [170].)

In its later stages the Corridor gained in richness and dignity; it lost in frivolity. The introduction of the patterned carpet, the bookshelves, the weightier central lustre brought from the Saloon, the painted and stained-glass doors at either end that contained the space, the stately tulip-shaped colza oil lamps on pedestals, the set of Indian 'Chippendale' furniture in sandalwood veneered in ivory (bought

170 The Corridor, c. *1820. From John Nash,* Views of the Royal Pavilion, Brighton
(1826). CAT. NO. 171.

171 The Corridor. By Augustus Pugin. 1822–4. CAT. NO. 172.

172 The Corridor, c. 1824. From John Nash, Views of the Royal Pavilion, Brighton (1826). CAT. NO. 174.

173 Design for a standard, the Corridor. 1815. CAT. NO. 175.   *174 Designs for standards, the Corridor. 1815.* CAT. NO. 176.

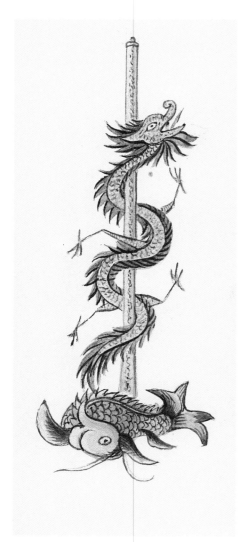

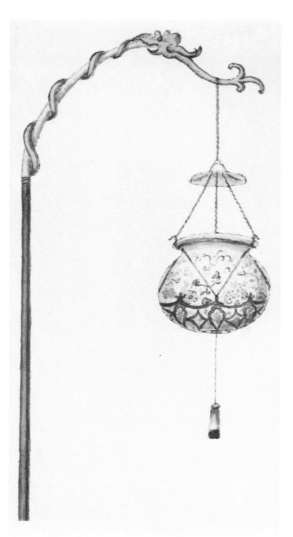

175 Design of dragon and fish,
possibly for a decorative standard.
By Frederick Crace. c. 1815.
CAT. NO. 177.

176 Design for a lantern and standard in
red, gold, and blue. Pobably 1802–4. CAT.
NO. 180.

177 Design for a banner and standard
in blue, yellow and pink. Probably
1802–4. CAT. NO. 182.

in 1819 by the Prince Regent from Queen Charlotte's sale), all contribute to the new sense of restraint and disciplined luxury. Still in place, however, are the simulated bamboo cabinets by Marsh and Tatham, with their scagliola tops, brass galleries, and pleated silk fronts, accompanied by benches and open cabinets; despite the oriental decorative detail, the French influence is strong, and one sees in the style of these cabinets the influence of Henry Holland. How far he controlled their production is another matter; some 'Holland' furniture made for Holland houses (at Southill, for instance) has deficiencies of design that give one doubts.

One conspicuous ornament of the first Corridor scheme that gave it much of its character was totally omitted from the second scheme – the splendidly decorated standards [170] from which depended the lanterns. These stand on either side of the Corridor in the early design [165]; a sketch for one of them, with the bamboo trellis lightly indicated, is perhaps earlier [173]. Other designs show them complete [174]. They are described in the accounts for the quarter ending October 1815 under 'preparing and painting 16 large ornamental carved standards – by Fricker and Henderson – 11 ft. high, highly enriched and varnished'.[114] The cost was £192. A little later in the same year £42 was charged for 'repainting and silvering in part . . . in consequence of alterations. . . .'[115] A standard that survives more or less complete, in the Royal Pavilion stores, appears to have been one of this group; it is interesting that some details of the workmanship, compared with the highly

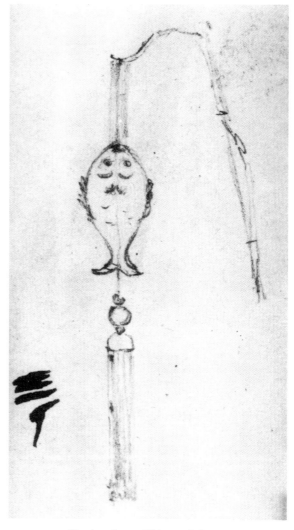

178 Design for a Chinese fish in silver, brown, pink, and green. Probably 1802–4. CAT. NO. 185.

179 Design for a Chinese fish. C. *1815.* CAT. NO. 186.

developed finish seen elsewhere, are crude, and did the account not exist one would be tempted to think that the standards, or at least some of their components, had been reused from an earlier scheme of decoration.

Two drawings from the Crace book [175, 183] may possibly be connected with designs for the standards, or for some similar decorative feature, and appear to belong to the same period. One is not so certain about four other designs [176, 177, 186, 187], some of which may date from an earlier period; [177] is for a banner.

Another arresting detail of the first phase of the Corridor is the series of life-size Chinese figures, clad in real robes, that stood in the niches. This theme, dear to the Prince's heart, had been rehearsed many times in different contexts, and in this instance the figures had, like the niches themselves, multiplied from the two to be found in the Entrance Hall of 1802. This was their final apotheosis, for they, also, were entirely to disappear from the final scheme for the Corridor.

From the rods in the hands of these figures hung an amusing miscellany of objects, principally fish – fishing was thought, for some reason, an appropriate occupation for a Chinaman. The fish ranged from the fearsome and fantastic [184] to the comparatively realistic, like the fish that tops the 'Drummer Boy' clock [178, 185]; the former may be an earlier design. A sketch for [185] seems to embody [179] a gently smiling caricature – of whom? If it is a caricature, it bears some resemblance to Mr Frederick Crace, whose tendency towards pomposity is known;

180 Design for a pedestal to carry a vase, perhaps for the corridor. 1815 or later. CAT. NO. 187.

it would be unlikely to be a self-caricature. An interesting pencil drawing from the Cooper-Hewitt collection [180] may perhaps be a preliminary design for the beautiful pedestals eventually used for the Chinese figures that stood either side of the central fireplace, seen most clearly in the aquatint [172].

In February 1816 Lady Ilchester wrote of the Corridor:

The evenings were not in the least formal. As soon as the Queen sat down to cards everybody moved about as they pleased, and made their own backgammon, chess or card party, but the walking up and down the gallery was the favourite lounge. All the rooms open into this beautiful gallery, which is terminated at each end by the lightest and prettiest Chinese staircases you can imagine, made of cast iron and bamboo, with glass doors beneath, which reflect the gay lanterns, etc., at each end. There are mandarins and pagodas in abundance, plenty of sofas, Japan and China. The centre of the gallery has a skylight . . .[116]

The design for this skylight exists still [188]; in the centre is the satyrish figure of 'Lin-shin, the God of Thunder, surrounded by his drums and flying. . . .'[117]

181 The Corridor. By Augustus Pugin. Before 1820. CAT. NO. 170.

Was the chubby little Chinese boy [192] meant for such a centrepiece? It is possible that such was the purpose of a strange half-bird, half-moth [190]; it displays the technique seen in many of the designs for glass, whereby the light is allowed to provide the highlights of the modelling, a technique seen in a similar form in the imported Chinese paintings on glass. This technique is very obvious in a design of two contorted dragons [193]; the opaque green and red limb, allied in colour to an abstracted scroll (see p. 108) on the same sheet (not illustrated), is an odd intrusion; one imagines it may have been made necessary by some structural consideration. The pretty dragon and bird design [194] shows how the contorted limbs of the dragon make sense when surrounded by fronds of vegetation; again, the dragon's scales and the bird's feathers show signs of having been destined for glass. Other skylight designs include one for the north staircase, which has a fantastic bird flanked by dragons [191], and a very pretty design [189] that has a central bird flanked by a decoration that appears again in the Crace Book [201].

182   The Corridor. By Augustus Pugin. 1822–4. CAT. NO. 173.

183 Design of dragon and pole, possibly for a decorative standard. By Frederick Crace. c. 1815. CAT. NO. 178.

184 Design for a Chinese fish, probably for the Corridor. By Frederick Crace. c. 1815. CAT. NO. 183.

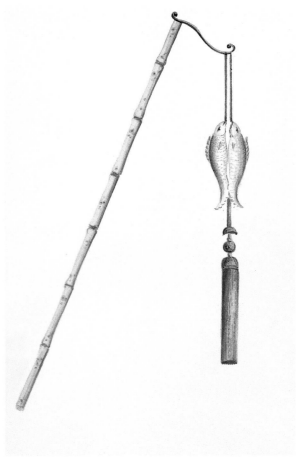

185 Design for a Chinese fish. By Frederick Crace. c. 1815. CAT. NO. 184.

186 Design for a lantern and standard. Probably 1802–4. CAT. NO. 179.

FAR RIGHT
187 Design for a lantern and standard. Probably 1802–4. CAT. NO. 181.

188 Design for a skylight, the Corridor. 1815. CAT. NO. 188.

189 Design for a skylight with an exotic bird, probably for the Corridor. 1815. CAT. NO. 190.

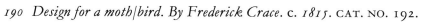

190 Design for a moth/bird. By Frederick Crace. c. 1815. CAT. NO. 192.

191 Design for a skylight, the Corridor. 1815. CAT. NO. 189.

*192 Design for a Chinese boy and flowers, probably for the
Corridor.* C. *1815.* CAT. NO. 191.

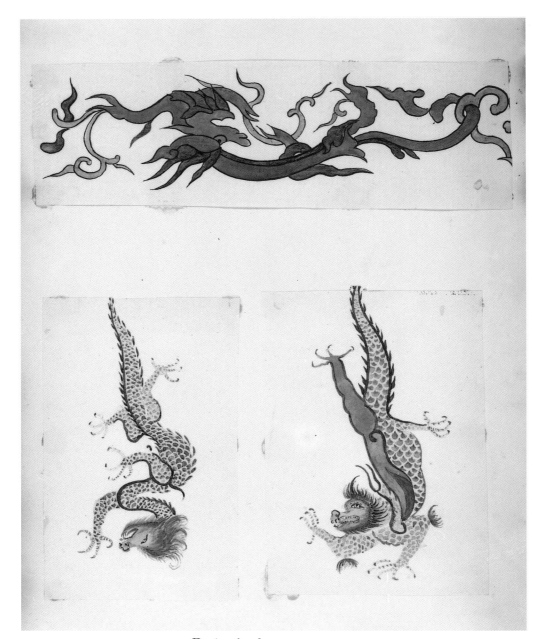

193 Design for dragons. CAT. NO. 193.

194 Design for a dragon and bird, with floral spray. By Frederick Crace. c. 1815. CAT. NO. 194.

195 Design for the skylight, the Corridor. Probably by Frederick Crace. 1815. CAT. NO. 195.

A most monstrous dragon occupies the centre circle of an executed design for the south staircase [195]; the bats that encircle it are seen also around a roundel enclosing an interlaced design [197]. The latter exists in somewhat more detail, and without its surrounding circle, in the Crace Book [196]. Obviously [196] is the original; [197] by a copyist.

There exists a whole group of designs probably meant for the Corridor: some perhaps intended to be painted on glass, others on walls. Three [198–200] are definitely designs for glass; the first two are designs for lustre or lantern glasses, the third for one of the larger and grander lustres, perhaps the 'umbrella' lustre from the Saloon, moved later to the Corridor. Others that are certainly or probably glass designs include [201] and [202] and the frets of [203] and [204] (see the border of [195]). More ambiguous are [205–209]. Of a rather different, and sufficiently extraordinary, character, is [210], which seems almost to anticipate, in its angular stylisation, certain 1930s designs.

196 Design for glass. By Frederick Crace.
C. *1815.* CAT. NO. *196.*

197 Design for glass. C. *1815.* CAT. NO. *197.*

*198 Design for a lantern glass. By Frederick
Crace.* C. *1815.* CAT. NO. *198.*

*199 Design, probably for a lantern glass. By
Frederick Crace.* C. *1815.* CAT. NO. *199.*

200 Design, probably for the edge of an 'umbrella' lustre. By Frederick Crace. C. 1815. CAT. NO. 200

201 Design with a grotesque head (detail for Corridor skylight). By Frederick Crace. C. 1815. CAT. NO. 201.

202 Design for a Chinese fret and leaves, possibly for glass. By Frederick Crace. C. 1815. CAT. NO. 202.

203 Chinese fret designs in green and yellow and in blue, possibly for glass. By Frederick Crace. C. 1815. CAT. NO. 203.

204 Chinese fret designs in lilac and in red, possibly for glass. By Frederick Crace. C. 1815. CAT. NO. 204.

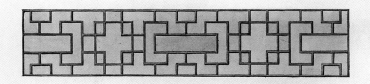

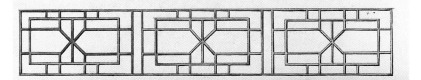

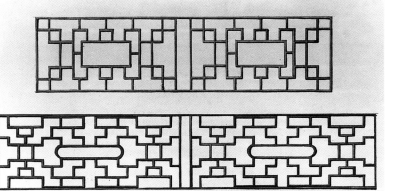

205 Two scroll designs. By Frederick Crace. c. 1815.
CAT. NO. 205.

206 Scroll design in lilac, yellow, and green. By
Frederick Crace. c. 1815. CAT. NO. 206.

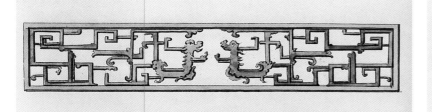

207 Design of Chinese fret in lilac and yellow. By
Frederick Crace. c. 1815. CAT. NO. 207.

208 Design of flowers and tendrils, possibly for glass. By
Frederick Crace. c. 1815. CAT. NO. 208.

209 Design of flowers and fruit. By Frederick Crace.
c. 1815. CAT. NO. 209.

210 Two repeat designs: fret and flowers, and Chinese
characters. By Frederick Crace. c. 1815. CAT. NO. 210.

211 Design of flowers and tendrils. By Frederick Crace. c. 1815. CAT. NO. 211.

212 Design of flowers and tendrils. By Frederick Crace. C. 1815. CAT. NO. 212.

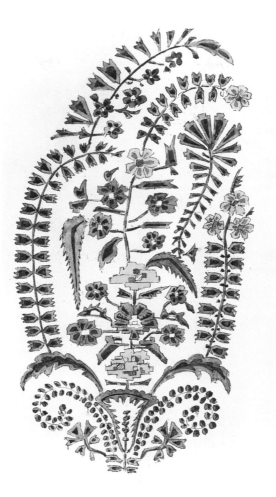

213 Design of ferns and flowers. By Frederick Crace. C. 1815. CAT. NO. 213.

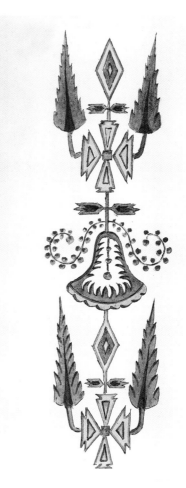

214 Design of leaves and geometric shapes. By Frederick Crace. C. 1815. CAT. NO. 214.

215 Chinoiserie design. By Frederick Crace. C. 1815. CAT. NO. 216.

216 Design for a wall decoration, possibly for the Corridor. c. *1815.* CAT. NO. 217.

217 Design for a chinoiserie decoration.
By Frederick Crace. c. *1815.* CAT. NO. 218.

218 Design for a chinoiserie decoration.
By Frederick Crace. c. *1815.* CAT. NO. 219.

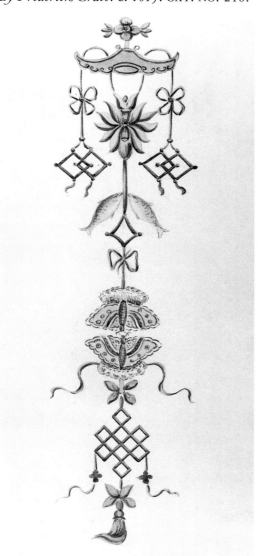

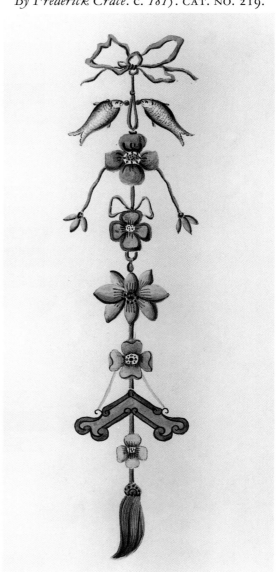

219 Design of chinoiserie scrolls, shapes, and flowers. C. *1815.* CAT. NO. 220.

There are also a small number of most charming naturalistic and semi-naturalistic designs, derived from Indian textile ornament, which were not used, and which breathe, in an undefinable way, a completely different spirit from that of the Pavilion. Such are [211–213] and, from a different source, [214]. (See also p. 224).

Two strange designs on the same page appear to be projects for the Corridor carpet [220]; that above, in the Corridor pink and cerulean blue, has a pattern derived from Tekke Türkmen designs (known to the carpet trade as 'Bokhara'), and since it is difficult to date Türkmen carpets, an English sketch of the early nineteenth century is of interest.[118] The pattern beneath it appears to be derived from tiles. The next design illustrated is, to the author, a mystery [215].

An idiosyncratic drawing for a wall decoration, perhaps in the hand of a copyist [216], gives a clue to the placing of other designs related to it (and discussed below); a blank central panel, obviously meant to carry some motif, is supported by a dado with a design of formal Chinese scrolls, and bordered on either side by upright panels bearing a design of fishes, moths, and decussated threads; (the latter is seen in colour in [217], and a simpler alternative (?) in [218]; it has affiliations also with designs for the Music Room).

OPPOSITE
220   Two designs for carpets, probably for the Corridor. By Frederick Crace. c. *1815.*
CAT. NO. 215.

221   Design of scrolls and flowers. c. *1815.* CAT. NO. 221.

222   Design for chinoiserie decoration. By Frederick Crace. c. *1815.* CAT. NO. 223.

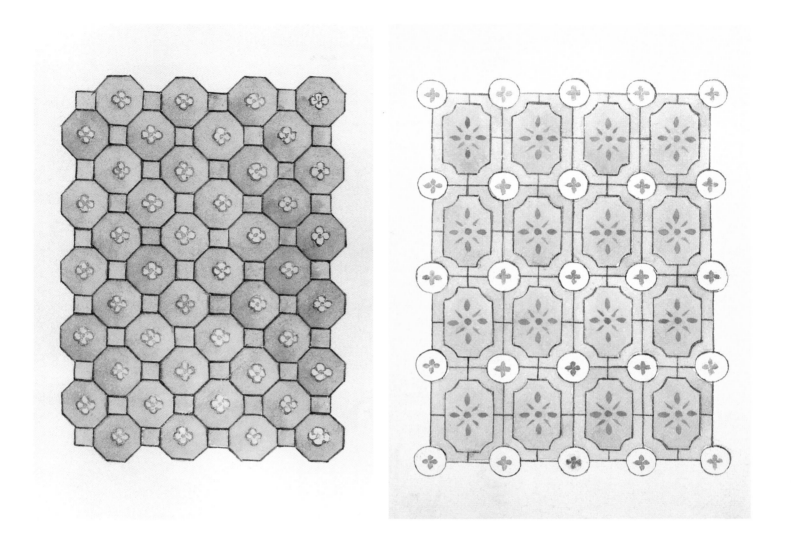

223 *Chinoiserie design in tones of blue. By Frederick Crace.* c. *1815.* CAT. NO. 222.

*224   Design for chinoiserie repeat pattern in green, pink, yellow, and blue. By Frederick
Crace. c. 1815.* CAT. NO. 224.

225   Design for chinoiserie repeat pattern. By Frederick Crace. c. 1815. CAT. NO. 225.

226   Design for chinoiserie repeat pattern. By Frederick Crace. c. 1815. CAT. NO. 226.

227 *Design for a panel.* c. *1815.* CAT. NO. 227.

The Banqueting Room

The Banqueting Room is nowhere mentioned in the surviving Crace ledgers; the details of its decoration given in the abstracted accounts make plain the important role played by Robert Jones and by Bailey and Saunders. The Royal Archives record that £173 15s 0d was paid to Jones for drawings for the Banqueting Room, and the large sum of £8,339 11s 0d was paid to him for work done within it.[121] Nowhere in that document is Crace mentioned. Of the few designs that appear to survive for it one is indubitably and another probably from the hand of Robert Jones (see also [257, 258]).

The Banqueting Room shares with the Music Room large flat surfaces, a deep coved ceiling, and a dome; it lacks the octagon canopy of the Music Room, and the absence of this capricious ingredient allows the spacious amplitude of the Empire style full expression, despite the flamboyantly exotic decoration.

A fine and large drawing [230] inscribed with the name of Robert Jones, for a fireplace wall, is close to the scheme installed, as may be seen by a comparison with the aquatint [233]. The cove and the framed chinoiserie paintings are much as executed, although as yet unevolved on the former is the truly remarkable sunflower, radiating light and with its centre made up of writhing serpent heads, that today adorns it; a variant of this design was to make up the silver and grey backgrounds of the chinoiserie paintings, and something allied to it, but lacking the arcane planetary symbolism, became the dragon 'damask' of the Red Drawing Room and the King's Apartments. The main difference between drawing and aquatint is the elimination of some of the dragons, the substitution of elaborately carved and gilded wooden overdoors, somewhat tinctured by Jones' Indian style, and the installation of chimneypieces with Chinese figures somewhat in the manner of the Carlton House chimneypiece recently placed in the North Drawing Room.

The magnificently vivid dragon [231], free and fiery, is not unlike those painted by Jones within the trompe l'œil satinwood panels of the Red Drawing Room doors and window shutters, and may be from his hand. It may have been meant for either Banqueting or Music Room.

The completed room in all its glory is shown in Pugin's drawing and in the aquatint [232, 233]; the engraving (not reproduced) is dated December 1 1824, although both Banqueting and Music Rooms had been substantially completed by the end of 1818; in October 1818 the Prince Regent had seen the gasoliers lit for the first time. Dazzling and magnificent as the room appears even now, bereft of its carpet and most of its rich furnishings, how much more must it have dazzled contemporaries. The reaction of such an experienced *femme du monde* as Princess Lieven, who had known the lavish interiors of Imperial Russia, is instructive: 'I do not believe that, since the days of Heliogabalus, there has been such magnificence and such luxury'. Of the Banqueting Room she wrote, 'We were shown a chandelier which cost eleven thousand pounds sterling — I write it out

230 Design for the Banqueting Room. By Robert Jones. C. *1816.* CAT. NO. 230.

in full because it is really incredible. The chandelier is in the form of a tulip held by a dragon.'[122] These gasoliers remain one of the most extraordinary features of the room, although Princess Lieven was wrong about the cost; the chandelier cost £5613 9s od.[123] And the Princess' tulips are lotus flowers. The dragon she mentions is a truly impressive creature; Bailey & Saunders' accounts mention 'To makg. & altg. at sundry times 2 Models of the Dragon as originally designed by Mr. Jones and under his superintendence'.[124] More dragons can be seen (on the right in both drawing and aquatint) attached to the 'very large and superbly decorated sideboard[s] made of very fine Rosewood, Snakewood and Satin Wood with 12 large Dragons and Ornamts. richly carved and double Gilt in the very best manner to Mr. Jones' design'.[125] The total cost of the sideboards' construction came to £2,760, although more legs and dragons were added later to the smaller ones (£223 18s od).[126] Similar dragons, in gilt bronze, can be seen on the dark-blue Spode columns of the torchères, also designed by Jones; the dolphins at the base of those in the window bay are obviously afterthoughts, since they are not ormolu but carved and gilded wood. (The bases of those on the opposite wall are enriched by the presence of the sideboards.) Or the dolphins may have been made as a model for gilt bronze that was for some reason not carried out.

The gilt wood columns at the angles of the room are in the form of fasces and lances entwined with serpents – almost symbols in themselves of the victory of orientalism over the classical tradition! The accounts of 1817 record their alteration, 'adding' (no doubt at the Regent's command) 'larger snakes'.[127]

The large Axminster carpet [232, 233] was designed by Jones, as were the two hearthrugs; the red semicircle in the foreground of the aquatint is possibly one of these rugs. The carpet, very broadly, echoed the design of the upper part of the room: in the centre was a dragon, corresponding to the dragon above; the greenish circle beyond the pink circle echoed the design of straight lines around the eyebrow windows. This regular pattern, well within eighteenth-century tradition, reinforces the impression made by the room of having a firm classical foundation.

Robert Jones' wall paintings – do they have distant influences from Boucher's designs for Beauvais? – are set on a wallpaper of blue and silver, an ambiguous design that is as much Gothick as anything else. The background to the lamps on the window wall is fluted silk.

The room is shown in the aquatint with the table, laden with silver gilt, set for dessert; the King sits in the centre facing the window. More magnificent silver gilt (all in the neo-classical, not Chinese, taste, although what appears to be a line of blanc de chine figures stands on the table) is displayed on the sideboards. A frequent visitor to the Prince's table compared his silver gilt unfavourably with the silver of the Duke of Wellington, which he considered lit up better; 'the whole aspect [of the latter's table] was of pure, glittering white; unlike the slightly shaded tinge which candles seem to cast from gold plate.'[128]

This splendour was carefully preserved in the absence of the Prince; the accounts record the manufacture of large numbers of brown holland covers lined in white calico, in which were muffled in melancholy darkness sideboards, torchères, chimneypieces, wine coolers, *et al.*

231 *Design of dragons, possibly for the Banqueting Room. Probably by Robert Jones.*
C. *1816.* CAT. NO. 231.

232 *The Banqueting Room. By Augustus Pugin.* c. *1820 or later.* CAT. NO. 232.

233 *The Banqueting Room. From John Nash,* Views of the Royal Pavilion, Brighton
(1826). CAT. NO. 233.

The Music Room

George IV was as susceptible to music as to the other arts, and its performance was, for him (as, it must be said, for his father also), inseparable from the enactment of the pomps of state or the convivialities of private occasions. Hence the importance in all his buildings of the 'Music Room', the room where a large group of people could be gathered together, in comfortable acoustic and physical conditions, to listen to the performance of music.

It will be remembered that it had been intended that the new south wing of the Pavilion erected in 1801 should bear the double role of Conservatory and Music Room; some sort of mysterious blight appears to have settled upon it, perhaps in the form of recurrent dry rot, for it appears to have been little used; the Crace ledgers make clear that from 1815 onwards, and probably well beforehand, it was the Dining Room to the north that doubled as a Music Room. When, therefore, the extensive Nash rebuilding commenced, and the Banqueting Room was moved south, it must have seemed axiomatic that the great balancing room to the north should be devoted to the purposes of making music.

Before moving to a detailed exposition of this room and the designs for it, three designs [234, 235, 241] should be considered. The reader will remember the discussion (see p. 151) of the ante room or lobby, north of the Egyptian Gallery, that connected the latter with the Dining Room, and the possibility that three designs [143–145] were associated with it. By 1815 this ante room was being described in the accounts as the 'Lobby from Music Room to Yellow Drawing Room' and, in common with that Music Room (not to be confused with Nash's later Music Room on part of the same site), was being redecorated. This redecoration is described in the Crace ledgers[129] as follows:

To Preparing and coloring small ceiling sky color.   12. 0

Do. do. the wood cornice and soffit yellow, red and black with Chinese railing over columns in various colors.   3. 5. 0

Preparing, repairing and varnishing the painting on walls in imitation of Green Marble and the 4 yellow Chinese columns and windows to Do.   2. 14. 0

Preparing, painting and graining in imitation of yellow satinwood and high varnished 3 pair of large folding doors – beads cut in brown, lining to doors etc. green.   10. 13. 4

This description is close to the scheme seen in [241], save that the marbling is blue rather than green; however, the green marbling is seen in [234]. [235] is obviously an alternative design for the same area. The room plainly has something, if not everything, in common with [143–145]. It is tempting to see [241] and [234], with their brilliant virtuoso marbling, as designs in something of the same idiom and from the same period as the brief green marbled phase of the

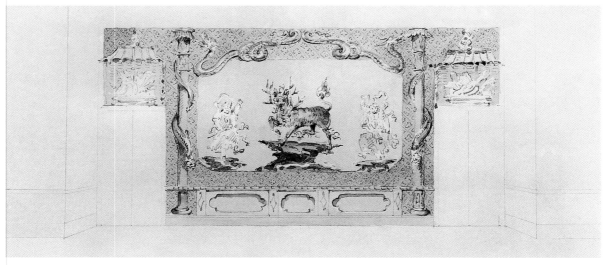

238 Design for the south wall, the Music Room. c. *1817.* CAT. NO. 240.

239 Design for the south wall, the Music Room. c. *1817.* CAT. NO. 242.

and serpents that anticipates elements of the completed scheme; the dado, also, begins to be delineated. Wreathed pilasters and interleaved serpents are seen again in a design for the south wall [238], but here a somewhat more convincing monster is supported on either side by warriors; again, one sees the repeat pattern wallpaper. It will be noticed that the cove is plain, lacking the bamboo that was later to appear.

The next design [245] is a more seemly confection, containing and combining motifs seen in the previous three; the beasts on rocks and clouds and on the hoop, in differently designed panels and with different dados – in that on the right, two dragons have contorted themselves into an almost Vitruvian pattern – are suspended on either side of an elaborately canopied chimney glass; beyond the beasts are warriors, very like those on the export Chinese paintings on glass that were inserted into the lanterns, who stamp menacingly on their pedestals.

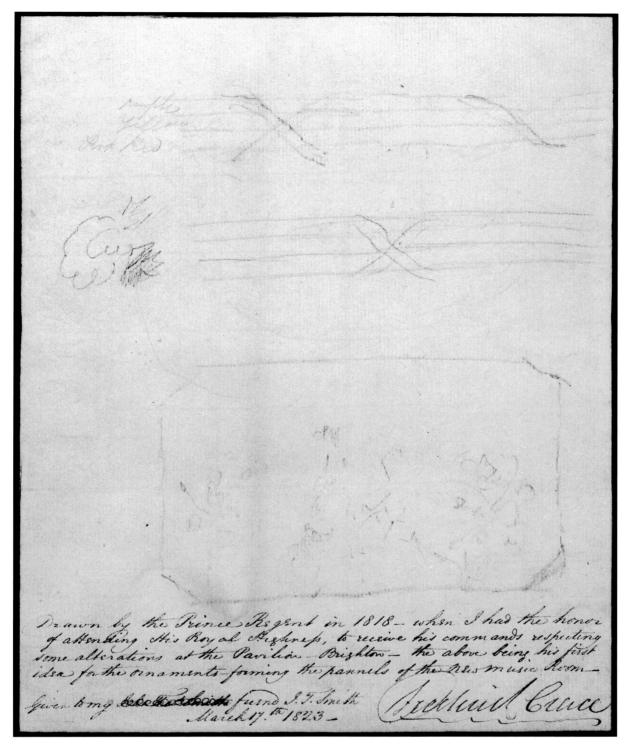

240 *Designs for the bamboo cove and a wall panel, the Music Room. By King George IV.*
C. *1817.* CAT. NO. 243.

Strides towards finality are seen in another design for the south wall [239]. The mood is weightier, although the high key and caprice of the earlier designs persist. Above the panels is seen the bamboo ceiling, wreathed with trompe l'œil ribbons, that was first sketched out in the King's own hand; the note to [240] reads, 'Drawn by the Prince Regent in 1818 – when I had the honor of attending His Royal Highness, to receive his commands respecting some alterations at the Pavilion Brighton – the above being his first idea for the ornaments forming the pannels of the New Music Room – Given to my friend J. T. Smith March 17th 1823 – Frederick Crace'. Within the panel sketched on [240] by the Prince may be seen very faint indications of the central beast of [239] and, on the left, a warrior holding a spear.

Above the bamboo ceiling of [239] is a light pencil sketch of the tent canopy, eyebrow window, and dome; the convex cove is not fully developed in the draw-

241 Design for a lobby, possibly the Ante Room to the Music Room, and close to a design installed in 1815. CAT. NO. 234.

ing, which may mean that the decorative schemes were being developed well before building work had been completed. However, the design that was to be employed on the convex cove, a combination of a variety of dog-tooth ornament and fleur de lys, is here put on the lower part of the dome; above is the line of pendants and cockleshells that exists today.

The next design [251] retains many of the features of earlier essays, but its effect is utterly different. Gone are the rococo gaiety and high spirits; in their place is an obsessively rich, intricately worked out and, to some, even sinister conception: the domicile of the Dowager Empress rather than of the Prince of the Pagodas. The eighteenth century has most decidedly been left behind. The colour scheme of 'Carmine, Lake, Vermilion, Crome, Yellow and other expensive colors'[130] reinforces this impression; the scarlet and gold landscapes offer entrance into a fabled and disturbing world; the dragons and serpents are beginning to come alive. An abstract of expenses incurred at Brighton during the year 1818 gives the largest sum, £453, to 'Mr. Lamberlet', and a sum of £116 to 'Mr. Fox';[131]

242 Design for a window, the Music Room. C. *1817.* CAT. NO. 247.

243 Design for an orchestra rail, the Music Room. C. *1817.* CAT. NO. 248.

a book of tracings by the latter after William Alexander exists still in the Royal Pavilion collections, and it seems likely that these were the two principal artists concerned with the execution of the wall paintings.

The vertical designs of the doors in [251] are somehow reminiscent, as are the interlaced circles, of the furniture from the Chinese Drawing Room at Carlton House; the former also remind one of the pencil drawing [216], as, very directly, does the wall panel to the right in [246], the last related also to designs from the Crace book – albeit in a very different palette [217].

A design for the wall adjacent to the bamboo tent ceiling [246] is in many respects close to that executed. The panel painting especially, with its immense coiled and iridescent snake and landscape in 'Carmine . . . in yellow etched in gold and highly varnished, and polished',[132] is not far removed from one erected; the completed work took '400 yards of fine cambric linen'.[133] It should be remarked that, as finally executed, the background diaper pattern was painted – not printed as seems to have been the case in the Banqueting Room. The bamboo ceiling,

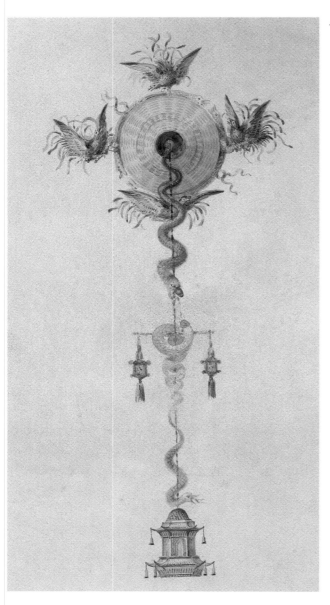

*244 Design, probably for the top of a gasolier, the
Music Room.* C. *1816.* CAT. NO. 238.

OPPOSITE
*246 Design for the wall and bamboo cove, the
Music Room. By Frederick Crace.* C. *1817.*
CAT. NO. 245.

245 Design for the west wall, the Music Room. C. *1817.* CAT. NO. 241.

247   Design, probably for the Orchestra, the Music Room.
c. *1817*. CAT. NO. 249.

here rainbow-hued to offer a choice, was to be the subject of a change of mind; 'painting in imitation of bamboo the reeded ceiling . . . and ornamenting the same with blue ribbons and highly varnished' was to be followed by 'Repainting the ribbons Lilac instead of blue, by order of His Majesty'.[134]

A design [250] for the west wall of the Music Room shows two variations for the area above the canopy. They are closely related to, but not as elaborate as, the executed work; pagoda'd pineapples were to replace the animals at the corner of the canopy (designed to hold the gasoliers) and entwined serpents were to occupy the blank spaces beneath the eyebrow windows. This carved, gilded, and painted work was to be of the highest technical quality; a subtle effect was achieved by the shading down of the 'green' (alloyed with silver) gold from the dome through 'yellow' gold to the 'regular' (pure gold) gilding used lower down; much of the work was water gilt and burnished. A note still exists, dated August 22 1818, of the amount of gold required; 68,500 sheets for cove ornaments, canopy, soffit, coves of spandrels and spandrels, and capitals and bases of columns.[135]. Amusingly enough, on the canopy real, thick, gilded rope was used as decoration: 'preparing and gilding 512 ft of cord and pole . . . £32'.[136] This canopy, with its

248 *Design of lamps and canopy, probably for the Music Room.* c. *1817.* CAT. NO. 250.

249 *Design of lamps and canopy, probably for the Music Room.* c. *1817.* CAT. NO. 251.

scales and bells, is not dissimilar to the canopy of the 'Drummer Boy' clock; the latter has palm-tree supports, not unlike, in their lower parts, the final version of the Music Room mirror frame – an early version is seen in [250]. The chimneypiece also is not the design chosen. The window design [242], with its giant moths (see also [190]), is close to one executed in 1818; a sum of twelve guineas was paid for 'working drawings for Messrs. Underwood and Foyle for the 8 stained glass windows';[137] the vivid yellow and purple glass (the moths were cold painted) was illuminated from behind at night, as is recorded in various bills – 'Men's time moving scaffolding the lighting up of windows while His Majesty was at Brighton . . . £24'.[138]

The design for the organ [252] is close to that actually followed, but is not identical with it; it is possible that the very dominant knops, which have elements in common with the existing top of the central gasolier, were erected and removed. In 1818 the Crace account mentions £12 for 'Making a Drawing of the Organ for the room and a design for the Orchestra'.[139] To 1820 belongs an account for making good 'in consequence of the alteration of the organ'.[140] However, the King was not yet satisfied, for in 1821 the Crace firm put in an account for again

250 Design for the west wall, the Music Room (alternative design concealed). By Frederick Crace.
c. 1817. CAT. NO. 246.

OPPOSITE

251 Design for the south wall, the Music Room. c. 1817. CAT. NO. 244.

252 Design for the north wall and organ, the Music Room. By Frederick Crace. c. 1817. CAT. NO. 252.

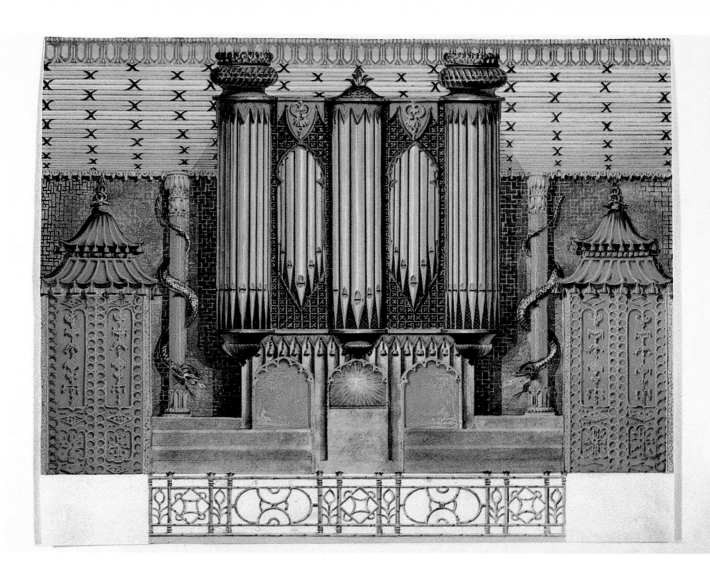

*253 Design, probably for a ceramic vase to be fitted
with ormolu mounts. By Frederick Crace. ?c. 1817.*
CAT. NO. 256.

'Making 3 designs for the alteration of the front of the Organ, by desire of His
Majesty'.[141] The fret decoration on the walls seen in [252], the door canopies,
and the door panels (again altered according to the accounts) are similar to the
final work, although the latter is, again, more elaborate than the design. The doors
especially, with their aventurine lacquer in the panels, were in the event superbly
finished. Not so, perhaps, at the first venture; the 'gold speckled to stiles of doors'
was later amended to green gold 'redone in consequence of the Gold speckling
not being approved of'.[142] The accounts of Bailey and Saunders record 'Ornamts.
very richly carved and Gilt for the front of the Organ to Mr. Crace's design'.[143]
    The orchestra rail is in the long, continuing bamboo fretwork idiom of the

Pavilion, not unlike that seen in the 1802 Saloon; it is not as executed, and indeed seems curiously unrelated to the new Music Room style. Another drawing for it [243] exists in the Crace collection in the Victoria and Albert Museum, together with a fascinating pen sketch [247]. The rail in the foreground of the latter probably indicates provision for an orchestra, with lamps for the use of the performers; this may well make sense of the two mysterious Cooper-Hewitt drawings [248, 249]. This drawing [247] relates in detail to the overdoors as completed, with their pagoda canopies, dragons, and pendants.

Two designs for the Music Room chimneypiece are still extant [254, 255]; they are unlike that proffered in [250], and are painted in a style other than that of Frederick Crace. An account of October 10 1822, to Westmacott, mentions 'A large Chimney Piece designed by W [sic] Jones Esqr. executed in Statuary Marble, of solid parts with a hearth slat of Statuary Marble 2 *in* thick. Including models for the Metalfounder . . . £380'.[144] The Crace firm was credited also with 'working drawings for Messrs. Vulliamy and Westmacot [sic]' for the chimneypieces, as early as 1818; presumably these were rejected.[145]

Westmacott's account emphasises the quality of the work, and it is indeed superb; the dragon with outspread wings and the mantelshelf (now in Buckingham Palace) are cut out of a single piece of white marble. Vulliamy's heavily gilded pillars are enwreathed with dragons. The stove front, as pictured in [255], is, again, in something of the idiom of the gilt bronze decoration on the Carlton House chimneypiece removed to the North Drawing Room. The final cost of the Music Room chimneypiece came to £1684 2s 6d.[146]

The clock depicted in [254] is not that eventually placed on the chimneypiece (as seen in the aquatint, [262]); this was the 'Rock Clock', of which the height, over forty-eight inches, gives some idea of the monumental size of the completed chimneypiece (the clock, now entirely gilt-bronze, had its rock work painted ultramarine and blue to harmonise with the Music Room).[147] The pagodas seen in [254] were never thus used, but a pair of large porcelain pagodas, with bases by Vulliamy, were placed on the floor on either side, giving something of the same effect.

The design for a 'vase on a pedestal' [256] is related to candelabra actually made, which may be seen in the aquatint [262] standing in the corner of the room; an account of 1818 from the Crace firm speaks of 'three designs for the bases of Chinese Jars and ornaments for lights to Do − £10'.[148] The same union of gilt bronze and ceramic ware is present in the Banqueting Room torchères and in the candelabra placed in the window of the North Drawing Room (see p. 139). A drawing [253], of a ceramic shape (colour notes beside), was meant probably as part of some such composite object.

Of the three curtain designs [257–259], the last is much the closest to that executed, although the central pagoda was omitted, and serpents were added to the company of the dragons; they were glazed in colours over silver leaf, with rich and enamelled effect. The account of Bailey and Saunders survives: '5 very large Window Curtains and Draperies to Mr Crace's design . . . 4 very richly carved Dragons with Superb entwining for the centre to support the Draperies at 2 Serpents at each extremity of the Windows, the whole silvered in the best manner to Mr Crace's design'.[149] The pleating, before which was placed six giant Yung Cheng pagodas, is much as was installed. The sweep of the curtains, which appear to have been composed of six different layers of 'blue and crimson satins, and yellow silks richly fringed',[150] became much bolder in the completed work than in the design.

254 *Design for the chimneypiece, the Music Room. Probably by Robert Jones.* C. *1820.* CAT. NO. 253.

255 *Design for the chimneypiece, the Music Room. Probably by Robert Jones.* C. *1820.* CAT. NO. 254.

256   *Design for vase and pedestal, the Music
Room. Probably by Robert Jones.* C. *1820.* CAT.
NO. 255.

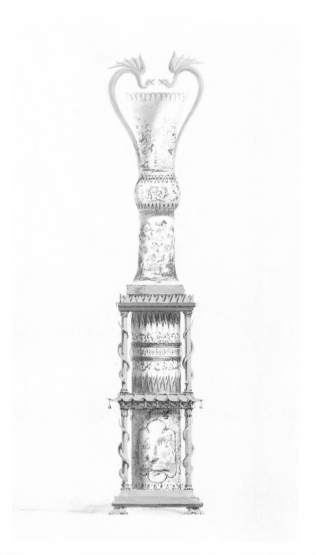

257   *Design for curtains, for either the Music
Room or the Banqueting Room.*
C. *1820.* CAT. NO. 257.

260 The Music Room. By Augustus Pugin. C. *1822.* CAT. NO. 261.

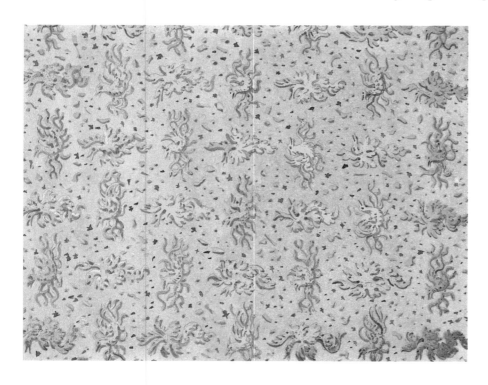

*261 Design for a carpet,
probably for the Music Room.*
C. *1820.* CAT. NO. 260.

262 The Music Room. From John Nash, Views of the Royal Pavilion, Brighton
(1826). CAT. NO. 262.

In these two pictures one can see the water-lily lustres, one of the strangest
inventions in the palace; by a happy conceit they are edged with 'pearls', like
huge drops of water – made of excessively thin blown and etched glass. The convex
cove shimmers with a silvery hue; this is an optical illusion (as was discovered
in a recent restoration, when the original bright cobalt blue and gold of the trellis
pattern were reproduced with some misgiving – one discovered, on the removal
of scaffolding, that seen from the floor the blue cooled the gold, and the gold
warmed the blue, in such a manner that the final effect became silvery). The whole,
completed, provoked astonishment and the use of superlatives. Brayley's slightly
sycophantic pen may be allowed to summarise: 'No verbal description, however
elaborate, can convey to the mind or imagination of the reader an appropriate
idea of the magnificence of this apartment; and even the creative delineations of
the pencil, combined with all the illusions of colour, would scarcely be adequate
to such an undertaking.'[155]

The Prince of Wales' Bedroom
and the King's Apartments

The royal sleeping apartments in the Pavilion are, despite their shift in 1819 to the north end of the building, here dealt with as one subject; there are sufficient connexions between the two to warrant this treatment.

A diary entry of the mid-1780s described the Prince of Wales' bedchamber as having the 'bed placed in a kind of niche or recess';[156] the plan of November 1787 (plan B), showing the bedchamber storey after Holland's rebuilding, still has such a niche in the Prince's bedchamber – in the south-east corner of the building. Obviously, few structural changes had been made in the upper storey of what had been the original farmhouse. The Prince may have found this arrangement of his bed in a niche, with service access beside it, congenial and convenient; thirty years later the same arrangement was repeated in the King's Bedroom (see p. 227).

There are various clues to the appearance of the Prince of Wales' Bedroom. The diary quoted above mentions that 'his sleeping apartment was hung with printed cotton, the bed of the same lined with a green and white check silk'; the *Sussex Advertiser* for July 9 1787 recorded that the Prince's bedchamber was hung in quilted chintz, with green and white silk; 'and near it is a glass, so situated as to afford the Prince an extensive view of the sea and Steine as he lies in bed'.[157] This statement is corroborated, as far as the chintz is concerned, by the accounts.[158] The liking for chintz continued. An account of June 1795 from N. Morel includes, amongst other items, mention of work in the Prince of Wales' Bedchamber at the Pavilion: 'Taking down the old furniture and putting up other Made out of some Chynts belonging to Carleton House'.[159]

The work done in 1795 has some significance, for it was in that year that thoughts were directed towards an alteration of the bedchamber storey in the Pavilion as a consequence of the Prince of Wales' marriage to Princess Caroline of Brunswick; a plan exists by Holland dated 'Sloane Place Feby. 1795' (plan D). It shows a complete rearrangement, with alterations picked out in pink, that would have given adjacent Bed Chambers for Prince and Princess, and adjoining dressing rooms. And indeed, when the Prince and Princess came to Brighton in June 1795 they had to stay at Mr Gerald Hamilton's house, since the Pavilion was still in the hands of the decorators.[160] The speedy deterioration of relations between Prince and Princess stultified the more ambitious scheme; one does not know whether any interior designs were produced for the work that was done, but it seems likely that they were.

The Prince's Bedroom was described, at a later period, as having been 'divided into three compartments; the centre enclosing, by sliding partitions, the bed, which was fitted up as a tent; around this were reflecting glasses, which enabled His Royal Highness, while reclining on his pillow, to see the promenade on the Steine

263 Design for an alcove with tent ceiling, probably for the Prince of Wales' Boudoir.
C. *1801–4.* CAT. NO. 263.

264 The King's Library. By Augustus Pugin. C. *1823.* CAT. NO. 265.

265 The King's Bedroom. By Augustus Pugin. C. *1823.* CAT. NO. 268.

very distinctly'.[161] This account is probably somewhat confused; there is no other reference to the centre compartment (known as the 'Boudoir') ever having enclosed the bed, although it may well have had sliding partitions between it and the Bedroom to the south, and between it and the Dressing Room to the north. The phrase 'three compartments' probably refers not to the Bedroom being divided into three compartments (without the northern niche, it measured twenty-four by twenty-five feet; not a large area to subdivide, although the Prince was not averse to small rooms, as Wyatville was later to lament). The 'compartments' are presumably the three rooms in sequence; and the centre room *is* shown as a tent room in the 1826 longitudinal section [1].

There are sufficient correspondences between these various descriptions and an existing design [263] to justify the latter's candidature as a design for the Prince's Bedchamber or Boudoir. The design itself belongs to the pre-chinoiserie phase of the Pavilion's existence; here, quite distinctly, is a chamber hung with chintz, with a tent ceiling of a simple kind, from the centre of which depends a tassel, and here are the sliding (and hinged) partitions enclosing a central area. One sees also a large convex mirror, of an orthodox variety, set in a sun-ray pleat, a mirror of a type said to have been once used in dining rooms to enable the man at the sideboard to see what was going on at the table without turning (and now used as a security device). A staircase, or possibly a piece of rattan furniture, may be glimpsed through the right-hand door of the drawing; if this staircase is that which lay between Bedroom and Dressing Room, it means that the drawing must date before 1801–2, when the staircase was removed during Holland's alterations (plan E). An earlier date is perfectly consistent with the style of decorations proposed, and the design could have been made, executed or unexecuted, for the alterations made by Morel early in 1795. But on balance it seems more likely that the design was meant for the Boudoir, which occupied the area formerly occupied by the staircase, and it may well have been executed during the 1802–4 period.

The Crace ledgers of 1802–4 are on the whole uninformative about the Prince's Bedroom and its contingent areas; they mention a large supply of 'yellow Satin Wood imitation and varnished'[162] and 'No. 10 Screen stands painted 4 oil Vermillion black beads and varnished', 'cutting out Flower pots for Do. and putting Do. on Screens'.[163] Satinwood appears to have remained in these rooms, for Brayley, writing after the death of George IV, and long after the King's Bedroom had been moved to the north of the Pavilion, remarked that in these apartments 'the furniture, which is mostly of satinwood is nearly in the same state as when used by the Prince'.[164]

Continuity, indeed, is an argument that favours the identification of [263] as the Boudoir; it has been mentioned above that the Boudoir is shown as a tent room in the Nash cross-section [1], and this room, 'His Majesty's [old] Boudoir', was described some time subsequent to the latest decorations in George IV's lifetime in the following terms: 'fluted blue silk on the walls and ceiling (entirely decaded/festooned and fringed with same silk, and white ground blue pattern convolvolus, calico blue silk ropes, tuft fringe – white silk ropes, bell tassels and tufted fringe – the center compartment having four fasces or standards – bamboo pattern – a convex mirror in a bamboo and blue painted frame with white scrolls opposite the window. . . . A banquet framed in 3 parts stuffed hair squab with feather top. . . .'[165]

By 1815 the rooms in the south-east corner of the building, now described as the 'Prince Regent's Bed-Dressing Room and Anti Room', were being redecorated in Chinese style in bamboo trellis and yellow satinwood. Obviously these decora-

266 The King's Library. By Augustus Pugin. c. *1823.* CAT. NO. 264.

tions did not proceed at the approved speed, for in October 1818 a letter to Mr Crace junior mentioned 'H.R.H. the Prince Regent is very anxious to have the Figures and Bamboo put in the pannels of his Bed Chamber . . . and will be very glad to know when he may expect to see you at the Pavilion. . . .'[166] Mr Crace came; in the accounts for the same year is 'attending the paper-hanger arranging the pannels for the bamboo trellis . . . Mr Crace's time and journey . . . £12.[167] It is recorded that at this time the bed was removed, perhaps in consequence of the Prince Regent's shifting to a lodging in Marlborough Row, 'no bigger than a parrot's cage', according to a happy simile of Princess Lieven.

It is probable that the decoration shown by the Nash longitudinal section as having been in the Prince Regent's Bedroom and Dressing Room should not be taken as an exact rendering. A large fragment of wallpaper survives in the Royal Pavilion Collections that was put up in the Bedroom, probably at some time between 1815 and 1819 (there were, as usual, changes of mind). The survival of so large a piece would be difficult to explain had it not been part of the final scheme. It does not correspond in detail with the schematic representation of the Bedroom in the Nash cross-section; its design is not, however, inconsistent with details given in the accounts. It contains bamboo trellis and panels; the latter, garlanded with and set upon an enchanting background of chinoiserie and *indienne* flowers, which may relate to [211] and [212], contain Chinese figures and scenes of kiosks set in landscapes, all depicted in silver upon an intense cerulean blue.

267 The King's Library, c. *1823. From John Nash,* Views of the Royal Pavilion,
Brighton *(1826).* CAT. NO. 266.

268 The King's Bedroom. By Augustus Pugin. C. *1823.* CAT. NO. 267.

Its occupant was soon to desert this bewitching scene. For mighty works were now in progress; in 1819 a whole new set of apartments was constructed at the north end of the Pavilion, comprehending a set of rooms and a bedroom for the Prince, a colonnade and balcony, and an harmonious and stately North Front (plan H).

This involved a greater segregation of the Prince's private apartments from the more public areas of the building: it meant also their removal to the ground floor. Old-fashioned formality was now much more possible than in the old Marine Pavilion, with its private apartments on the first floor; the Prince, of whom it was said that 'PRIDE' dominated his nature, 'not only the pride of the Monarch, but the pride of the man . . . ever and anon glimmered forth some sparklings of the ruling passion, which threw a reserve and a coldness over his society',[168] would have been fully aware of the privileged meaning of admission to the private apartments. More than the considerable enlargement of the building, more than its fretted and domed skyline and grandiloquent new State Apartments, the creation of this enfilade of rooms signified the conversion of the Marine Pavilion into a royal Palace.

The apartments, as seen in the Pugin drawings [264–266, 268] and the aquatints [267, 269], are intimate in scale and in decoration; they lack the flamboyance and grandeur of other parts of the palace. One has nonetheless an impression, standing in these rooms, that orientalising eclecticism is nowhere as mature or as perfectly integrated as here. Chinese, Indian, even hints of Egyptian and Gothick are blended into a perfect harmony of form and decoration; the slight submarine quality given by the dominant greens and the deeply overhanging balcony outside intensify the sense of restraint and apartness, and the balcony would have given the privacy needed in such a context.

The Library is pictured in a Pugin drawing [266] and watercolour [264], and in an aquatint [267]. It consisted of two rooms, that at the south end very small and connected by folding doors to the larger room to the north. It seems that the watercolour was the first in the sequence, before the carpet was laid, or the more elaborate white marble chimneypiece of [266] installed; it was painted also from a very slightly different vantage point. The line engraving (not reproduced) is dated January 1824.

The smaller room, seen through the simple rectangular opening at the south end of the Library, bears on its white marble chimneypiece ornaments that signal a new sobriety: an Empire ormolu clock with an Apollo, and a pair of Empire bronze and ormolu candelabra. This apartment, like the larger room and the Bedroom beyond, is papered with Jones' dragon pattern wallpaper; in January 1822 he charged £125 for designing 'pattern and attendance for casting blocks for Dragon Paper'.[169] This paper has the appearance of a trompe l'œil damask (see p. 229).

The ceilings of the Library were skied, the plasterwork having been executed by Francis Bernasconi.[170] It was not until October 1823 that Jones put in his account for 'painting in difft [different] greens and relieved tints the Ornamts. in the Cieling of the Library'[171] and for painting the sky itself. He also designed and decorated the woodwork of the columns, of the capitals, and of the mirror frame over the chimneypiece, which has composition ornaments. Bailey & Saunders did most of the decoration; they supplied the 'superb Brussels Carpet' and the 'Yellow Marino Damask Window Curtains', with their 'Worsted Fringe' and 'Twisted Rope',[172] silk fringe, silk, lace, and tassels. The simulated bamboo chairs were covered also in 'Yellow marino', and were supplied with loose covers of brown holland.

269 The King's Bedroom, c. 1823. From John Nash, Views of the Royal Pavilion,
Brighton *(1826).* CAT. NO. 271.

The four bookcases in the recesses were made of 'His Majesty's Japan and Metal
Columns and wrought Caps and bases to Design';[173] lining the wall are Regency
cabinets in Japanese lacquer; recognisable on the top of that on the extreme left
is a pair of black Sèvres vases decorated with gold and gilt bronze dragons, bought
by George IV in 1812.[174] On the chimneypiece is a large Boulle clock of Régence
design. The superbly restrained French desk, of oak veneered with purplewood,
had been bought by the Prince of Wales in 1783.[175] The whole ensemble, with
the rays of the winter afternoon sun penetrating the muslin curtains, is grave and
dignified in the extreme.

The Bedroom is shown in a similar sequence. As with the Library, the watercolour [265] is earlier than the drawing [268]; the latter and the aquatint [269]
have the alcove furnished by Bailey & Saunders with a 'Canopy Bed Furniture
of His Majesty's Yellow silk fringed and decorated with our silk Fringe, lace
etc.'.[176] Underneath was a 'Very large Mahogany bedstead richly carved . . .
Covered with his Majesty's silk . . . and our strong French Castors . . .'. The bed
had a 'thick flock and hair mattress in a fine white bordered Cover', together with
another, thinner one, 'covered with His Majesty's white Satin'; a 'fine large white
fustian bolster filled with the best Dantzick feathers', two down pillows, all
covered with 'His Majesty's white satin'; and four 'large very superfine swanskin
blankets'. The accounts mention also a 'furniture for above [the bed] of His
Majesty's Lilac silk, decorated with rich deep fringe lace etc.';[177] this sounds like
some kind of tent ceiling within the recess. Or was it a treatment of the alcove
like that in the South Drawing Room, unrecorded pictorially because it was done
too late?

Beside this magnificent bed, and seen in the illustrations, are two mahogany pot cupboards; another and interesting utilitarian piece, which has somewhat lost its details in the aquatint but is clear in the watercolour, is a 'Mahogany Washing Table fitted up with Wedgewood Ware';[178] the blue and white pottery appears to be let into the side of the table. A 'Mahogany Cheval Screen with brass Ornaments'[179] leans against the wall next to the fireplace; the King changed his mind and had the yellow silk in this replaced with green. In the corner of the room is a humble 'Mahogany folding airing horse';[180] two cheval mirrors complete the 'working' furniture of the room, apart from the barometer and thermometer beside the door.

Apart from the desk – and a more striking contrast would be difficult to find, for this splendid piece by François-Honoré Jacob-Desmalter, in pollard elm with martial ornaments at each end, is one of the most majestic things imaginable – the only considerable piece of furniture in the room is the Boulle cabinet on the right; on it stand two oil-burning lamps with lotus tops (omitted in the watercolour) of which there were many in the Pavilion.

An amusing metamorphosis has overcome the object on the chimneypiece. In the watercolour it is a clock in a glass case, somewhat ambiguously doubled in the mirror behind; in the drawing it is indubitably a clock unambiguously reflected. In the etching (not illustrated) it has become a hollow object with a clock face upon it; in the aquatint it is a shiny hollow object, something like a coal scuttle, and the clock face has become decoration. The Brussels carpet (not shown in the watercolour) is of apparently the same pattern as that in the Library, but with a more colourful pattern. Above it is the most Gothick ceiling in the building, similar in detail to that designed for the Nash Dining Room in Carlton House, with pink dragons, painted by Jones, on a green background.

Beyond the Bedroom was a bathroom; it contained a white marble bath, sixteen feet long by ten feet wide, and six feet deep, which was supplied with salt water from the sea and heated by a great oven in the basement.

The Red Drawing Room

The Red Drawing Room, adjacent to the Entrance Hall (plan H), was added by Nash; a certain degree of improvisation may have obtained since, unusually for the Pavilion, the ground floor outer wall is of flimsy construction. According to Brayley it was used principally as a Breakfast Room; in the Brighton Account Book it is called the 'Ladies' Drawing Room'; a plan of the 1840s calls it the 'Equerries Room'.[181]

No designs for this room appear to survive, but it is seen in a Pugin watercolour [271] and in the aquatint [270]. The motif used, of Chinese paintings applied directly to the wall as decoration, is one used extensively in the early chinoiserie years of the Pavilion; the Red Drawing Room had its more primitive precursor in the Ante Room adjacent to the Saloon, which also displayed paintings stuck directly on a red wall. Here they were given trompe l'œil bamboo frames, and the background was the magnificent 'red damask' dragon pattern, designed by Jones and used also in the King's Apartments. There it was block-printed; here it was painted freehand, and it seems possible that the decision to use it in the King's Apartments was a result of its successful employment in the Red Drawing Room. Indeed, some surviving Chinese paintings, detached from their places, have fragments of the same design on their backs in yellow, which indicates that it may have been tried elsewhere also.

The accounts survive for the Red Drawing Room only in the Brighton abstract, not in the Crace ledgers. There is a possibility that Jones did all the decorative work for this quite small room. His name occurs in the Crace ledgers where the work was apportioned between himself and the Crace firm; the lack of mention of the Red Drawing Room therein is negative evidence that at times he worked independently of the Craces, as is the non-survival of any designs for the room in the Crace collection.

Together with the Corridor, the Red Drawing Room preserves a flavour of the lighthearted, unstrained gaiety of the earlier years that disappeared with the new regality. Its fanciful wooden pillars and pendants in the Indian style (the former concealing cast iron) are glazed in quite strong colours, greens shading to red, on top of a lighter base. The compartmentalism of the ceiling, where there is no structural need to compartmentalise, makes a charming effect; it is possible that decorative lessons had been learned from the ceiling of the Blue Drawing Room. It has affinities also with the ceiling of the Nash Dining Room at Carlton House.

The accounts give Jones as 'Painting graining and varnishing door Window Shutters linings architraves etc.';[182] they do not mention the most extraordinary feature of this graining, which is unique in the Royal Pavilion to this room, and perhaps unique anywhere. The graining, which is somewhat like simulated satinwood, carries within it, as it were part of the grain, figures of flame-like dragons;

270 The Red Drawing Room, c. *1823. From John Nash,* Views of the Royal Pavilion,
Brighton *(1826).* CAT. NO. 271.

it is not obtrusive, and can easily be missed, so well is it done. It is, however,
one of the minor masterpieces of the building, and it strikes one as a probably
wholly spontaneous reaction of the artist to his surroundings.

The furniture shown in the aquatint is simple, of the export Chinese bamboo
type found everywhere in the building in its earlier phases; it is extraordinarily
flimsy (the accounts are full of repairs) and it seems likely that it was exported
in flat sections and made up in this country. The green silk curtains, and the simply
patterned green carpet, provoke a frisson in their contiguity with the complementary red, the frisson that one feels everywhere in the Royal Pavilion – lilac and
yellow, blue and yellow, pink and blue, yellow and pink; the permutations are
played with infinite skill.

271 The Red Drawing Room. By Augustus Pugin. C. *1822.* CAT. NO. 270.

272 The South Galleries. By Augustus Pugin. C. *1822.* CAT. NO. *273.*

The South Galleries

The South Galleries were two rooms on the upper floor that led to bedrooms on either side; those to the east were occupied by the Prince until the building of the King's Apartments. They led also to the Corridor staircase. They are shown in the Pugin drawing and watercolour and in the aquatint [272–274]; no designs survive. A design (not illustrated) of columns similar to those on either side of the doors indicates the continuity of this particular motif; it almost certainly dates from the 1802–4 period, and of course the columns themselves may well have been reused from an earlier scheme.

The fret decoration on the walls was created from block-printed wallpapers (of which samples survive), from which the lines composing the fret patterns were cut in strips, being then stuck directly on to a painted wall – in this case blue – in the chosen pattern. The method allowed improvisation. The carpet is somewhat in the idiom of another surviving carpet design [68].

The furniture is of the simple Chinese export type; on the tables at the end of the gallery stand two ivory Chinese junks in glass cases. It will have been noticed that throughout the Pavilion the clocks are similarly encased; the one really sumptuous article in this unpretentious but charming apartment is the unencased gilt bronze cartel clock above the sofa. These galleries were used as breakfast rooms for guests who stayed at the Pavilion; Mme de Boigne, daughter of the then French ambassador, described how 'I was much astonished when I came out of my room to find the table laid upon the staircase landing. But what a landing and what a staircase! The carpets, the tables, the chairs, the porcelain, the china were as exquisite as luxury and good taste could possibly find. The Prince attached more importance to the perfection of this meal for the reason that he never appeared to share it, and was anxious that none of his careful precautions for the comfort of his guests should be neglected.'[183]

273 The South Galleries. By Augustus Pugin. c. *1822.* CAT. NO. 272.

274 The North and South Galleries.
From John Nash, Views of the Royal Pavilion, Brighton *(1826).* CAT. NO. 274.

The Portico
and the Octagon Hall

275 The Portico. By Augustus Pugin. c. *1820.* CAT. NO. 275.

276 The Octagon Hall. From John Nash, Views of the Royal Pavilion, Brighton *(1826).* CAT. NO. 276.

The drawing by Augustus Pugin of the Portico [275] might perhaps be thought to belong more properly with the views of the exterior than here, save that it is designed as a vignette and that it acts so perfectly as an introduction to the Octagon Hall that lay within. The horseman who raises his hat in a gallant gesture is King George IV.

No designs seem to exist for the Octagon Hall – that enchanting prelude to the glories of the Pavilion – but its interior is depicted in the aquatint [276] (the splendid brass fireplace is still in situ.) Its decoration is recorded in the Crace ledgers for 1820: 'Preparing and painting the ornamental ceiling in shades of light peach blossom colour and moulding cut in to Do'; the walls and skirting were treated in the same manner, and the woodwork to the windows was painted 'in imitation of the Pollard Oak, the mouldings cut in dark and high varnished'.[184] The original watercolour for the aquatint exists in a private collection.

The Kitchen

No designs exist for the Great Kitchen; it is, however, given the honour of a plate in the Nash book [278]. The etching, which is dated April 2 1820, does not show the palm-tree tops to the pillars; these were added in April 1820 by Palmer, ironmonger, at a cost of £80,[185] and the detail was painted into the aquatint.

The Prince's love of good food was the subject of many cruel jests; the Great Kitchen of the Pavilion (called 'Great' because smaller kitchens lay to the south of it) was, in its day, a conspicuous example of advanced utilitarian design. In Croker's often quoted words, 'The kitchens and larders are admirable – such contrivances for roasting, boiling, baking, stewing, frying, steaming and heating; hot plates, hot closets, hot air and hot hearths, with all manner of cocks for hot water and cold water, and warm water and steam, and twenty saucepans all ticketed and labelled, placed up to their necks in a vapour bath'.[186] The spits before the great fireplace were rotated by means of a fan in the chimney, itself turned by hot air from the fire. The Prince himself took a great interest in the kitchens: 'if . . . he happened to meet any new-comers to the pavilion, he took a delight in showing them over the palace itself, a special point being his kitchens, which were entirely steam-heated by a system at that time new, with which he was charmed.'[187]

Two interesting plans of the kitchen, reproduced here, give some idea of how it was equipped. The first [277] has details of the walls attached in the form of flaps; the list of 'contrivances' includes 'Steam Boiler', 'Iron ovens', 'Scouring Tables', 'Washing Sinks Heated by steam', 'Hot Closets', 'Hot Tables heated by Steam'. The second plan [279], which seems to be of a later date, has as elaborate a list of equipment, together with some details of the water supply, which was carried in copper pipes. Shown in addition, to the west of the 'Passage', are a 'Pastry Room' and a 'Pastry Kitchen'.

237

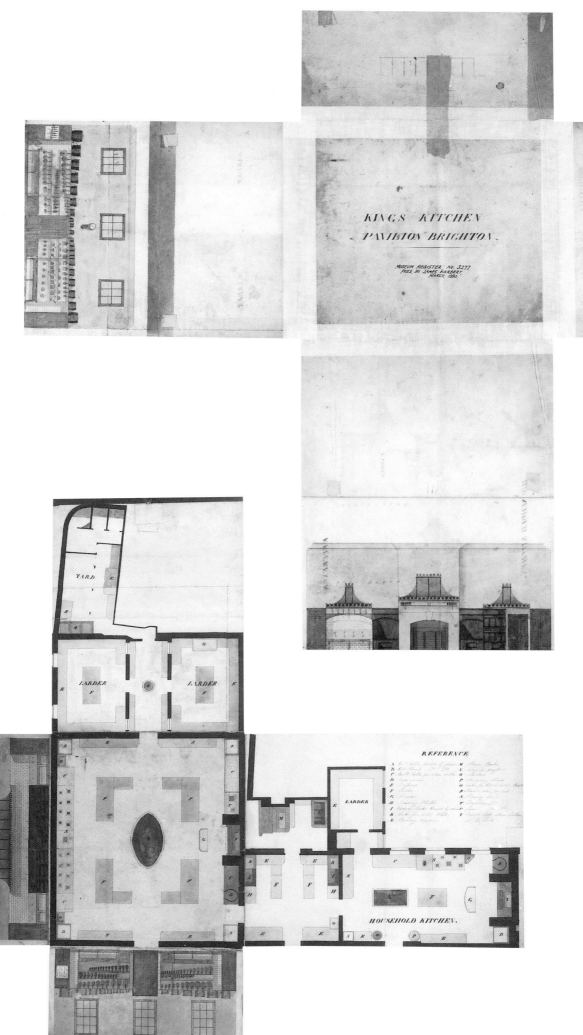

277 The Kitchen: plan. CAT. NO. 278.

238

278 The Kitchen. From John Nash, Views of the Royal Pavilion, Brighton *(1826)*. CAT. NO. 277.

279 The Kitchen: plan. CAT. NO. 279.

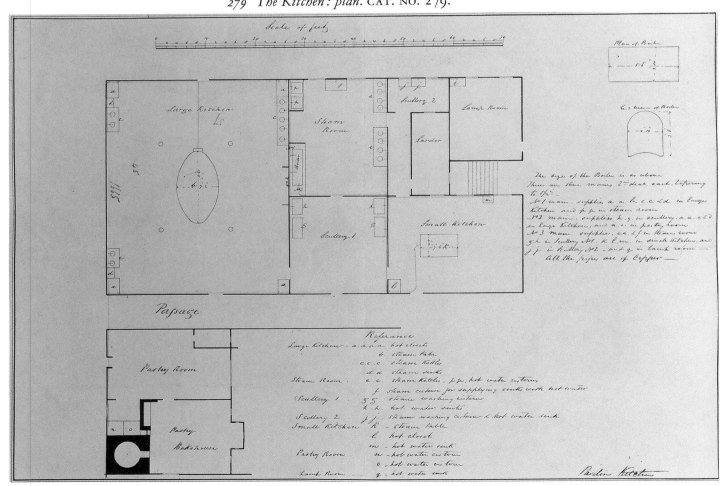

Miscellaneous Designs

280 Designs for fretwork panels. Probably c. *1802–4.* CAT. NO. 280.

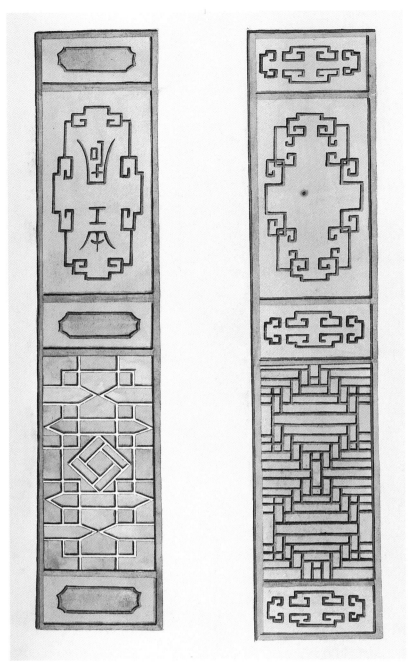

281 Designs for fretwork panels. By Frederick Crace. c. *1815.* CAT. NO. 286.

Various designs remain, which appear to fit into no particular context, but which are of interest and beauty.

The first are six sheets [280, 283–286, 292] of vigorous designs, in the deep suffused colours of the 1802–4 period, for vertical fretwork panels and dadoes. Another six sheets [281, 282, 287–289], from the Crace book, show the difference between the earlier and the later manner; they appear to be from the Blue and Yellow Drawing Rooms period, and may reflect essays for these rooms. Associated with them are three designs [290, 291, 293], apparently for mirror frames; the peculiar lack of any bottom rail is common to pier glasses in the Pavilion, so designed that the furniture that stood beneath them concealed what was often a raw mirror edge. It is interesting to see [293] the orthodox Regency design of side pilasters, with enclosed plate above the mirror plane, here translated into a chinoiserie vocabulary.

282 Designs for fretwork panels. By Frederick Crace. c. 1815. CAT. NO. 287.

This concludes the present survey of designs made for the Pavilion at Brighton; they make up in total a group of extraordinary originality and beauty, and in their freshness and immediacy enable one to catch something of the excitement and interest that must have attached to the task of creating that eccentric masterpiece. The use of exotic styles acts always as a catalyst in releasing one from the inhibitions of one's own period and time, and is meant to do so; in this case the existence of a more than ordinarily uninhibited and adventurous patron led to a result that still awakens an astonished response in an age that has been jaded by repeated marvels. These designs, as a record of the pilgrimage towards perfection and as works of art in their own right, evoke not only admiration, but an uneasy nostalgia for a period that could, with unhesitating self-confidence, create such a building for its amusement and delectation, and that could in doing so overcome national reticence and conjure up, in 'the pale gleam of the sea, shrouded from time to time in fog,'[188] the most important exotic monument in Europe.

283 Designs for fretwork panels. Probably c. *1802–4.* CAT. NO. 281.

284 Designs for fretwork panels. Probably c. *1802–4.* CAT. NO. 282.

285 Designs for fretwork panels. Probably c. *1802–4.* CAT. NO. 283.

286 Designs for fretwork panels. Probably c. *1802–4.* CAT. NO. 284.

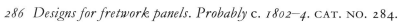

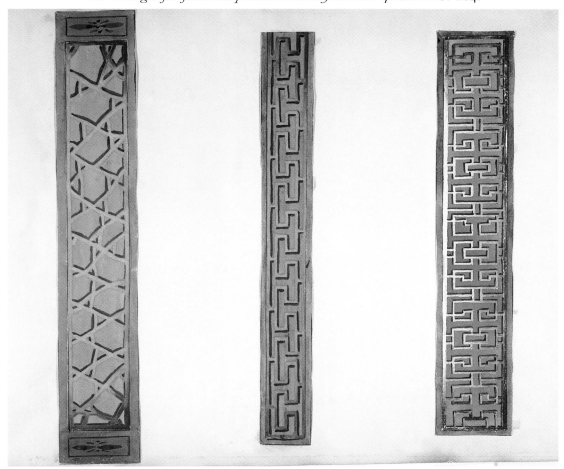

287

288

287–289 Designs for fretwork panels. By Frederick Crace. C. *1815.* CAT. NOS 288–290.

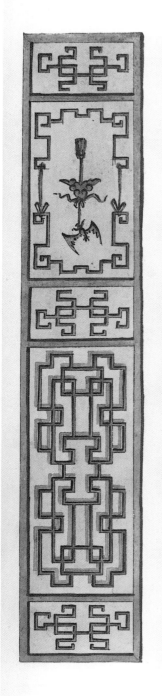

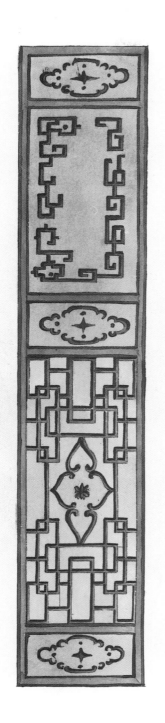

289

290

290 Design, probably for a mirror frame. By Frederick Crace. C. *1815.* CAT. NO. 291.

291   293

291–293 *Two designs, probably for mirror frames. By Frederick Crace.* C. *1815.* CAT. NOS 292–293

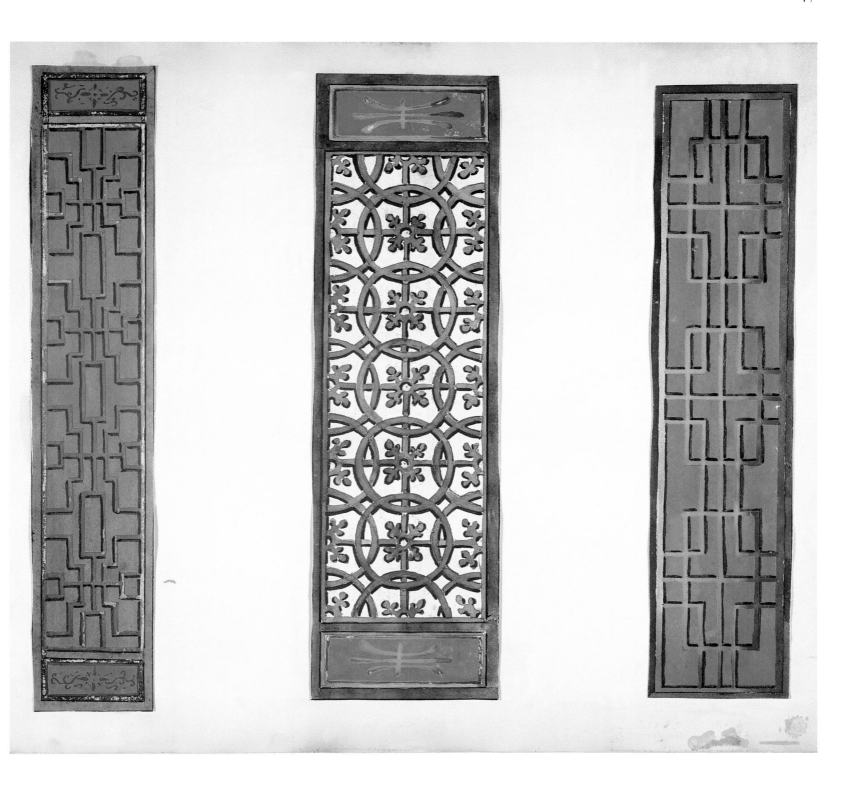

292 Designs for fretwork panels. Probably c. *1802–4.* CAT. NO. 285

References

Authorities given in the 'List of Sources and Short Bibliography' are cited either under the abbreviations listed there or under the author's surname or other short title.

THE PATRON

1   *Croker Papers*, ed. L.J.Jennings, London, John Murray, 1885, p. 290
2   Ibid., p. 431, Sept. 1828
3   Huish, Robert, *Memoirs of George IV etc.*, London, T.Kelly, 1830, p. 251
4   British Library, 1857-5-20-87
5   Huish, op. cit., p. 268
6   Praz, Mario, *An Illustrated History of Interior Decoration*, Zurich, Conzett and Huber, 1964, p. 23
7   By Nathaniel Wraxall: see catalogue of the exhibition, 'George IV and the Arts of France', The Queen's Gallery, Buckingham Palace, 1966, p. 1
8   Jesse, Captain, *The Life of Beau Brummell*, London, John C. Nimmo, 1886, p. 66
9   Thackeray, W.M., *The Four Georges*, London, Smith, Elder, 1861, p. 178.
10 Willett, C. and P.Cunnington, *Handbook of English Costume in the Nineteenth Century*, London, Faber, 1959, p. 35
11 Greville, C.C., *Journal of the Reigns of King George IV and King William IV*, London, Longmans, 1874, p. 221
12 Huish, op. cit., pp. 10–11
13 Bellaigue et al., pp. 104–5
14 Greville, op. cit., p. 240
15 Huish, op. cit., p. 272
16 Lieven, Princess, *Unpublished Diary*, ed. Harold Temperley, London, Cape, 1930, p. 119
17 Lieven, Princess, *Private Letters to Prince Metternich 1820–26*, ed. Peter Quennell, Frome, Butler and Tanner, 1948, p. 308, June 14 1826
18 Gower, Lord Granville Leveson (1st Lord Granville), *Private Correspondence 1781–1821*, ed. Castalia, Countess Granville, 1916, II, p. 120, letter dated Oct. 9 1805; quoted by Sir Francis Watson, 'George IV as an Art Collector', *Apollo*, June 1966, p. 410
19 Illustrated by Bellaigue et al., pp. 144, 145
20 'George IV and the Arts of France', op. cit., p. 24

21 Trollope, Anthony, *The Warden*, 1855
22 Thackeray, W.M., *Vanity Fair*, 1847 (London, Zodiac Press, 1967, p. 398: 'tawdry and beautiful, and, thirty years ago, deemed as precious as works of real genius')
23 John, Brother, *The Yacht for the R———t's B———m———*, 1816, British Library, C.131.d. 6. (15)
24 'Designs for the Private Apartments at Windsor Castle by Sir Jeffry Wyatville', catalogue, Sotheby and Co., Apr. 9 1970
25 Farington, Joseph, *Diary*, ed. J.Greig, London, Hutchinson, 8 vols, 1922–8, vol. VIII, entry for Jan. 9 1819
26 RA 25258
27 Bellaigue, G. de, lecture given to the Furniture History Society, 1978
28 Brougham, Lord, *Historical Sketches of Statesmen*, London, C. Knight & Co., 1839–43, p. 1
29 Anon., *An Historical Account of the Public and Domestic Life and Reign of George the Fourth etc*, Harrogate, Wm Blackburn, 1830
30 Anon., *A Review of the Conduct of the Prince of Wales etc*, London, 1797, British Library, 1102 i S2
31 Mingay, G.E., *English Landed Society in the 18th Century*, London, Routledge, 1963, p. 19
32 Ibid., p. 151
33 Thompson, F.L.M., *English Landed Society in the 19th Century*, London, Routledge, 1963, pp. 88–91
34 Summerson, p. 157
35 Roberts, p. 126
36 *Correspondence of George, Prince of Wales*, ed. A. Aspinall, 8 vols, London, Cassell, 1963, vol. I, Oct. 27 1784
37 *The Letters of King George IV*, ed. A. Aspinall, 3 vols, Cambridge University Press, 1938, vol. II, p. 158
38 Musgrave, p. 92

THE EXTERIOR

HENRY HOLLAND AND THE MARINE PAVILION

1   Pasquin, Anthony, *The New Brighton Guide*, 6th ed., 1796
2   RA 34218
3   Croly, Rev. George, *The Personal History of . . . George IV*, London, Colburn, 1841, p. 111
4   Stendhal, *Memoirs of an Egotist*, trans. David Ellis, London, Chatto and Windus, 1975, p. 98
5   *Correspondence of George, Prince of Wales*, ed. A. Aspinall, 8 vols, London, Cassell, 1963, vol. I, Nov. 7 1783
6   RA 33513
7   Stroud, p. 73
8   *Chambers Cyclopaedia*, 1727–41; quoted in *Oxford English Dictionary* under 'Pavilion'
9   RA 34216–34219
10 *Correspondence of George, Prince of Wales*, op. cit., vol. III, Jul. 28 1795
11 Brayley, p. 2
12 RA 33526
13 From a letter by D.Metcalfe, Oct. 16 1801 (archives of the Royal Pavilion, Brighton)
14 RA 33530
15 RA 33529
16 Musgrave, p. 28
17 RA 33528
18 Roberts, p. 30
19 RA 33528
20 CL, p. 46
21 Roberts, pp. 72–3
22 Ibid., p. 82

PORDEN'S CHINESE DESIGNS AND THE ROYAL STABLES

23 Musgrave, p. 46
24 Roberts, p. 63
25 Conner, P., 'Unexecuted Designs for the Royal Pavilion', *Apollo*, Mar. 1978, p. 195
26 Brayley, p. 16
27 Hope, Thomas, *Household Furniture and Interior Decoration*, 1807, reprinted London, Tiranti, 1970
28 Musgrave, p. 46
29 Repton, p. VI
30 Musgrave, p. 96
31 Brayley, p. 16
32 Musgrave, pp. 45–6
33 Farington, Joseph, *Diary*, ed. J. Greig, London, Hutchinson, 8 vols, 1922–8, vol. III, entry for Jul. 20 1804
34 Roberts, p. 65
35 RA 33591
36 RA 33593–33594
37 RA 33652

HUMPHRY REPTON'S 'DESIGNS FOR THE PAVILLON AT BRIGHTON'

38 British Library Add. Ms 62112 1058A, pp. 85–6
39 Ibid., p. 88
40 Ibid., unpaginated
41 Summerson, p. 40. But see A.P.Oppé, *English Drawings at Windsor Castle*, London, Phaidon, 1950, cat. entry 489, p. 82
42 Details of Walsh Porter's 'Egyptian Hall' at Craven Cottage, Fulham, *c.* 1805–6, are given in the catalogue *The Inspiration of Egypt*, ed. Patrick Conner for the Royal Pavilion and Museums, Brighton, Croydon Printing Co., 1983, p. 53
43 British Library Add. Ms, op. cit., p. 216
44 Ibid., p. 224
45 Brayley, p. 2
46 British Library Add. Ms, op. cit., p. 215
47 Ibid., p. 226
48 Ibid., p. 228
49 Ibid., unpaginated
50 Repton, H., *Observations on the Theory and Practice of Landscape Gardening*, London, 1803, chap. XI
51 Stroud, pl. 43
52 British Library Add. Ms, op. cit., p. 214
53 Repton, H., *Fragments on the Theory and Practice of Landscape Gardening*, London, 1816, fragment XIII

JOHN NASH AND THE REBUILDING OF THE PAVILION

54 Pueckler-Muskau, Prince, *Tour of England, Ireland and France 1826, etc.*, Massie, 1940, entry for Oct. 5 1826
55 Summerson, p. 90
56 Knighton, Lady, *Memoirs of Sir William Knighton*, vol. II, p. 161, Jul. 6 1830
57 PRO, Works 19 1/2
58 Ibid.
59 RA 34216–34219
60 Price, Sir Uvedale, *Sir Uvedale Price on the Picturesque with additions by Sir. Thos. Lauder Bart*, Edinburgh and London, 1842, p. 83
61 RA 34218–34219
62 RA 34219
63 RA 34066–34067
64 RA 34069
65 *The Builder*, 1 [1843], p. 289; information from Sir J.Summerson in Royal Pavilion archives
66 Parlt Papers, vol. 16, pp. 272–3
67 Roberts, p. 211
68 Price, op. cit., p. 132
69 RA 3383
70 By Mr Roy Bradley
71 RA 33931
72 RA 33961
73 RA 34062–34063

THE INTERIOR

THE CRACE FIRM

1 Roberts, p. 43
2 Unattributed quotations in the following account are taken from the Crace genealogy, of which there is a copy in the Crace Papers, Victoria and Albert Museum, London (uncatalogued)
3 RA 33513
4 Bloch, Maurice, 'Regency Styling, the Prince and the Decorator', *Connoisseur*, June 1953, CXXXI, no. 531, p. 130. The document quoted remained, with others, at the Cooper Union when the separation occurred from the Cooper-Hewitt Museum (information from the latter). An inquiry of the former elicited the response, 'the correspondence . . . if in fact we have it at the Cooper Union – is uncatalogued and inaccessible. . . .'
5 A of A, facing p. 7
6 CB
7 Denon, Baron, *Voyage dans la Basse et la Haute Egypte*, Paris, 1802. This romanticism appears in Bonaparte's own words: 'In Egypt . . . I dreamed all sorts of things, and I saw how all I dreamed might be realised. I created a religion: I pictured myself on the road to Asia, mounted on an elephant, with a turban on my head, and in my hand a new Koran, which I should compose . . .': Mme de Remusat, *Memoirs*, London, Sampson Lowe, 1880, vol. 1, p. 149
8 RA 27723
9 Rogers, Samuel, *Recollections*, ed. W. Sharpe, 1859, p. 84
10 *Gazette of Fashion*, 1822, vol. 2, p. 82

THE SALOON

11 PRO, H.O.73.26
12 Stroud, p. 88; the reference is to Thomas Rowlandson and Henry Wigstead, 'An Excursion to Brighthelmstone', 1790
13 RA 33513
14 PRO, H.O.73.23(2)
15 CL, p. 43
16 CL, p. 1
17 CL, p. 19, Midsummer-Christmas 1803
18 CL, p. 1
19 RA 33529
20 CL, p. 20
21 CL, p. 42
22 CL, p. 1
23 CL, p. 6
24 CL, p. 2
25 CL, p. 56
26 CL, p. 20
27 CL, p. 61
28 CL, p. 81; last entry for new work in the Saloon
29 CL, pp. 68, 80
30 CL, p. 80
31 CL, p. 100
32 CL, p. 61
33 CL, p. 68
34 CL, p. 75
35 CL, p. 105
36 PRO, LC9/42
37 A of A, facing p. 17
38 RA 25382
39 PRO, LC1/42, p. 45
40 RA 25371

THE DRAWING ROOMS BEFORE 1815

41 CL, p. 24; '*Glass Passage* between Breakfast and Music Rooms'
42 CL, p. 43
43 Bishop, J.G., *The Brighton Pavilion and Its Royal Associations*, Brighton, J.G.Bishop, 1884, pp. 9–10
44 Walker, C., *Brighton and its Environs*, London, Townsend, Powell and Co., 1809, p. 25
45 CL, pp. 2–3
46 CL, p. 16
47 CL, pp. 48–9, 55–6
48 RA 27723
49 RA 28455
50 See, for example, Charles C. Oman and Jean Hamilton, *Wallpapers*, London, Sotheby, 1982, cat. no. 153 – a border of 1806 with a design of Egyptian motifs and a strip of edging made for Crawley House, Bedfordshire
51 Catalogue, *The Inspiration of Egypt*, ed. Patrick Conner for the Royal Pavilion and Museums, Brighton, Croydon Printing Co., 1983, cat. no. 89, p. 49
52 CL, p. 24
53 RA 33530
54 CL, pp. 24, 25
55 CL, p. 29
56 CL, p. 55
57 CL, p. 71
58 CL, p. 88
59 CL, p. 24
60 CL, pp. 11–12
61 CL, pp. 23–4
62 CL, p. 4
63 CL, pp. 21–2

THE BLUE/SOUTH DRAWING ROOM

64 CL, p. 69
65 CL, p. 79
66 CL, p. 78
67 CL, pp. 68–71
68 CL, p. 71
69 CL, p. 69
70 CL, p. 70
71 CL, p. 69
72 CL, p. 70
73 CL, p. 75
74 CL, p. 90
75 CL, p. 92

76   CL, p. 105
77   Illustrated Bellaigue et al., pp. 120–26
78   Illustrated Pyne, W.H., *The History of the Royal Residences*, London, 1819, A. Dry, facing p. 63
79   CL, p. 133

THE YELLOW/NORTH DRAWING ROOM

80   CL, p. 78
81   CL, pp. 67–8
82   CL, p. 75
83   CL, p. 67
84   CL, p. 68
85   CL, p. 88
86   CL, p. 106
87   CL, p. 131
88   A of A, p. 128 and page facing p. 128
89   CL, pp. 131–2
90   A of A, facing p. 23
91   Bellaigue, G. de, 'The Furnishings of the Chinese Drawing Room, Carlton House', *Burlington Magazine*, vol. CIX, Sept. 1967, p. 518

THE CONSERVATORY/MUSIC ROOM
AND THE DINING ROOM

92   CL, pp. 8–9
93   CL, p. 48
94   Crookes, C., *The Royal Visit; . . . a full and circumstantial account of everything connected with the King's visit to Ireland*, Dublin, 1821
95   CL, p. 3
96   CL, p. 42
97   Ibid.

THE ENTRANCE HALL

98   CL, pp. 14–15
99   CL, p. 22
100   CL, p. 48
101   CL, pp. 12–13
102   CL, p. 13
103   Bishop, op. cit., p. 10
104   Sickelmore, R., *Epitome of Brighton*, Brighton, W. Fleet for the author, 1815, p. 38
105   CL, p. 71
106   CL, p. 72
107   CL, p. 76
108   CL, pp. 119–20
109   CL, p. 119
110   CL, p. 123
111   Brayley, p. 6

THE CORRIDOR

112   CL, p. 60
113   CL, p. 66
114   CL, p. 60
115   CL, p. 74
116   Quoted by Musgrave, p. 86
117   Brayley, p. 7
118   Information from Mrs J. McDowell
119   Brayley, p. 7
120   Ibid.

THE BANQUETING ROOM

121   RA 34224
122   Quoted by Musgrave, pp. 90, 92
123   RA 34224
124   A of A, p. 8
125   Ibid.
126   A of A, facing p. 10
127   A of A, p. 9
128   Rush, Richard, *The Court of London 1819–25*, London, Bentley, 1873, p. 354

THE MUSIC ROOM

129   CL, p. 67
130   CL, p. 94
131   Crace Papers, op. cit.
132   CL, p. 110
133   CL, p. 112
134   CL, p. 110
135   Crace papers, op. cit.
136   CL, p. 109
137   CL, p. 94
138   CL, p. 116
139   CL, p. 95
140   CL, p. 115
141   CL, p. 134
142   CL, p. 115
143   A of A, p. 8
144   A of A, facing p. 130
145   CL, p. 94
146   RA 34223: £440 to Vulliamy, £1244 2s 6d to Westmacott
147   CL, p. 117
148   CL, p. 95
149   A of A, p. 7
150   Brayley, p. 8
151   Brayley, p. 9
152   A of A, p. 7
153   CL, p. 116
154   *Croker Papers*, ed. L. J. Jennings, London, John Murray, 1885, p. 125
155   Brayley, p. 8

THE PRINCE OF WALES' BEDROOM
AND THE KING'S APARTMENTS

156   Roberts, p. 49; the date given, 1785, is impossibly early
157   Ibid., p. 27
158   Ibid., p. 29
159   PRO, HO.73.20 pt i (1)
160   Musgrave, Clifford, *Life in Brighton*, London, Faber and Faber, 1970, p. 119
161   Bishop, op. cit., p. 9
162   CL, p. 15
163   CL, p. 28
164   Brayley, p. 6
165   Inventory of the contents of the Royal Pavilion, p. 99
166   From a letter in the Cooper-Hewitt collection
167   CL, p. 98
168   Huish, Robert, *Memoirs of George IV etc*, London, T. Kelly, 1830, p. 192
169   A of A, p. 71

170 Crace Papers, op. cit.
171 A of A, p. 75
172 A of A, facing p. 15
173 A of A, p. 15
174 Illustrated Bellaigue et al., p. 125
175 Bill in Royal Archives, June 20 1783, from J. Walker; information kindly supplied by Mr Geoffrey de Bellaigue
176 A of A, p. 18
177 A of A, p. 22
178 A of A, p. 19
179 Ibid.
180 Ibid.

THE RED DRAWING ROOM
AND SOUTH GALLERIES
181 RA 18964
182 A of A, p. facing p. 71
183 *Memoirs of the Comtesse de Boigne*, ed. Charles Nicoullaud, 3 vols, London, Heinemann, 1908, vol. III, p. 252

THE PORTICO AND THE OCTAGON HALL
184 CL, p. 119

THE KITCHEN
185 A of A, p. 99
186 *Croker Papers*, op. cit., p. 126
187 *Memoirs of the Comtesse de Boigne*, op. cit., loc. cit.
188 Praz, Mario, *An Illustrated History of Interior Decoration*, Zurich, Conzett and Huber, 1964, p. 245. (It should be remarked that Praz does less than justice to the excellent Brighton weather, but the poetic image is irresistible, and it is perhaps appropriate that the last quotation in this book should come from his pen.)

Catalogue of Illustrations

Most of the designs are untitled, and in these cases the titles given in the catalogue and the captions have been devised by the author. However, even where titles do exist (for example, in plates reproduced from Nash's *Views*) these have, in most instances, been altered by the author in order to give a more useful description of what is shown.

The illustrations are listed here in approximate chronological order within each section – conforming basically to the order in which they are discussed in the text. The title, or description, is given first, followed by the artist's name (if known), date, published source (if relevant), medium, dimensions, the text of any inscriptions, any note by the author, the location of the work (with museum or other reference number) and the number of the illustration in the present book. Dimensions are not given for entries taken from the Crace Book, the pages of which all measure 21.2 × 13.4 cm. The following abbreviations are used to indicate the locations:

CB	Crace Book (Mrs J.F.Crace)
CH	Cooper-Hewitt Museum, New York
RL	Royal Library, Windsor
RP	Royal Pavilion, Art Gallery and Museums, Brighton
V & A	Victoria and Albert Museum, London

Full details of the volume by John Nash, *Views of the Royal Pavilion, Brighton*, 1826 (published 1827), are given in Roberts, pp. 153–9; other details and topographical views are given in John and Jill Ford, *Images of Brighton*, Richmond upon Thames, St Helena Press, 1981.

Some considerations that need to be taken into account in attributing the 'Crace' designs are mentioned in the text (pp. 79–80), but they need here to be enlarged upon. The three main sources are the Cooper-Hewitt Museum, the Royal Pavilion, and the Crace Book (in private possession). The designs in the Cooper-Hewitt are the most finished and elaborate of all those that survive; they include examples from the whole chinoiserie period, from 1801 or earlier to the 1820s. The designs in the Royal Pavilion fall into several groups. First comes a large number of loose, small designs, mostly in pencil, few of which are illustrated here; many duplicate the coloured versions in the Crace book and seem to be by Frederick himself, others are of a more miscellaneous nature. Second comes a group of designs that had been pasted into a bound book; the book has been split up for display purposes but the page sequence and binding have been preserved. These designs are often accompanied by brief pencil descriptions, in the same hand, which appear to have been added probably at the time of compilation; designs that appear to date from an early, probably 1802–4, period, are promiscuously intermingled with designs

of an indubitably 1815 or post-1815 date. The collection has the appearance of
a compilation made, perhaps, for reference purposes, and the author's guess is
that this was done in or about 1815. The book was given to the Royal Pavilion
collections by a member of the Crace family, Mr John Crace, in the early 1950s.
The third Pavilion group, a very small group, is of designs by Robert Jones of
which the provenance is unknown. The designs in the Crace Book, given by early
family authority to Frederick Crace himself, are all in one hand – accomplished
and meticulous – which there is no reason to doubt is that of Frederick. The
book was not bound at a later period; the studies were painted directly into it.

A small group of watercolour chinoiserie designs exists in the Cooper-Hewitt
Museum, none of which has been illustrated or referred to in the text. These are
of kiosks and similar little buildings, with Chinese perspective, that were probably
copied directly from, or very closely influenced by, original Chinese paintings.
It is the author's opinion that these were probably used as sources for buildings
depicted on the 'Chinese' paintings and panels that were liberally used in the
Pavilion decorations between 1802 and 1804, and 1815 and 1817.

One important design for the Saloon carpet, obviously by Robert Jones, has
proved impossible to trace. It is illustrated in Bertram Jacobs, *Axminster Carpets*,
Leigh-on-Sea, F.Lewis, 1970, pl. 19, as from the collection of Sir Reginald Whitty,
who died in 1960.

The Crace firm employed a large-number of journeymen painters; many of the
designs in the Royal Pavilion collections, and some of those in the Cooper-Hewitt
collection, appear to be in the hands of copyists of varying skills. This has no
particular significance in the problem of placing the designs in context, but it com-
plicates that of attribution. There is, moreover, the possibility of artists having
influenced each other, and the fact that the task of evolving a unified decorative
scheme must have meant that individual idiosyncracies were subordinated to the
needs of the scheme as a whole has also to be taken into account.

In the catalogue below no attempt has been made to attribute the designs here
ascribed to the 1802–4 period; the evidence is too scanty, and too many hands
are involved (the temptation to imagine that the more refined and imaginative
designs are by the youthful Frederick – and some do approach his later style and
technique – is here resisted in the face of lack of evidence). Certain of the other
early designs are somewhat crude and unsophisticated.

For the period 1815 and after, no attempt has been made to distinguish between
copyists, but Frederick Crace and Robert Jones are identified where possible.
Augustus Pugin's watercolour hand is different from Charles Moore's, but pencil
drawings by them may prove to be virtually indistinguishable.

Where undated items have been dated, the attributed date is the author's.

A   Plan of the ground floor of the Marine
    Pavilion, as built by Henry Holland
    1787
    Watercolour and ink on paper
    42.4 × 66.6
    Inscribed: 'General Plan of Brighton
    House.'
    RP 102527

B   Plan of the first floor of the Marine Pavilion,
    as built by Henry Holland
    1787
    Watercolour and ink on paper
    32.5 × 40.5
    Inscribed: 'Plan of the Chamber Story at
    Brighton . . . Hertford Street Nov. 1787'
    RP 102528

C   Plan of the ground floor of the Marine
    Pavilion, with alterations proposed by
    Henry Holland
    1795
    Watercolour and ink on paper
    39.5 × 50.6
    Inscribed: 'General Plan of Brighton, with
    Alteration . . . Sloane Place Feby. 1795.'
    RL 18954
    Reproduced by Gracious Permission of
    H.M. The Queen

D   Plan of the first floor of the Marine Pavilion,
    with alterations proposed by Henry
    Holland
    1795
    Watercolour and ink on paper
    25.5 × 39.2
    Inscribed: 'Plan of the Bed Chamber Story
    at Brighton, with Alteration . . . Sloane
    Place Feby. 1795'
    RL 18955
    Reproduced by Gracious Permission of
    H.M. The Queen

E   Plan of the ground floor of the Marine
    Pavilion, with alterations
    1801
    Watercolour and ink on paper
    13.3 × 17.5 within margins
    Inscribed: 'HH Sloane Place July 1801.'
    RL 18957
    Reproduced by Gracious Permission of
    H.M. The Queen

F   Plan of the first floor of the Marine Pavilion,
    with alterations
    1801
    Watercolour and ink on paper
    13.3 × 17.5 within margins
    Inscribed: 'Plan for the Bed-Chamber Story
    . . . HH Sloane Place.'
    RL 18958
    Reproduced by Gracious Permission of
    H.M. The Queen

G   Plan of the ground floor of the Pavilion and
    east front elevation, as before January 1815
    Published Nash, *Views*, pl. 2
    Inscribed: 'A. Pugin delt. . . . G. Gladwin
    sculpt. . . . Pavilion previous to the
    alterations.'
    RP 100683
    A watercolour for the depiction here of the
    1787 Pavilion, by Pugin, exists in the Royal
    Pavilion collections
    RP 102671

H   Plan of the ground floor of the Pavilion, as
    rebuilt by Nash 1815–22, and a design for
    the Gardens
    Augustus Pugin
    Ink and pencil on paper
    24.6 × 30.3
    RP 100683

THE EXTERIOR

1   The Marine Pavilion, East Front
1788
Watercolour and pencil on paper
13.3 × 29.2
Inscribed in pencil: 'Pavillion'
Related to aquatint in Ford, op. cit.,
     no. 381, p. 296
RP 101362
Illustration 2

2   The Marine Pavilion, West Front
1788
Watercolour and pencil on paper
13.3 × 29.2
Inscribed in pencil: 'Pavillion'
RP 101363
Illustration 3

3   Design for the Marine Pavilion
1795
Watercolour and ink on paper
29.2 × 43.4 including painted margin
Inscribed: 'Elevation for the Front next
     the Steene at Brighton'
RL 18956
Illustration 4
Reproduced by Gracious Permission of
     H.M. The Queen

4   The Marine Pavilion, East Front
Henry Holland
1801
Watercolour and ink on paper
13.2 × 17.4 within border
Inscribed: 'Elevation to the Steyne as
     executing'; dated Jul. 1801 on cover of
     little book containing also RL 18957,
     18958, and 18960 (see no. 5)
RL 18959
Illustration 5
Reproduced by Gracious Permission of
     H.M. The Queen

5   Design for the East Front of the Marine
     Pavilion in chinoiserie style
Henry Holland
Watercolour and ink on paper
13.2 × 17.4 within border
Inscribed: 'A Design for the Elevation to
     the Steyne'
RL 18960
Illustration 6
Reproduced by Gracious Permission of
     H.M. The Queen

6   Designs for a house and stables adjoining
     the Pavilion
Henry Holland
1802
Watercolour and pencil on paper
31.6 × 18.2 within margins
Inscribed: 'Brighton Pavilion: Elevation
     towards the Steyne for the House
     adjoining the Pavilion: Elevation for

decorating the front of the Stable
building in the Garden: H H Sloane
Place Nov. 1802'
RP 101343
Illustration 7

7   Design for the Pavilion in chinoiserie style
William Porden
Watercolour and ink on paper
58 × 107.5 within mount
RP 101348
Illustration 8

8   Design for the Pavilion in chinoiserie style
William Porden
Watercolour and ink on paper
61.5 × 110.5 within mount
Inscribed: 'Design for embellishing the
     East Front of the Pavilion in the Chinese
     Style with the Upper Part of the New
     Apartments in the West Front appearing
     over it'
RP 101338
Illustration 12

9   Design for the Pavilion in chinoiserie style
William Porden
Watercolour and ink on paper
62 × 111
RP 101339
Illustration 9

10   The Stables, the Garden Front
Nash, *Views*, pl. 25; outline etching
     published 1824
Aquatint
19.2 × 33.5
A pencil drawing for this view by
     Augustus Pugin exists in the Royal
     Pavilion collections
RP
Illustration 10

11   The Stables and Riding House, seen from
     Church Street
Nash, *Views*, pl. 27
Aquatint
11 × 17.8
RP
Illustration 11

12   The Stables; the 'Rotunda'
Augustus Pugin
Pencil on paper
24.8 × 31.6
Inscribed: '70'
The figures were probably added by James
     Stephanoff
RP 100716
Illustration 13

13   The Stables; the 'Rotunda'
Augustus Pugin
Watercolour and pencil on paper
25.1 × 31.8
Inscribed: '69'

A similar watercolour at Windsor (RL 18160) is inscribed: 'Charles Moore del'; Moore's name is given on the etching in Nash's *Views*. No. 13 has all the marks of Pugin's hand
RP 100715
Illustration 14

14 The Riding House
Nash, *Views*, pl. 27
Aquatint
11 × 19
RP
Illustration 15

15 Design for a Conservatory
Watercolour, pencil, and pen on paper
26.6 × 55.5
RL 17090
Illustration 16
Reproduced by Gracious Permission of H.M. The Queen

16 Ground plan of the Pavilion
From Humphry Repton's manuscript of 'Designs for the Pavillon at Brighton', 1805
Watercolour and pencil on paper
51.4 × 35.2 with irregularly shaped flap
RL 18070
Illustration 17
Reproduced by Gracious Permission of H.M. The Queen

17 Ground plan of the Pavilion
From Humphry Repton, *Designs for the Pavillon at Brighton*, London, Stadler, 1808
RP
Illustration 18

18 View of the Stable Front, seen from the garden
From Repton's manuscript, op. cit., 1805
Watercolour and ink on paper
21.1 × 27.1 with flap (closed)
RL 18071
Illustration 21
Reproduced by Gracious Permission of H.M. The Queen

19 As no. 18, with flap open
From Repton's manuscript, op. cit., 1805
RL 18071
Illustration 24
Reproduced by Gracious Permission of H.M. The Queen

20 View from the Dome
From Repton's manuscript, op. cit., 1805
Watercolour and ink on paper
43.3 × 33.5; below flap 27.6 × 27.2
RL 18071 C
Illustration 22
Reproduced by Gracious Permission of H.M. The Queen

21 As no. 20, with flap open
From Repton's manuscript, op. cit., 1805
RL 18071 D
Illustration 25
Reproduced by Gracious Permission of H.M. The Queen

22 West Front of the Pavilion
From Repton's manuscript, op. cit., 1805
Watercolour and ink, monochrome, on paper
40.8 × 26.6
RL 18076
Illustration 19
Reproduced by Gracious Permission of H.M. The Queen

23 West Front of the Pavilion
From Repton, *Designs for the Pavillon at Brighton*, 1808, op. cit.
Aquatint
27 × 44.5
RP
Illustration 20

24 The Dining Room
From Repton's manuscript, op. cit., 1805
Watercolour, monochrome, on paper
20 × 24.4
RL 18077
Illustration 27
Reproduced by Gracious Permission of H.M. The Queen

25 General view from the Pavilion
From Repton's manuscript, op. cit., 1805
Watercolour on paper
34.3 × 64 with two irregularly shaped flaps (closed)
RL 18079
Illustration 23
Reproduced by Gracious Permission of H.M. The Queen

26 As no. 25, but with flaps open
From Repton's manuscript, op. cit., 1805
RL 18079
Illustration 26
Reproduced by Gracious Permission of H.M. The Queen

27 The West Corridor
From Repton's manuscript, op. cit., 1805
Watercolour on paper
17.2 × 27.5
RL 18080
Illustration 28
Reproduced by Gracious Permission of H.M. The Queen

28 The Orangery: winter
From Repton's manuscript, op. cit., 1805
Watercolour and ink on paper
18.5 × 26 including mount
RL 18081
Illustration 29
Reproduced by Gracious Permission of H.M. The Queen

29   As no. 28: summer
    1805
    RL 18081
    Illustration 32
    Reproduced by Gracious Permission of
      H.M. The Queen

30   The Pheasantry
    From Repton's manuscript, op. cit., 1805
    Watercolour and ink on paper
    34.7 × 28
    RL 18082
    Illustration 35
    Reproduced by Gracious Permission of
      H.M. The Queen

31   The East Front
    From Repton's manuscript, op. cit., 1805
    Watercolour and ink on paper
    15.6 × 27 plus flap (closed)
    RL 18083
    Illustration 30
    Reproduced by Gracious Permission of
      H.M. The Queen

32   As no. 31, with flap open
    1805
    RL 18083
    Illustration 33
    Reproduced by Gracious Permission of
      H.M. The Queen

33   View of the West Front
    From Repton's manuscript, op. cit., 1805
    Watercolour on paper
    32.4 × 47.5 plus flap
    RL 18084
    Illustration 31
    Reproduced by Gracious Permission of
      H.M. The Queen

34   As no. 33, with flap open
    1805
    RL 18084
    Illustration 34
    Reproduced by Gracious Permission of
      H.M. The Queen

35   View of the North Front
    From Repton's manuscript, op. cit., 1805
    Watercolour and ink on paper (fully
      extended)
    23 × 71.6 plus two flaps (here closed)
    RL 18085
    Illustration 36
    Reproduced by Gracious Permission of
      H.M. The Queen

36   As no. 35, with flaps open
    1805
    RL 18085
    Illustration 37
    Reproduced by Gracious Permission of
      H.M. The Queen

37   Longitudinal section of the Pavilion
    Nash, *Views*, pl. 28
    Aquatint

31.8 × 88
Inscribed: 'A Pugin delt'
RP
Illustration 1

38   Design for the Steine Front, the Pavilion
    Nash, *Views*, pl. 2; outline etching
      published Feb. 1825
    Aquatint
    18.3 × 30.2
    Inscribed: 'Steyne Front as Originally
      Designed'
    RP
    Illustration 40

39   Plan and section of the Pavilion
    1815
    ?John Nash
    Pencil on paper
    C-H 1948-40-1
    Illustration 41
    Courtesy of the Cooper-Hewitt Museum,
      the Smithsonian Institution's National
      Museum of Design

40   The West Front, the Pavilion
    Augustus Pugin
    Pencil and watercolour on paper
    15.2 × 34.5
    Inscribed on the reverse: '2 Imperial
      White'
    RP 10068
    Illustration 42

41   The West Front, the Pavilion
    Augustus Pugin
    Watercolour and pencil on paper
    13.3 × 21.2
    Inscribed on verso: 'West Front/Pavilion'
    RP 102667
    Illustration 43

42   The West Front, the Pavilion
    Nash, *Views*, pl. 7; outline etching
      published June 2 1823
    Aquatint
    20.6 × 35
    Inscribed on mount: 'A. Pug. delt'
    RP
    Illustration 38

43   The East Front, the Pavilion
    Nash, *Views*, pl. 5; outline etching
      published Apr. 1824
    Aquatint
    20.3 × 32.2
    Inscribed: 'A. Pugin delt.'
    RP
    Illustration 39

44   The East Front, the Pavilion
    Augustus Pugin
    Watercolour and pencil on paper
    21.8 × 35
    Inscribed in ink: 'Augst. Pugin 1823'
    RP 100684
    Illustration 45

45 The Entrance Portico and West Front, the
      Pavilion
   Augustus Pugin
   Watercolour and pencil on paper
   23 × 33.5
   A pencil drawing for this view, by
      Augustus Pugin, exists in the Royal
      Pavilion collections
   RP 102672
   Illustration 46

46 The King's Apartments, the Pavilion
   Charles Moore
   Watercolour and pencil on paper
   23.5 × 31
   A pencil drawing for this view, by
      Augustus Pugin, exists in the Royal
      Pavilion collections
   RP 102673
   Illustration 47

47 The North Front, the Pavilion
   Augustus Pugin
   Watercolour and pencil on paper
   18.8 × 33
   Inscribed in ink, with crossings out:
      'North End of Pavilion'; in pencil: '19'
   RP 100688
   Illustration 44

48 Design for a conservatory
   ?John Nash
   c. 1824
   Ink and wash on paper
   31.2 × 51.3
   RL 18968
   Illustration 48
   Reproduced by Gracious Permission of
      H.M. The Queen

49 Design for a conservatory
   ?John Nash
   c. 1824
   Ink and wash on paper
   24.6 × 44.5
   RL 18969
   Illustration 49
   Reproduced by Gracious Permission of
      H.M. The Queen

THE INTERIOR

THE SALOON

50 Design for the Saloon
   1787
   Watercolour and ink on paper
   35.5 × 40.4
   Inscribed: 'Brighton, Pavilion. This
      Design for the Great Saloon was
      received from M. Lignereux'
   V & A 2216.37
   Illustration 52

51 Design for the Saloon
   1787
   Watercolour and ink on paper
   21.5 × 40.2
   V & A 2216.4
   Illustration 53

52 The Saloon
   Thomas Rowlandson
   c. 1790
   Watercolour and ink on paper
   22 × 29.4
   RP 102268
   Illustration 54

53 The Saloon
   ?Frederick Crace
   c. 1815
   Watercolour and pencil on paper
   52.7 × 34.6
   Two sheets laid down on a mount: the
      lower portion, silhouetted, 26.6 × 29.8;
      the chandelier, 21.1 × 13.7
   C-H 1948-40-25 A & B
   Illustration 50
   Courtesy of the Cooper-Hewitt Museum,
      the Smithsonian Institution's National
      Museum of Design

54 Design for the Saloon
   1802–4
   Watercolour and ink on paper
   12.3 × 31.3
   Inscribed: 'The Cornice of the Saloon
      Brighton Pavilion'
   Attached to the same sheet is RP 100396, a
      detail of the Corridor skylight design RP
      100378 (see 190)
   RP 100395
   Illustration 55

55 Design for a cornice: dragons chasing a
      fabulous beast
   1802–4
   Watercolour and ink on paper
   13 × 27 (irregular shape)
   Attached to the same sheet is RP 100394,
      possibly a design connected with the
      Conservatory/Music Room
   RP 100393
   Illustration 56

56 Designs using bamboo motifs
   1802–4
   Watercolour and ink on paper
   26 × 37
   The three designs are attached to one
      mount
   RP 100421
   Illustration 57

57 Design for a wall with three Gothic arches
   ?1801
   Watercolour and pencil on paper
   24.4 × 38
   C-H 1948-40-43
   Illustration 62

Courtesy of the Cooper-Hewitt Museum,
the Smithsonian Institution's National
Museum of Design

58   Design for a wall with three Gothic arches
and Chinese lantern
? 1801
Watercolour and pencil on paper
23.8 × 38.9
C-H 1948-40-42
Illustration 63
Courtesy of the Cooper-Hewitt Museum,
the Smithsonian Institution's National
Museum of Design

59   Design for a door and overdoor with
fantastic bird
1802 or earlier
Watercolour and pencil on paper
16 × 5
C-H 1948-40-21
Illustration 58
Courtesy of the Cooper-Hewitt Museum,
the Smithsonian Institution's National
Museum of Design

60   Design for a blue and silver wall
decoration
1802 or earlier
Watercolour and ink on paper
16.7 × 18.1
C-H 1948-40-64
Illustration 64
Courtesy of the Cooper-Hewitt Museum,
the Smithsonian Institution's National
Museum of Design

61   Designs for lanterns
Probably 1802–4
Watercolour on paper
Each 19 × 10.5 (corners clipped), lantern
bodies themselves cut out and attached;
mounted
RP 100436, 100437
Illustration 59

62   Design for a lantern
Probably 1802–4
Watercolour and pencil on paper
68 × 25.5 (corners clipped); mounted
RP 100338
Illustration 65

63   Design for the central chandelier, the
Saloon
? Frederick Crace
1815 or earlier
Watercolour and pencil on paper
29.3 × 21.2
Inscribed in pencil: 'watermark 1814 cut
off': 'why? and by whom? C.M.'
RP 100340
Illustration 60

64   Design for a lantern, perhaps for the
Saloon
? Frederick Crace

1815 or earlier
Pencil on paper
19 × 13
RP 102536
Illustration 61

65   Design for a lantern, perhaps for the
Saloon
? Frederick Crace
1815 or earlier
Pencil on paper
19.2 × 13.2
RP 102535
Illustration 71

66   Design for a lantern
? Frederick Crace
1815 or earlier
Pencil on paper
31.8 × 22.8
Inscribed in pencil: 'Lanthorn for the
Saloon Brighton'
RP 100388
Illustration 72

67   Design for a chandelier, probably for the
Saloon
? Frederick Crace
1815 or earlier
Pencil on paper
20 × 13
A sketch for 68
RP 102542
Illustration 73

68   Design for a chandelier, probably for the
Saloon
? Frederick Crace
1815 or earlier
Watercolour and pencil on paper
28.7 × 21.7
Related to 67
RP 100341
Illustration 66

69   Design for a chandelier, probably for the
Saloon
? Frederick Crace
1815 or earlier
Pencil on paper
21 × 12.9
Inscribed: '5 OClock HL [HH?] wishes to
see Mr. C . . . respecting the detail of the
Drawings. will call again this Eveng.'
A sketch for 70
RP 102541
Illustration 74

70   Design for a chandelier, probably for the
Saloon
? Frederick Crace
1815 or earlier
Watercolour and pencil on paper
29.2 × 21.3
Related to 69
RP 100339
Illustration 75

71 Design for a lantern, surmounted by a bird
1815 or earlier
Pencil on paper
19 × 13
RP 102534
Illustration 76

72 The Saloon, 1817
Augustus Pugin
Before 1822
Pencil on paper
27.5 × 31.5
RP 100701
Illustration 69

73 The Saloon, 1817
Augustus Pugin
Before 1822
Watercolour on paper
25.6 × 31.2
All the watercolours RL 18154–18161 have
a 'worked over' surface, possibly due to
varnish. It seems possible that some may
have been painted over etching.
However, Pugin's typical technique is
discernible in this item as in the others
RL 18161
Illustration 67
Reproduced by Gracious Permission of
H.M. The Queen

74 Design for a carpet, probably for the
Saloon
? Frederick Crace
c. 1815
Watercolour on paper
24.5 × 34.5 (irregular shape)
C-H 1948-40-90
Illustration 68
Courtesy of the Cooper-Hewitt Museum,
the Smithsonian Institution's National
Museum of Design

75 Design of naturalistic flowers and foliage
c. 1815
Watercolour on paper
21 × 13.3
CB
Illustration 70

76 Design for the Saloon
Robert Jones
c. 1816–22
Watercolour and pencil on paper
34.8 × 28.1
Inscribed: 'design for the door recess at
each end of the Saloon'
RP 100889
Illustration 51

77 Design for the curtains, the Saloon
Robert Jones
1823
Watercolour and pencil on paper
39 × 49.3
Inscribed: 'Design for the Curtain Cornice

etc – from the Saloon – approved by His
Majesty 3 July 1823 – R. Jones'
RP 100888
Illustration 77

78 The Saloon
Augustus Pugin
c. 1823
Pencil on paper
23.2 × 21
Inscribed: '44'
RP 100702
Illustration 78

79 The Saloon
1823
Nash, *Views*, pl. 18; outline etching
published June 2 1823
Aquatint
26.3 × 31.9
RP
Illustration 79

80 The Saloon
Augustus Pugin
c. 1823–4
Watercolour on paper
25.7 × 31.4
See note to 73
RL 18158
Illustration 81
Reproduced by Gracious Permission of
H.M. The Queen

81 The Saloon
Nash, *Views*, pl. 18; drawn by Augustus
Pugin, etched by Jas. Tingle; dated
June 2 1823
RP
Illustration 80

THE DRAWING ROOMS BEFORE 1815

82 Rough plan of rooms south of the Saloon,
including the Conservatory/Music
Room, and designs for a passage with a
canopy
? King George IV
1803 or earlier
Pencil on paper
19 × 30.3
The obverse of 84
RP 102529
Illustration 83

83 Designs for a passage with a canopy,
probably an unexecuted design for the
Glass Passage
1803 or earlier
Watercolour, ink, and pencil on paper
23.2 × 17
C-H 1948-40-65
Illustration 82
Courtesy of the Cooper-Hewitt Museum,
the Smithsonian Institution's National
Museum of Design

84   Designs of chinoiserie motifs
        1803 or earlier
        Watercolour, ink, and pencil on paper
        19 × 30.3
        The obverse of 82
        RP 102529
        Illustration 84

85   Designs for scrolling patterns in lilac,
            yellow, and two shades of pink
        1801–4
        Watercolour, gouache, and ink on paper
        Various sizes, 26.2 × 37 mounted
        RP 100427
        Illustration 85

86   Design for a passageway, possibly the
            Glass Passage
        1803 or earlier
        Watercolour and ink on paper
        12.7 × 10
        C-H 1948-40-50
        Illustration 91
        Courtesy of the Cooper-Hewitt Museum,
            the Smithsonian Institution's National
            Museum of Design

87   Design for fretwork, perhaps for the Glass
            Passage
        1803 or earlier
        Watercolour and ink on paper
        9.2 × 21.2
        C-H 1948-40-51
        Illustration 92
        Courtesy of the Cooper-Hewitt Museum,
            the Smithsonian Institution's National
            Museum of Design

88   Designs for a passageway, perhaps for the
            Glass Passage
        ?King George IV
        1803 or earlier
        Pencil on paper
        19.5 × 30.4
        RP 102530
        Illustration 90

89   Designs for glass panels and framework
        Probably 1802–4
        Watercolour, ink, and pencil on paper
        26.3 × 7.5, 27 × 8.2 attached to mount
        RP 100419, 100420
        Illustration 86

90   Design for a room with Chinese wallpaper
        1802 or earlier
        Watercolour, gouache, and ink on paper
        16.3 × 25.5
        C-H 1948-40-52
        Illustration 93
        Courtesy of the Cooper-Hewitt Museum,
            the Smithsonian Institution's National
            Museum of Design

91   Design for a window alcove with curtains
        1802 or earlier
        Watercolour and gouache on paper
        18.3 × 24.9 (silhouetted)

        C-H 1948-40-67
        Illustration 94
        Courtesy of the Cooper-Hewitt Museum,
            the Smithsonian Institution's National
            Museum of Design

92   Design for a window alcove
        1802 or earlier
        Watercolour and gouache on paper
        13.2 × 16.4
        C-H 1948-40-66
        Illustration 87
        Courtesy of the Cooper-Hewitt Museum,
            the Smithsonian Institution's National
            Museum of Design

93   Design for curtains
        1802 or earlier
        Gouache, ink, and pencil on paper
        17.9 × 18.6
        C-H 1948-40-76
        Illustration 88
        Courtesy of the Cooper-Hewitt Museum,
            the Smithsonian Institution's National
            Museum of Design

94   Design for a chimneypiece wall with
            chinoiserie landscapes, possibly for the
            Library
        1802
        Watercolour and pencil on paper
        10.9 × 23.5
        The Library (see plan E) was also known
            as the Breakfast Room or the Small
            Drawing Room
        C-H 1948-40-47
        Illustration 95
        Courtesy of the Cooper-Hewitt Museum,
            the Smithsonian Institution's National
            Museum of Design

95   Design for a window wall, possibly for the
            Library
        1802
        Watercolour and pencil on paper
        22.2 × 46.7
        See note on 94
        C-H 1948-40-48
        Illustration 96
        Courtesy of the Cooper-Hewitt Museum,
            the Smithsonian Institution's National
            Museum of Design

96   Design for a doorway and bookcase,
            possibly for the Library
        1802
        Watercolour and pencil on paper
        10.3 × 18.8
        See note on 94
        C-H 1948-40-45
        Illustration 97
        Courtesy of the Cooper-Hewitt Museum,
            the Smithsonian Institution's National
            Museum of Design

97   Design for an aperture and curtains,
            possibly for the Library

1802
Gouache on paper
10.9 × 18.5
See note on 94
C-H 1948-40-77
Illustration 89
Courtesy of the Cooper-Hewitt Museum,
the Smithsonian Institution's National
Museum of Design

98 Design for a wall with doorway, possibly
for the Library
1802
Watercolour and pencil on paper
10.8 × 22.2
This design is for the same wall as 99. See
note on 94
C-H 1948-40-49
Illustration 98
Courtesy of the Cooper-Hewitt Museum,
the Smithsonian Institution's National
Museum of Design

99 Design for a wall with doorway, possibly
for the Library
1802
Watercolour and pencil on paper
10.8 × 22.1
See note on 94
C-H 1948-40-46
Illustration 99
Courtesy of the Cooper-Hewitt Museum,
the Smithsonian Institution's National
Museum of Design

100 Design (incomplete) for a wall with
doorway, probably for the Ante Room
1802 or earlier
Watercolour, gouache, and ink on paper
11.3 × 23.5
C-H 1948-40-44
Illustration 100
Courtesy of the Cooper-Hewitt Museum,
the Smithsonian Institution's National
Museum of Design

101 Designs for implements of war
Probably 1801–4
Watercolour and ink on paper
  (a) 'A Chinese Battle-axe and Helmet'
      11.8 × 15.5
  (b) A shield
      14 × 14
  (c) A flag
      17.2 × 13
RP 100343, 100342, 100345
Illustration 101a–c

THE BLUE/SOUTH DRAWING ROOM
102 The Blue Drawing Room
Augustus Pugin
Before 1821
Watercolour and pencil on paper
24.3 × 34
Inscribed: '77'

RP 100703
Illustration 105

103 The Blue Drawing Room
c. 1820
Nash, *Views*, pl. 30; drawn by Augustus
Pugin, etched by T.Kearnan; dated Dec.
1 1824
Etching
22 × 30.5
RP
Illustration 102

104 Design for a door and overdoor
Watercolour, gouache, and ink
16.9 × 10.2
C-H 1948-40-59
Illustration 108
Courtesy of the Cooper-Hewitt Museum,
the Smithsonian Institution's National
Museum of Design

105 Design for a door and overdoor
Watercolour, gouache, and ink
16.8 × 10.2
C-H 1948-40-60
Illustration 103
Courtesy of the Cooper-Hewitt Museum,
the Smithsonian Institution's National
Museum of Design

106 Design for a wall decoration
Watercolour and pencil on paper
10.7 × 9
C-H 1948-40-61
Illustration 104
Courtesy of the Cooper-Hewitt Museum,
the Smithsonian Institution's National
Museum of Design

107 Design for a wall decoration
Watercolour and pencil on paper
11 × 9.3
C-H 1948-40-62
Illustration 109
Courtesy of the Cooper-Hewitt Museum,
the Smithsonian Institution's National
Museum of Design

108 Design for a wall decoration
? Robert Jones
c. 1820
Pencil on paper
22.9 × 29.3
Inscribed: 'Gallery next the Dining Room
color Yellow Pannel to be raised & a
dado the same as the other Gallery'
C-H 1948-40-32
Illustration 106
Courtesy of the Cooper-Hewitt Museum,
the Smithsonian Institution's National
Museum of Design

109 Design for a wall decoration
? Robert Jones
c. 1820
Pencil on paper

27.2 × 39
C-H 1948-40-23
Illustration 107
Courtesy of the Cooper-Hewitt Museum,
　　the Smithsonian Institution's National
　　Museum of Design

110　Design for a mirror frame
　　　c. 1820
　　　Pen, pencil and watercolour on paper
　　　39.1 × 29.6
　　　Inscribed: 'Banquetting Room Gallery'
　　　V & A (no cat. no.)
　　　Illustration 110

111　Design for a mirror frame
　　　c. 1820
　　　Pen, pencil and watercolour on paper
　　　37.1 × 29.5
　　　Inscribed: 'Banquetting Room Gallery'
　　　V & A (no cat. no.)
　　　Illustration 111

112　The South Drawing Room
　　　Augustus Pugin
　　　1821 or later
　　　Pencil on paper
　　　14.3 × 21.8
　　　RP 100706
　　　Illustration 112

113　The South Drawing Room
　　　Augustus Pugin
　　　1821 or later
　　　Watercolour and pencil on paper
　　　20.3 × 30.5
　　　Inscribed: '47'
　　　RP 100704
　　　Illustration 114

114　The South Drawing Room
　　　Augustus Pugin
　　　1821 or later
　　　Watercolour and pencil on paper
　　　20.3 × 30.4
　　　Inscribed: '48'
　　　RP 100705
　　　Illustration 115

115　The South Drawing Room
　　　1823
　　　Nash, *Views*, pl. 19
　　　Aquatint
　　　19.8 × 30.6
　　　Inscribed on the mount: 'A Pugin delt'
　　　RP
　　　Illustration 113

THE YELLOW/NORTH DRAWING ROOM

116　The Yellow Drawing Room
　　　Augustus Pugin
　　　Before 1821
　　　Pencil on paper
　　　20.3 × 30.5
　　　Inscribed: '80'
　　　RP 100699
　　　Illustration 117

117　The Yellow Drawing Room
　　　Augustus Pugin
　　　Before 1821
　　　Watercolour and pencil on paper
　　　17.8 × 31.2
　　　Inscribed: '79'
　　　RP 100698
　　　Illustration 116

118　Design for a wall decoration
　　　c. 1815
　　　Watercolour and pencil on paper
　　　13.3 × 29.9
　　　C-H 1948-40-19
　　　Illustration 118
　　　Courtesy of the Cooper-Hewitt Museum,
　　　　the Smithsonian Institution's National
　　　　Museum of Design

119　Design for a wall decoration
　　　c. 1815
　　　Watercolour and pencil on paper
　　　18.2 × 30.4
　　　C-H 1948-40-18
　　　Illustration 122
　　　Courtesy of the Cooper-Hewitt Museum,
　　　　the Smithsonian Institution's National
　　　　Museum of Design

120　Design for a wall decoration surmounted
　　　　by an exotic bird, and for a wall
　　　　decoration of frames for pictures
　　　c. 1815
　　　Watercolour, ink, and pencil on paper
　　　36 × 25.3
　　　RP 100390
　　　Illustration 124

121　Chinese dog
　　　Ink on paper
　　　32.4 × 23.6 (corners clipped)
　　　RP 100444
　　　Illustration 119

122　Design for an exotic bird
　　　c. 1815
　　　Ink on paper
　　　21.6 × 26.2
　　　Inscribed: 'Royal Bird Foo hum'
　　　RP 100450
　　　Illustration 120

123　Design for an exotic bird
　　　c. 1815
　　　Watercolour and ink on paper
　　　18.3 × 24
　　　Inscribed in pencil: 'The Royal Bird –
　　　　Calld Foo hum'
　　　RP 100447
　　　Illustration 127

124　Design for an exotic bird
　　　c. 1815
　　　Watercolour, ink, and pencil on paper
　　　17.8 × 25.5
　　　Inscribed in pencil: 'The Royal Bird Foo
　　　　hum'

RP 100448
Illustration 123

125 Design for an exotic bird
c. 1815
Watercolour and ink on paper
27 × 21 (corners clipped)
Inscribed in pencil: 'The Royal Bird Foo
    hum'; inscription gone over at a later
    date
RP 100445
Illustration 129

126 Design for a wall decoration
? Robert Jones
c. 1820
Pencil on paper
24.8 × 29.3
Inscribed: 'Gallery next the Music Room,
    Lalic'
C-H 1948-40-20
Illustration 121
Courtesy of the Cooper-Hewitt Museum,
    the Smithsonian Institution's National
    Museum of Design

127 The North Drawing Room
Augustus Pugin
1821 or later
Pencil on paper
18.4 × 25.6
RP 100700
Illustration 125

128 The North Drawing Room
Augustus Pugin
1821 or later
Watercolour and pencil on paper
19.7 × 31.4
Inscribed: '42'
RP 100697
Illustration 128

129 The North Drawing Room
c. 1823
Nash, *Views*, pl. 17; the outline etching is
    undated
Aquatint
20.2 × 29.4
RP
Illustration 126

THE CONSERVATORY/MUSIC ROOM
AND THE DINING ROOM

130 Design for a wall decoration, probably for
    the Conservatory/Music Room
1802 or earlier
Watercolour, gouache, and ink on paper
17.6 × 22.6
C-H 1948-40-63
Illustration 131
Courtesy of the Cooper-Hewitt Museum,
    the Smithsonian Institution's National
    Museum of Design

131 Design for a ceiling, probably for the
    Conservatory/Music Room

1802 or earlier
Watercolour, gouache, and ink on paper
17.5 × 31.1
C-H 1948-40-68
Illustration 132
Courtesy of the Cooper-Hewitt Museum,
    the Smithsonian Institution's National
    Museum of Design

132 Design for a lantern
1803–4
Watercolour, ink, and pencil on paper
Inscribed: 'A Lanthorn for the Old Music
    Room Brighton. And Fel down on Mr.
    F. Crace on the Night of the first grand
    entertainment.' This inscription must
    have been added after the Nash
    rebuilding had begun, or after the
    Conservatory/Music Room had fallen
    into disuse.
RP 100386
Illustration 140

133 Design for a ceiling (detail), probably for
    the Conservatory/Music Room, or
    perhaps for the Dining Room
1802 or earlier
Watercolour and ink on paper
15.4 × 30.3
C-H 1948-40-70
Illustration 130
Courtesy of the Cooper-Hewitt Museum,
    the Smithsonian Institution's National
    Museum of Design

134 Design for a ceiling, probably for the
    Conservatory/Music Room, or perhaps
    for the Dining Room
1802 or earlier
Watercolour and ink on paper
9.2 × 16.5
C-H 1948-40-69
Illustration 133
Courtesy of the Cooper-Hewitt Museum,
    the Smithsonian Institution's National
    Museum of Design

135 Design for a ceiling
c. 1820
Watercolour and ink on paper
40.3 × 35
The watermark, 'J. Whatman', is similar to
    that on the paper of 158
C-H 1948-40-71
Illustration 139
Courtesy of the Cooper-Hewitt Museum,
    the Smithsonian Institution's National
    Museum of Design

136 Design for a ceiling
c. 1820
Watercolour and ink on paper
40.1 × 35.3
C-H 1948-40-72
Illustration 134
Courtesy of the Cooper-Hewitt Museum,

the Smithsonian Institution's National
Museum of Design

137 Design for a ceiling (detail), perhaps for
the Conservatory/Music Room or
Dining Room
1802 or earlier
Watercolour and ink on paper
16.4 × 25.2
C-H 1948-40-182
Illustration 135
Courtesy of the Cooper-Hewitt Museum,
the Smithsonian Institution's National
Museum of Design

138 Design for a ceiling
1801 or earlier
Watercolour and ink on paper
17.2 × 24
C-H 1948-40-179
Illustration 136
Courtesy of the Cooper-Hewitt Museum,
the Smithsonian Institution's National
Museum of Design

139 Design for a ceiling
1801 or earlier
Watercolour and ink on paper
17.6 × 24.5
C-H 1948-40-180
Illustration 137
Courtesy of the Cooper-Hewitt Museum,
the Smithsonian Institution's National
Museum of Design

140 Alternative designs for a ceiling
1801 or earlier
Watercolour and ink on paper
25.5 × 19.6
C-H 1948-40-181
Illustration 138
Courtesy of the Cooper-Hewitt Museum,
the Smithsonian Institution's National
Museum of Design

141 Design for a wall with chimneypiece,
probably for the Dining Room
1802 or earlier
Watercolour, gouache, and ink on paper
17.7 × 26.9
C-H 1948-40-27
Illustration 141
Courtesy of the Cooper-Hewitt Museum,
the Smithsonian Institution's National
Museum of Design

142 Design for a window, probably for the
Dining Room
1802 or earlier
Watercolour and ink on paper
17.5 × 13.4
C-H 1948-40-93
Illustration 142
Courtesy of the Cooper-Hewitt Museum,
the Smithsonian Institution's National
Museum of Design

143 Design for a doorway, possibly for the
Lobby or its vicinity south of the Dining
Room
1802 or earlier
Watercolour and ink on paper
12.5 × 13.3
C-H 1948-40-56
Illustration 143
Courtesy of the Cooper-Hewitt Museum,
the Smithsonian Institution's National
Museum of Design

144 Design for a window, possibly for the
Lobby or its vicinity south of the Dining
Room
1802 or earlier
Watercolour and ink on paper
12.6 × 11.6
C-H 1948-40-58
Illustration 144
Courtesy of the Cooper-Hewitt Museum,
the Smithsonian Institution's National
Museum of Design

145 Design for a wall decoration, possibly for
the Lobby or its vicinity south of the
Dining Room
1802 or earlier
Watercolour and ink on paper
12.6 × 9.7
C-H 1948-40-57
Illustration 145
Courtesy of the Cooper-Hewitt Museum,
the Smithsonian Institution's National
Museum of Design

THE ENTRANCE HALL

146 Design for the Entrance Hall, the west wall
1802
Watercolour, gouache, and ink on paper
26 × 29.8
C-H 1948-40-6
Illustration 150
Courtesy of the Cooper-Hewitt Museum,
the Smithsonian Institution's National
Museum of Design

147 Design for a wall decoration, perhaps for
a corridor
1802
Watercolour and ink on paper
11.4 × 24.7
C-H 1948-40-40
Illustration 147
Courtesy of the Cooper-Hewitt Museum,
the Smithsonian Institution's National
Museum of Design

148 Design for a wall decoration and door,
with columns
1802
Watercolour and ink on paper
11.4 × 29.4
C-H 1948-40-41
Illustration 151

Courtesy of the Cooper-Hewitt Museum, the Smithsonian Institution's National Museum of Design

149 Design for a stove
c. 1801–4
Pen and wash on paper
24 × 15
RP 100404
Illustration 146

150 Design for the Entrance Hall, the east wall
Probably 1802 or earlier
Watercolour and ink on paper
22.4 × 27.2; hinged alternative design
22.3 × 27.1
Inscribed on the sheet beneath the addition: 'Sky'
C-H 1948-40-35 A/B
Illustration 156
Courtesy of the Cooper-Hewitt Museum, the Smithsonian Institution's National Museum of Design

151 Design for the Entrance Hall, the east wall
Probably 1802 or earlier
Watercolour and ink on paper
20.9 × 27.3
C-H 1948-40-34
Illustration 154
Courtesy of the Cooper-Hewitt Museum, the Smithsonian Institution's National Museum of Design

152 Design for the Entrance Hall, the north wall
Probably 1802 or earlier
Watercolour and ink on paper
22.3 × 25.3
C-H 1948-40-38
Illustration 155
Courtesy of the Cooper-Hewitt Museum, the Smithsonian Institution's National Museum of Design

153 Design for the Entrance Hall, the north wall
Probably 1802 or earlier
Watercolour and pencil on paper
26.5 × 33
Inscribed: 'Brighton Pavilion. Decoration for one side of the Hall'; in another hand: 'For Mr. Crace'
C-H 1948-40-39
Illustration 148
Courtesy of the Cooper-Hewitt Museum, the Smithsonian Institution's National Museum of Design

154 Design for the Entrance Hall, the west wall
Probably 1802 or earlier
Watercolour and ink on paper
22.3 × 27.1
C-H 1948-40-36
Illustration 149
Courtesy of the Cooper-Hewitt Museum,

the Smithsonian Institution's National Museum of Design

155 Design for the Entrance Hall, the west wall
Probably 1802 or earlier
Watercolour and ink on paper
22.2 × 27.3
C-H 1948-40-37
Illustration 160
Courtesy of the Cooper-Hewitt Museum, the Smithsonian Institution's National Museum of Design

156 Design for the Entrance Hall, the south wall
Probably by Frederick Crace
1815
Watercolour and pencil on paper
25 × 31.9
C-H 1948-40-33
Illustration 161
Courtesy of the Cooper-Hewitt Museum, the Smithsonian Institution's National Museum of Design

157 Design for the Entrance Hall, the east wall
Probably by Frederick Crace
1815
Watercolour, ink, and pencil on paper
24.8 × 31.9
C-H 1948-40-29
Illustration 162
Courtesy of the Cooper-Hewitt Museum, the Smithsonian Institution's National Museum of Design

158 Design for the Entrance Hall, the south wall
? Robert Jones
c. 1820
Pencil on paper
34 × 50.1
C-H 1948-40-3
Illustration 152
Courtesy of the Cooper-Hewitt Museum, the Smithsonian Institution's National Museum of Design

159 Design for the Entrance Hall, the east wall
? Robert Jones
c. 1820
Pencil on paper
33.2 × 44.9
C-H 1948-40-28
Illustration 153
Courtesy of the Cooper-Hewitt Museum, the Smithsonian Institution's National Museum of Design

160 Design for the Entrance Hall, the south wall
? Robert Jones
c. 1820
Pencil on paper
32.6 × 50.8
C-H 1948-40-4
Illustration 157

Courtesy of the Cooper-Hewitt Museum,
   the Smithsonian Institution's National
   Museum of Design

161   Design for the Entrance Hall, the east wall
      ? Robert Jones
      c. 1820
      Pencil on paper
      34.6 × 47.6
      C-H 1948-40-30
      Illustration 158
      Courtesy of the Cooper-Hewitt Museum,
         the Smithsonian Institution's National
         Museum of Design

162   Design for the Entrance Hall, the south
      wall
      ? Robert Jones
      c. 1820
      Pencil on paper
      35.5 × 48.9
      C-H 1948-40-2
      Illustration 159
      Courtesy of the Cooper-Hewitt Museum,
         the Smithsonian Institution's National
         Museum of Design

163   The Entrance Hall
      Augustus Pugin
      c. 1820
      Watercolour and pencil on paper
      19 × 29.5
      Inscribed: '25'
      RP 100690
      Illustration 163

164   The Entrance Hall
      c. 1820
      Nash, *Views*, pl. 12; the outline etching is
         undated
      Aquatint
      19 × 29.2
      RP
      Illustration 164

THE CORRIDOR

165   Design for the Corridor
      Probably by Frederick Crace
      1815
      Watercolour, ink, and pencil on paper
      26 × 29.8
      C-H 1948-50-5
      Illustration 165
      Courtesy of the Cooper-Hewitt Museum,
         the Smithsonian Institution's National
         Museum of Design

166   Design for a wall decoration below a
         skylight
      Frederick Crace
      1815
      Watercolour and ink on paper
      CB
      Illustration 166

167   Design of flowers and leaves in pink and
         blue, possibly for the Corridor
      Frederick Crace

1815
Watercolour and ink on paper
CB
Illustration 167

168   Design derived from Chinese characters in
         pink and green, probably for the
         Corridor
      Frederick Crace
      1815
      Watercolour on paper
      CB
      Illustration 168

169   The Corridor
      Augustus Pugin
      Before 1820
      Pencil on paper
      20.3 × 29.3
      Inscribed: '32'
      RP 100693
      Illustration 169

170   The Corridor
      Augustus Pugin
      Before 1820
      Watercolour and pencil on paper
      20.4 × 30
      Inscribed: '31'
      RP 100692
      Illustration 181

171   The Corridor
      c. 1820
      Nash, *Views*, pl. 14; outline etching
         published Apr. 2 1820
      Aquatint
      20.4 × 30
      RP
      Illustration 170

172   The Corridor
      Augustus Pugin
      1822–4
      Pencil on paper
      21.6 × 31.6
      Inscribed: '36'
      RP 100695
      Illustration 171

173   The Corridor
      Augustus Pugin
      1822–4
      Watercolour and pencil on paper
      21.9 × 28.7
      Inscribed: '35'
      RP 100694
      Illustration 182

174   The Corridor
      c. 1824
      Nash, *Views*, pl. 15; outline etching
         published Dec. 1 1824
      Aquatint
      21.5 × 29.8
      RP
      Illustration 172

175 Design for a standard, the Corridor
1815
Pencil on paper
18 × 13.2
RP 102590
Illustration 173

176 Designs for standards, the Corridor
1815
Watercolour and ink on paper
31 × 10.5, 31 × 10.5; mounted
Inscribed in pencil on both: 'Standards for
the Long Gallery'
RP 100383
Illustration 174

177 Design of dragon and fish, possibly for a
decorative standard
Frederick Crace
c. 1815
Watercolour and ink on paper
CB
Illustration 175

178 Design of dragon and pole, possibly for a
decorative standard
Frederick Crace
c. 1815
Watercolour and ink on paper
CB
Illustration 183

179 Design for a lantern and standard
Probably 1802–4
Watercolour, ink, and pencil on paper
34.9 × 24.3 (corners clipped)
RP 100432
Illustration 186

180 Design for a lantern and standard in red,
gold, and blue
Probably 1802–4
Watercolour and ink on paper
19.2 × 13.4 (corners clipped)
RP 100431
Illustration 176

181 Design for a lantern and standard
Probably 1802–4
Watercolour and ink on paper
32.2 × 23.2
RP 100433
Illustration 187

182 Design for a banner and standard in blue,
yellow, and pink
Probably 1802–4
Watercolour and ink on paper
31.6 × 22
RP 100403
Illustration 177

183 Design for a Chinese fish, probably for the
Corridor
Frederick Crace
c. 1815
Watercolour and ink on paper
CB

Illustration 184

184 Design for a Chinese fish
Frederick Crace
c. 1815
Watercolour and ink on paper
CB
Illustration 185

185 Design for a Chinese fish in silver, brown,
pink, and green
Probably 1802–4
Watercolour and ink on paper
22.2 × 12.8
RP 100399
Illustration 178

186 Design for a Chinese fish
c. 1815
Pencil on paper
11 × 5
RP 102539
Illustration 179

187 Design for a pedestal to carry a vase,
perhaps for the Corridor
1815 or later
Pencil on paper
C-H 1948-40-188
Illustration 180
Courtesy of the Cooper-Hewitt Museum,
the Smithsonian Institution's National
Museum of Design

188 Design for a skylight, the Corridor
1815
Watercolour and ink on paper
14 × 28
Inscribed in pencil: 'The Drawing for the
Great Sky Light in Long Gallery
Brighton Pavilion'
RP 100376
Illustration 188

189 Design for a skylight, the Corridor
1815
Watercolour and ink on paper
19.2 × 33.8
Inscribed in pencil: 'Drawing for the Sky
Light on the North Staircase'
RP 100380
Illustration 191

190 Design for a skylight with an exotic bird,
probably for the Corridor
1815
Watercolour and ink on paper
21 × 32.8
See 54, 197
RP 100378
Illustration 189

191 Design for a Chinese boy and flowers,
probably for the Corridor
c. 1815
Pencil on paper
10.2 × 9.7
RP 102582

Illustration 192

192 Design for a moth/bird
Frederick Crace
c. 1815
Watercolour and ink on paper
CB
Illustration 190

193 Design for dragons
Watercolour and ink on paper
15.6 × 19.8, 15.8 × 11.2
RP 100406, 100407
Illustration 193

194 Design for dragon and bird, with floral
spray
Frederick Crace
c. 1815
Watercolour, ink, and pencil on paper
CB
Illustration 194

195 Design for a skylight, the Corridor
Probably by Frederick Crace
1815
Watercolour and ink on paper
21 × 27.5
Inscribed on mount: 'Drawing for the
Skylight – South Staircase'
RP 100381
Illustration 195

196 Design for glass
Frederick Crace
c. 1815
Watercolour and ink on paper
CB
Illustration 196

197 Design for glass
c. 1815
Watercolour and ink on paper
19.2 × 25.8
Related to 196
RP 100439
Illustration 197

198 Design for a lantern glass
Frederick Crace
c. 1815
Watercolour and ink on paper
CB
Illustration 198

199 Design, probably for a lantern glass
Frederick Crace
c. 1815
Watercolour and ink on paper
CB
Illustration 199

200 Design, probably for the edge of an
'umbrella' lustre
Frederick Crace
c. 1815
Watercolour and ink on paper
CB
Illustration 200

201 Design with a grotesque head (detail for
Corridor skylight)
Frederick Crace
c. 1815
Watercolour and ink on paper
See 54, 190
CB
Illustration 201

202 Design of Chinese fret and leaves, possibly
for glass
Frederick Crace
c. 1815
Watercolour and ink on paper
CB
Illustration 202

203 Chinese fret designs in green and yellow
and in blue, possibly for glass
Frederick Crace
c. 1815
Watercolour and ink on paper
CB
Illustration 203

204 Chinese fret designs in lilac and in red,
possibly for glass
Frederick Crace
c. 1815
Watercolour and ink on paper
CB
Illustration 204

205 Two scroll designs
Frederick Crace
c. 1815
Watercolour and ink on paper
CB
Illustration 205

206 Scroll design in lilac, yellow, and green
Frederick Crace
c. 1815
Watercolour and ink on paper
CB
Illustration 206

207 Design of Chinese fret in lilac and yellow
Frederick Crace
c. 1815
Watercolour and ink on paper
CB
Illustration 207

208 Design of flowers and tendrils, possibly for
glass
Frederick Crace
c. 1815
Watercolour and ink on paper
CB
Illustration 208

209 Design of flowers and fruit
Frederick Crace
c. 1815
Watercolour and ink on paper
CB
Illustration 209

210 Two repeat designs: fret and flowers, and
   Chinese characters
   Frederick Crace
   c. 1815
   Watercolour and ink on paper
   Influenced by the 'meandering stem' of
   Ottoman embroidery
   CB
   Illustration 210

211 Design of flowers and tendrils
   Frederick Crace
   c. 1815
   Watercolour and ink on paper
   CB
   Illustration 211

212 Design of flowers and tendrils
   Frederick Crace
   c. 1815
   Watercolour and ink on paper
   CB
   Illustration 212

213 Design of ferns and flowers derived from
   Indian embroidery
   Frederick Crace
   c. 1815
   Watercolour and ink on paper
   CB
   Illustration 213

214 Design of leaves and geometric shapes
   derived from Turkoman carpets
   Frederick Crace
   c. 1815
   Watercolour and ink on paper
   CB
   Illustration 214

215 Two designs for carpets, probably for the
   Corridor
   Frederick Crace
   c. 1815
   Watercolour and ink on paper
   CB
   Illustration 220

216 Chinoiserie design
   Frederick Crace
   c. 1815
   Watercolour and ink on paper
   CB
   Illustration 215

217 Design for a wall decoration, possibly for
   the Corridor
   c. 1815
   Pencil on paper
   27.6 × 37.7
   C-H 1948-40-183
   Illustration 216
   Courtesy of the Cooper-Hewitt Museum,
   the Smithsonian Institution's National
   Museum of Design

218 Design for a chinoiserie decoration
   Frederick Crace

c. 1815
Watercolour and ink on paper
CB
Illustration 217

219 Design for a chinoiserie decoration
   Frederick Crace
   c. 1815
   Watercolour and ink on paper
   CB
   Illustration 218

220 Design of chinoiserie scrolls, shapes, and
   flowers
   c. 1815
   Watercolour and ink on paper
   18.3 × 35
   RP 100409
   Illustration 219

221 Design of scrolls and flowers
   c. 1815
   Watercolour and ink on paper
   24.5 × 36
   RP 100426; reverse of RP 100427
   Illustration 221

222 Chinoiserie design in tones of blue
   Frederick Crace
   c. 1815
   Watercolour and ink on paper
   CB
   Illustration 223

223 Design for chinoiserie decoration
   Frederick Crace
   c. 1815
   Watercolour and ink on paper
   CB
   Illustration 222

224 Design for chinoiserie repeat pattern in
   green, pink, yellow, and blue
   Frederick Crace
   c. 1815
   Watercolour and ink on paper
   CB
   Illustration 224

225 Design for chinoiserie repeat pattern
   Frederick Crace
   c. 1815
   Watercolour and ink on paper
   CB
   Illustration 225

226 Design for chinoiserie repeat pattern
   Frederick Crace
   c. 1815
   Watercolour and ink on paper
   CB
   Illustration 226

227 Design for a panel: heron with a rose in its
   beak, Chinese clouds, etc
   c. 1815
   Watercolour and ink on paper
   21 × 22.2

RP 102649
Illustration 227

228 Design for a panel: dragon with Chinese
     clouds, etc
     c. 1815
     Watercolour and ink on paper
     25.2 × 19.1
     RP 100446
     Illustration 228

229 The staircase, the Corridor
     Nash, *Views*, pl. 11; inscribed: 'A. Pugin
     delt.'; outline etching undated
     Aquatint
     13 × 17.8
     RP
     Illustration 229

THE BANQUETING ROOM

230 Design for the Banqueting Room
     Robert Jones
     c. 1816
     Watercolour and pencil on paper
     25.2 × 42.6
     Inscribed in ink: 'R. Jones'
     RP 100890
     Illustration 230

231 Design of dragons, possibly for the
     Banqueting Room
     Probably by Robert Jones
     c. 1816
     Pencil on paper
     28.2 × 31.8
     C-H 1948-40-24
     Illustration 231
     Courtesy of the Cooper-Hewitt Museum,
       the Smithsonian Institution's National
       Museum of Design

232 The Banqueting Room
     Augustus Pugin
     c. 1820 or later
     Pencil and watercolour on paper
       (extended)
     25.4 × 38.4
     Figures probably by James Stephanoff;
       outline etching dated Dec. 1 1824
     RP 100707
     Illustration 232

233 The Banqueting Room
     Nash, *Views,* pl. 20
     Aquatint
     26.2 × 31
     RP
     Illustration 233

THE MUSIC ROOM

234 Design for a lobby, possibly the Ante
       Room to the Music Room
     Probably close to a design installed in 1815
     Watercolour and ink on paper
     15.3 × 14.4
     C-H 1948-40-54
     Illustration 241

Courtesy of the Cooper-Hewitt Museum,
  the Smithsonian Institution's National
  Museum of Design

235 Design for a lobby, possibly the Ante
       Room to the Music Room
     Probably close to a design installed in 1815
     Watercolour and ink on paper
     17 × 13.5
     C-H 1948-40-53
     Illustration 234
     Courtesy of the Cooper-Hewitt Museum,
       the Smithsonian Institution's National
       Museum of Design

236 Design for a lobby, possibly the Ante
       Room to the Music Room
     Watercolour and ink on paper
     15.5 × 13.6
     C-H 1948-40-55
     Illustration 235
     Courtesy of the Cooper-Hewitt Museum,
       the Smithsonian Institution's National
       Museum of Design

237 Design for the west wall, the Music Room
     c. 1817
     Pencil on paper
     30.5 × 51.6
     C-H 1948-40-22
     Illustration 236
     Courtesy of the Cooper-Hewitt Museum,
       the Smithsonian Institution's National
       Museum of Design

238 Design, probably for the top of a gasolier,
       the Music Room
     c. 1816
     Pencil and watercolour on paper
     45.4 × 31.2
     V & A (no cat. no.)
     Illustration 244

239 Design for the west wall, the Music Room
     c. 1817
     Watercolour and pencil on paper
     33.8 × 52.2
     C-H 1948-40-14
     Illustration 237
     Courtesy of the Cooper-Hewitt Museum,
       the Smithsonian Institution's National
       Museum of Design

240 Design for the south wall, the Music Room
     c. 1817
     Watercolour and pencil on paper
     21.2 × 28.8
     C-H 1948-40-12
     Illustration 238
     Courtesy of the Cooper-Hewitt Museum,
       the Smithsonian Institution's National
       Museum of Design

241 Design for the west wall, the Music Room
     c. 1817
     Watercolour and ink on paper
     32.5 × 51.8

C-H 1948-40-13
Illustration 245
Courtesy of the Cooper-Hewitt Museum,
the Smithsonian Institution's National
Museum of Design

242 Design for the south wall, the Music Room
c. 1817
Watercolour and pencil on paper
33.2 × 48.7
C-H 1948-40-11
Illustration 239
Courtesy of the Cooper-Hewitt Museum,
the Smithsonian Institution's National
Museum of Design

243 Designs for the bamboo cove and a wall
panel, the Music Room
King George IV
c. 1817
Pencil on paper
Inscribed: 'Drawn by the Prince Regent in
1818 – when I had the honour of
attending his Royal Highness, to receive
his commands respecting some
alterations at the Pavilion Brighton – the
above being his first idea for the
ornaments forming the pannels of the
New Music Room – Given to my Friend
J.T.Smith March 17th 1823 – Frederick
Crace'
British Library
Illustration 240

244 Design for the south wall, the Music Room
c. 1817
Watercolour and gouache on paper
30.9 × 49.8
C-H 1948-40-8
Illustration 251
Courtesy of the Cooper-Hewitt Museum,
the Smithsonian Institution's National
Museum of Design

245 Design for the wall and bamboo cove, the
Music Room
Frederick Crace
c. 1817
Gouache on paper
38 × 31.2
C-H 1948-40-10
Illustration 246
Courtesy of the Cooper-Hewitt Museum,
the Smithsonian Institution's National
Museum of Design

246 Design for the west wall, the Music Room
Frederick Crace
c. 1817
Watercolour and gouache on paper
33.7 × 51.3 with hinged addition to show
an alternative design
C-H 1948-40-9 A and B
Illustration 250
Courtesy of the Cooper-Hewitt Museum,
the Smithsonian Institution's National
Museum of Design

247 Design for a window, the Music Room
*c.*1817
Watercolour and ink on paper
32.8 × 22.7
C-H 1948-40-89
Illustration 242
Courtesy of the Cooper-Hewitt Museum,
the Smithsonian Institution's National
Museum of Design

248 Design for an orchestra rail, the Music
Room
c. 1817
Pencil, watercolour and gouache on paper
watermarked 'J. WHATMAN 1816'
20.4 × 45.1
V & A (no cat. no.)
Illustration 243

249 Design, probably for the orchestra, the
Music Room
c. 1817
Pencil on paper
43.5 × 32.1
V & A (no cat. no.)
Illustration 247

250 Design of lamps and canopy, probably for
the Music Room
c. 1817
Pencil on paper
31.6 × 25.6
C-H 1948-40-31B
Illustration 248
Courtesy of the Cooper-Hewitt Museum,
the Smithsonian Institution's National
Museum of Design

251 Design of lamps and canopy, probably for
the Music Room
c. 1817
Pencil on paper
32.2 × 26.8
C-H 1948-40-31A
Illustration 249
Courtesy of the Cooper-Hewitt Museum,
the Smithsonian Institution's National
Museum of Design

252 Design for the north wall and organ, the
Music Room
Frederick Crace
c. 1817
Gouache and watercolour on paper
27.2 × 32.8
C-H 1948-40-17
Illustration 252
Courtesy of the Cooper-Hewitt Museum,
the Smithsonian Institution's National
Museum of Design

253 Design for the chimneypiece, the Music
Room
Probably by Robert Jones
c. 1820
Watercolour and pencil on paper
28.1 × 30.5

C-H 1948-40-74
Illustration 254
Courtesy of the Cooper-Hewitt Museum,
the Smithsonian Institution's National
Museum of Design

254 Design for the chimneypiece, the Music
Room
Probably by Robert Jones
c. 1820
Watercolour and pencil on paper
26.1 × 33.2
C-H 1948-40-73
Illustration 255
Courtesy of the Cooper-Hewitt Museum,
the Smithsonian Institution's National
Museum of Design

255 Design for vase and pedestal, the Music
Room
Probably by Robert Jones
c. 1820
Watercolour and pencil on paper
47.8 × 30.8
C-H 1948-40-75
Illustration 256
Courtesy of the Cooper-Hewitt Museum,
the Smithsonian Institution's National
Museum of Design

256 Design, probably for a ceramic vase to be
fitted with ormolu mounts
Frederick Crace
?c. 1817
Ink on paper
CB
Illustration 253

257 Design for curtains, for either the Music
Room or the Banqueting Room
? Robert Jones
c. 1820
Watercolour and pencil on paper
30.5 × 43.5
C-H 1948-40-15
Illustration 257
Courtesy of the Cooper-Hewitt Museum,
the Smithsonian Institution's National
Museum of Design

258 Design for curtains, for either the Music
Room or the Banqueting Room
? Robert Jones
c. 1820
Watercolour on paper
30.8 × 46.1
C-H 1948-40-16
Illustration 258
Courtesy of the Cooper-Hewitt Museum,
the Smithsonian Institution's National
Museum of Design

259 Design for curtains for the Music Room
1820
Watercolour and pencil on paper
30.9 × 48.7
Inscribed in pencil: 'Music Room'

C-H 1948-40-17
Illustration 259
Courtesy of the Cooper-Hewitt Museum,
the Smithsonian Institution's National
Museum of Design

260 Design for a carpet, probably for the Music
Room
c. 1820
Watercolour on paper
9.5 × 12.3
C-H 1948-40-91
Illustration 261
Courtesy of the Cooper-Hewitt Museum,
the Smithsonian Institution's National
Museum of Design

261 The Music Room
Augustus Pugin
c. 1822
Watercolour and pencil on paper
26.8 × 34.5
Inscribed: '39'
RP 100696
Illustration 260

262 The Music Room
Nash, *Views*, pl. 16; inscribed: 'A. Pugin
Delt'; outline etching published Jan.
1824
Aquatint
26.4 × 34.5
RP
Illustration 262

THE PRINCE OF WALES' BEDROOM
AND THE KING'S APARTMENTS

263 Design for an alcove with tent ceiling,
probably for the Prince of Wales'
Boudoir
c. 1801-4
Watercolour and ink on paper
20.3 × 27.9
C-H 1948-40-26
Illustration 263
Courtesy of the Cooper-Hewitt Museum,
the Smithsonian Institution's National
Museum of Design

264 The King's Library
Augustus Pugin
c. 1823
Pencil on paper
20.8 × 30.3
Inscribed: '58'
RP 100711
Illustration 266

265 The King's Library
Augustus Pugin
c. 1823
Watercolour on paper
21.8 × 31.2
Inscribed: '57'
RP 100710
Illustration 264

266 The King's Library
c. 1823
Nash, *Views*, pl. 22; inscribed: 'A Pugin
    Delt.'; outline etching dated Jan. 1824
Aquatint
20.2 × 30.2
RP
Illustration 267

267 The King's Bedroom
Augustus Pugin
c. 1823
Pencil on paper
19 × 30.7
Inscribed: '54'
RP 100709
Illustration 268

268 The King's Bedroom
Augustus Pugin
c. 1823
Watercolour on paper
15.3 × 24.8
Inscribed: '53'
RP 100708
Illustration 265

269 The King's Bedroom
c. 1823
Nash, *Views*, pl. 21; outline etching dated
    June 1824
Aquatint
19 × 30.4
RP
Illustration 269

THE RED DRAWING ROOM
270 The Red Drawing Room
Augustus Pugin
c. 1822
Watercolour and pencil on paper
14.8 × 21.3
Inscribed: '28'
Mounted with 272
RP 100712
Illustration 271

271 The Red Drawing Room
c. 1823
Nash, *Views*, pl. 13; inscribed: 'A. Pugin
    delt.'; outline engraving published Jul.
    1823
Aquatint
19 × 29.9
RP
Illustration 270

THE SOUTH GALLERIES
272 The South Galleries
Augustus Pugin
c. 1822
Watercolour and pencil on paper
25 × 33
Inscribed: '28'
Mounted with 270

RP 100712
Illustration 273

273 The South Galleries
Augustus Pugin
c. 1822
Pencil and some watercolour on paper
20.5 × 30.4
Inscribed on the mount: '61'
RP 100713
Illustration 272

274 The North and South Galleries
Nash, *Views*, pl. 23; outline etching dated
    June 2 1823
Aquatint
20.8 × 30.5
RP
Illustration 274

THE PORTICO AND THE OCTAGON HALL
275 The Portico
Augustus Pugin
Figures probably by James Stephanoff
c. 1820
Pencil and brown wash on paper
15.2 × 12.7
Inscribed on verso: 'Entrance to the
    Pavillion'
RP 102670
Illustration 275

276 The Octagon Hall
Nash, *Views*, pl. 11; outline etching
    published Apr. 1824
Aquatint
9.3 × 11
RP
Illustration 276

THE KITCHEN
277 The Kitchen
Nash, *Views*, pl. 24; outline etching
    published Apr. 2 1821
Aquatint
22 × 30
RP
Illustration 278

278 The Kitchen: plan
Ink and watercolour on paper
Maximum dimensions 75 × 72
Inscribed: 'Kings Kitchen Pavilion
    Brighton'
RP 102648
Illustration 277

279 The Kitchen: plan
Ink on paper
24.3 × 35.9
Inscribed: 'Pavilion Kitchen', etc
RL 23445
Illustration 279
Reproduced by Gracious Permission of
    H.M. The Queen

MISCELLANEOUS DESIGNS

280   Designs for fretwork panels
      Probably *c.* 1802–4
      Watercolour, gouache, pencil, and ink,
         mounted on paper
      37 × 26.5
      281 is on the reverse
      RP 100415
      Illustration 280

281   Designs for fretwork panels
      Probably *c.* 1802–4
      Watercolour, gouache, pencil, and ink,
         mounted on paper
      37 × 26.5
      280 is on the reverse
      RP 100414
      Illustration 283

282   Designs for fretwork panels
      Probably *c.* 1802–4
      Watercolour, gouache, pencil, and ink,
         mounted on paper
      37 × 26.5
      283 is on the reverse
      RP 100410
      Illustration 284

283   Designs for fretwork panels
      Probably *c.* 1802–4
      Watercolour, gouache, pencil, and ink,
         mounted on paper
      37 × 26.5
      282 is on the reverse

RP 100411
Illustration 285

284   Designs for fretwork panels
      Probably *c.* 1802–4
      Watercolour, gouache, pencil, and ink,
         mounted on paper
      37 × 26.5
      RP 100416
      Illustration 286

285   Designs for fretwork panels
      Probably *c.* 1802–4
      Watercolour, gouache, pencil, and ink,
         mounted on paper
      37 × 26.5
      RP 100412
      Illustration 292

286–
290   Designs for fretwork panels
      Frederick Crace
      c. 1815
      Watercolour and ink on paper
      CB
      Illustrations 281, 282, 287–289

291,
292,
293   Three designs, probably for mirror frames
      Frederick Crace
      c. 1815
      Watercolour and ink on paper
      CB
      Illustrations 290, 291, 293

Index

The list of 'Contents' provides an index to the principal stages in the evolution of the Royal Pavilion and its most important interiors. Those stages are detailed in the Index, but glancing references are given only where they carry significant information. The same principle is followed with the main architects, decorators, and motifs concerned. Numbers in italics refer to illustrations.